The Perfect Other

The
Perfect Other

A Memoir of My Sister

Kyleigh Leddy

An Imprint of HarperCollinsPublishers

HarperCollins books may be purchased for educational, business,
or sales promotional use. For information, please email the Special
Markets Department at SPsales@harpercollins.com.

FIRST EDITION

Designed by Emily Snyder

Library of Congress Cataloging-in-Publication Data has been applied for.
ISBN 978-0-358-46934-6 (hardcover)

22 23 24 25 26 LSC 10 9 8 7 6 5 4 3 2 1

This book is for the estimated 970 million people world-wide who suffer from a mental health disorder. This book is for their suffering, and for those who love them.

All I can hope is that it helps, even just a single person, even just for a moment.

Author's Note

While writing this book, I kept returning to the part of the Hippocratic Oath that instructs, "Do no harm." My intention was genuine and transparent — I wanted to help break the stigma surrounding mental illness and assist others in all the ways that I failed to save my sister. There was also, in all honesty, a quality of penance to the undertaking as well, as if by seeking to prevent future tragedies, my guilt over the past could be lessened.

The opportunity to share my family's story fell into place in a way that I can only describe as divine luck. The unlikely events aligned like a string of runway lights, setting the way forward, and for the first time in my overly anxious, constantly second-guessing mind, the path before me was undeniable. Every morning I woke with a burning urge to get the words down on paper, and every night before bed, I was kept awake with the fear that I wouldn't have the chance to finish or remedy it. I took to sending my most recent draft to my email, writing down my password, and reminding my mom to forward it to my editor if something should happen to me. I was almost scary in my single-minded, ceaseless determination, possessed by my mission to an unhealthy degree. After years of uselessly standing by as my sister's battle with her mental health spiraled to new lows, I finally had a chance to *do something*, to *help*. The effect was dizzying.

Then, inevitably, once the first draft was committed to the page, this conviction shook loose. Part of my fear was born as a natural extension of the subject I chose to write about: Mental health is complicated and inherently personal. No single experience is exactly the same, and while there is power in relating to an individual perspective, there is also a great deal of danger. After all, how can one person, from a comparatively privileged subset of our population, speak for a world of diverse experiences?

The answer is she can't.

It is important to acknowledge that the story you are about to read centers around a girl who, despite her mental illness and according to the many problematic standards of our society, was immensely privileged: She was white, heterosexual, cisgender, physically attractive, smart, capable, and fiercely loved. She attended a well-funded school district, had a family that was eager to help her in any way they could, and had safety nets in place that kept her from falling into homelessness or prison. She possessed the financial luxury to attend rehabilitation centers, therapy, experimental treatments, and group homes, and the healthcare coverage to be prescribed antipsychotic medication. She was an anomaly, the peak of fortune, and yet none of this was enough to save her.

According to the United States HHS Office of Minority Health, Black Americans are more likely to report persistent symptoms of emotional distress than white Americans, but only one in three Black adults who need mental healthcare receive it. There are countless systemic reasons why this is true: intergenerational trauma, higher rates of cyclical poverty, and limitations in access to healthcare resources. There is the nature of the prison industrial system, microaggressions, the stress and physical trauma of racism, the lack of diversity in mental healthcare providers, and many, many more tragic factors.

There is also an incredible burden on the LGBTQ community: higher rates of trauma, hate crimes, bullying, depression, anxiety, and substance abuse. According to the CDC, queer youth are *twice* as likely to attempt suicide as their heterosexual peers are.

In 2018, 19.1 percent of the United States reported a mental illness (this is 47.6 *million* people, or one in five adults). Of these cases, schizophrenia is purported to affect 1.5 million U.S. citizens. Furthermore, 37 percent of incarcerated adults and 20.1 percent of individuals experiencing homelessness have been diagnosed with a mental illness. In the United States, suicide is the second leading cause of death for people ages ten to thirty-four, and depression is the leading disability worldwide. The weight of knowing I will doubtlessly fail to capture and recognize these innumerable experiences left me frequently paralyzed.

It is also worth mentioning that diagnosis isn't a straight line — it's possible for a treatment to be worse than the ailment itself, or for that very same ailment to be an unlikely source of enjoyment. For my sister, the disease's progression was a deterioration, a lessening of who she was rather than a means by which she expanded. This is not the case for everyone, and I would hate if my sharing of my limited perspective, my very microscopic story in a universe of macrocosms, meant anyone else felt invalidated.

The Nigerian writer and public speaker Chimamanda Ngozi Adichie said it best: "The single story creates stereotypes, and the problem with stereotypes is not that they are untrue, but that they are incomplete. They make one story become the only story." This book is a single rock in the void. We need more voices, more stories, and we need them now.

Rarely will you be the first in all of human history to experience anything, but you will experience it all your own just the same. I know there are thousands, millions, billions of stories that my own will never touch. I also know that somewhere out there is a family suffering as ours did, voiceless and afraid.

The Perfect Other

On January 8, 2014, my sister, Kait, was wearing a red North Face jacket when she disappeared.

That is a fact among others. None of them makes much sense to me.

A girl walks to the peak of the Benjamin Franklin Bridge. A girl in a red North Face jacket and high winter boots. A girl walks, and then, poof, gone.

My sister walks to the peak of the Benjamin Franklin Bridge.

Kait walking.

Kait, and then, poof, gone.

I repeat this mantra in my head. When I say it aloud, the words solidify, become something permanent. When I write it, the block letters stare back at me —formal and official like the autopsy report we never received.

My sister on the Benjamin Franklin Bridge.

On January 8, 2014, my sister walked the Benjamin Franklin Bridge.

My sister disappeared.

How? Why?

I never viewed the security photographs myself. I didn't ask to. Is it really her? Are we sure? Perhaps it was easier not to know, not to have the defini-

tive proof of seeing it for myself. The image in my head is thus one of my own creation.

A girl walking.
  Kait walking.
  Poof, gone.

Prologue

When I was twenty years old, I went to a psychic in lieu of going to a therapist.

The decision was made in a semi-desperate strait, the way I assume most people find themselves at an ostensible mystic's door: half believing, half skeptical, morbidly curious, and almost always looking for some elusive answer that proved absent elsewhere.

I had worn down the alternative path already, tried on different therapists like Goldilocks, never finding one that fit "just right." In the last few years, I sat before men and women, young and old, austere and analytical, flowery and bohemian. They always meant well, but it was as if they could taste my hunger in the air, my desperation to be pardoned and validated. My carnal need for an excuse vibrating between us. I sometimes wondered if they could see into my very brain. Could they tell that my nerves were all bundled and splintered, like necklaces tangled in the bottom of a drawer?

I knew well the interior of a therapist's office. I knew the scratchy couches and the patient stares. I once sat before my sister's old therapist, sweated nervously as we both cried. Stood in the basement of a beach home with my mom's therapist, the shell-lined driveway slightly visible above me like a thin layer of frosting. Everything in the world upside down.

I knew the process by now, and I could predict the same well-intentioned half-truth I was always told: "It's not your fault."

It was a phrase therapists liked to return to in the pauses and gentle stutters that lingered in the stale air. *It's not your fault.* The words, once so welcome, were memorized, rehearsed, stuck in my mind like that hit song on the radio that started out catchy but has now turned torturous: a ceaseless loop, resurfacing late at night when you're an inch from sleep.

Hearing this was never enough, because the clinicians only knew what I told them: the omissions I made, backtracks. There was only one person who could truly exonerate me, and she was unreachable. When I strip my reasoning for going to the psychic that day, this is the essence at its core. This was the reassurance I sought.

Crystal rocks were scattered on the window shelves. Geodes reflected the neon purple lights of the storefront's sign. A Buddha sculpture sat in the corner, its arms folded and its eyes closed. There were sun gods, moon gods, a diagram of the Hindu concept of chakras: the seven colors illuminated from the head of the body down to the base of the spine — a gradient scale from lavender to blue, green, yellow, and finally red.

A sweet, suffocating incense spread from a series of burning candles. It made the collar around my neck feel tight and restricting.

I had dragged my friend Devin here with me. For her, I assumed the outing was silly: a fun, spontaneous Sunday break from the mundane obligations of student life. She wanted to know if the guy she was seeing was her soulmate. She wondered if she was moving toward the right career path. For me, the visit represented something darker, more desperate, more intense.

"I can only take one of you right now. Who wants to go?" the psychic asked.

Suddenly panicked, I shot Devin a look that meant to say, *You go.*

The woman wasn't the Hollywood stereotype I was expecting. She sounded more like a Real Housewife of New Jersey, nasal and thick. Her hair was straight and glossy, and her smooth, tanned face was covered by what seemed to be a fresh application of makeup. On her website she was described as a "natural-born, third generation psychic."

Devin and I stood in momentary paralysis. I watched her blond head swivel in confusion. We backed away slightly, as if to retreat to-

ward the exit. My hands were clammy and slick with nerves. This was
a bad idea.

Before we could decide who should go first, the woman pointed in my
direction.

"You," she said. "Come with me. This will be fast."

As little girls, my sister and I invented our own religion.

Growing up, we went to mass on holidays, received our First Commu-
nions and our Confirmations. We would say the occasional Hail Mary
as little girls on Christmas Eve in our PJs, but God was a distant concept who lived in the clouds and never deigned to appear in our common
lives. Instead, we invented rituals of our own: Kait passing rules, and
then amending them with exceptions and revisions of her own.

Some were common childhood parables: "If you step on a crack, you'll
break your mother's back." We crossed to the other side of the street,
jumped slabs of concrete to avoid the fractures in walkways. Others I believed were universal but over time discovered were an invention of my
sister's imagination.

*If you're walking with someone, and anything separates you — a pole, an
awning, whatever — you have to immediately kiss something blue or your relationship will be doomed.*

I learned to be creative, sly even, kissing the sleeve of my blue T-shirt
as if I were only brushing my hair from my face, or discreetly touching
my lips to the back of my hand where my veins wound blue. If a friend
and I were walking together and she went on one side of a telephone
pole, I would follow behind, determined not to let it separate us.

By the time I was five or six, Kait and I had also developed a Morse
code of knocks between the walls of our bedrooms.

One knock: Hello. Two knocks: Are you awake? There was language
in the gentle, rhythmic patterns. Her knocks were always more intricate
than mine, more complex. They became miniature songs that made me
giggle.

Three knocks: See you in the morning.

Four knocks: The time — 11:11 p.m. Make a wish.

Every day, twice a day, Kait would wait for the clock to strike the hour eleven and the minute eleven. At lunch, she watched as the hand of the clock ticked the seconds from 11:10 a.m. to 11:11 a.m. The minute was as slow as the hum of bees until the four ones clicked together in rhythmic bliss.

It's time to make a wish! she announced to whoever was near.

Squeezing her eyes shut, holding her little fingers pressed into her palms, creating crescent-shaped indentations in the skin like half-moons, she made her two wishes of the day.

When I remember these rituals, I wonder what we were really attempting — where was the anxiety born from? What were we so afraid of, even then?

Looking back, I think of our shared practices as equated to a man kneeling beside his bed to recite his nightly prayers or a professional athlete wearing the same pair of lucky socks to the season opener. We wanted to impose a set of rules onto the way the world should be — a naïve faith that if you wished hard enough, maintained a certain discipline, colored within the lines, the universe would reward you. You would be protected. Even then, I suppose, even before, we suspected that there was something to be protected from.

So we waited for 11:11 to hit the clocks. We avoided cracks in the sidewalk, and telephone poles. We kissed something blue. And we hoped everything would be okay.

There's a painting hanging on the wall of my family's living room. In its gilded, rectangular frame is the image of two children on a pale Massachusetts beach. One is shorter and blonder with nearly platinum hair. The other is taller with dirty-blond strands, tangled and wild and curly. Both are wearing matching print bathing suits outlined against the ocean, their expressions obscured from the viewer. The younger girl is chasing after the older one, straining to keep up.

The painting holds an ephemeral quality to it; every line a soft cloud like a Monet, the colors bleeding into one another until it is impossible to determine precisely where one figure begins and the other ends. The shaky quality reminds me of memory itself—how it wiggles from underneath us. As soon as we think we've caught it, it vibrates and writhes, as treacherous as quicksand.

This is how I spent my childhood and adolescence, leaning in to superstition, trying to catch up to my sister. I lived in her footsteps, her shadow, her religion, until, days before my seventeenth birthday, she disappeared from me altogether.

Now, three years later, I found myself at the psychic's shop, looking for a sign, a confirmation, a pardoning. I was the same little girl in the painting, still striving to know my sister, to get closer, and still failing all the same. I needed Kait to know that I loved her—that I was sorry. I knew it was illogical and possibly weak to want such a thing. I had made mistakes, and I deserved to suffer for those mistakes. And yet I craved the comfort just the same, the way you reach for your baby blanket or the soothing, hushed reassurance that *everything is going to be okay* in the face of undeniable impending disaster.

I needed my sister to tell me that it wasn't my fault.

My hands hung numb and slack at my sides as I followed the psychic behind a beaded curtain, and Devin took a seat on a white leather couch in the entryway.

The day outside was bright and sunny; too cheery to stand among the neon lights of the psychic's shop. I almost wished it were raining instead.

The psychic gestured for me to sit at a rounded table. She took a seat before me.

"Today we will do a quick read of the Celtic Cross."

Symbols of moons, stars, astrological figures, and horoscopes jumped out from the patterned sheet that clothed the table before us. The mystic spread a series of gold cards, each displaying variations of the same key themes: knives, weeping women, lovers, and a hermit.

"This is the Celtic Cross. It's one of the oldest tarot card readings, representing the past, future, present, subconscious hopes, and eventual outcome. There is nothing more descriptive."

I pursed my lips, my eyes fixated on the cards before me. Knives hung above the outline of a girl sleeping in bed, the sharp tips of the blades threatening to penetrate her. Two women were on a boat, hunched forward as more swords pierced the mast in vertical lines. A decrepit old man leaned on his sapper for support, staring out at a mountain in loneliness. More knives. A naked man and a woman reaching across to each other. A crumbling tower. Knives again.

Cheery stuff.

"I detect in your palms and in your cards that you had a difficult upbringing: loss, trauma, and family struggle." She looked to me for confirmation.

I looked at the table instead.

"You have insomnia. You're tired. You're an anxious person, always waiting for the next catastrophe. But . . . I think I was sent here today to tell you that all of the bad stuff, the past trauma, it's over. The future is going to be bright. Stop waiting for the next tragedy."

I felt a humming deep within my chest, a loss of breath.

The woman was right — the last ten years had been consumed by a consistent, brutal storm: each day a new crisis. And yet that could have only been a lucky guess. I needed more.

This was my third psychic — in the last three years, I had visited two others.

The first was in Manayunk, Pennsylvania, across the street from the Starbucks where I was having a college interview with a Dartmouth alumnus. I sat near a window, shaking the interviewer's hand and watching the lights of the storefront glow in the snowfall like a beacon. My mom came with me that day. The psychic told her there was an angry angel over her shoulder. We cried on the walk back to the parking lot.

There was Donna, in Avalon, New Jersey, where I was visiting my college roommate the summer after our freshman year. Donna's shop jutted out onto the sandy streets. She told me I would get engaged at twenty-seven but never mentioned marriage or children. The omission made me wonder, seeping into my consciousness like a slow poison in strange and surprising ways. She attempted to sell one of my friends a rose quartz and prophesized the other would meet the love of her life in the next six months (she didn't). Every stranger we met on the street that day looked shiny with potential.

But no psychic had ever mentioned Kait. I knew it was desperate to wish they would. I knew it was silly, and fruitless, and immature, but grief is desperate and fruitless too. I had left logic behind long ago.

I didn't truly believe the psychics, and neither did I expect a miracle. I knew their tricks. I studied "cold" and "hot" readings — how they guess at random or look you up beforehand. But I still walked into the shop that day hoping against hope that Kait would somehow show herself. I had spent most of my life with my sister — and all of my life without her — searching for signs and patterns in the universe. Wishes, messages from beyond. I was growing tired, desperate.

The light filtered through the window of the psychic's store, touching the shelves and illuminating the layer of dust that hugged the array of spiritual objects. I could easily imagine Kait here — amid the sculptures and the tarot cards. It was eclectic and bright, colorful and disorganized, just like she was.

As the psychic began to read the cards in front of her, she suddenly stopped, staring at the dust particles dancing and hanging in the faded light. She seemed to see something there, her smooth face twisting with confusion.

"I'm receiving a message from someone . . . someone looking for you."

There are moments that freeze you still, take your laugh and shrivel it. My throat went dry, my eyes opened wider, my heart tugged to my knees. I didn't dare breathe.

"What does the number eleven mean to you?" the psychic asked.

I watched the past fall apart and stitch itself back together again.

Phase I, Prodromal

Blue Beginnings

One

I was willed into existence by my sister. My life began with a prayer uttered on the hard wood of a church pew by a five-year-old girl in a bright Sunday dress. My sister begged for a baby sister, pretended her dolls *were* her baby sister. Convinced all good things came in two, Kait was obsessed with the television twins Mary-Kate and Ashley Olsen. I was designed to be just that for her — a sister to complete her duo, to make us whole.

My life was ordained in her two tiny palms pressed together — in the moment her head cast down and her delicate features fixed in concentration. I was born on January 11 as a playmate, a best friend. Some little girls want a puppy or the newest Barbie DreamHouse, but Kait wanted *me*.

Driving by a church, she would peek her head out the window and shout:

"Stop the car! I need to run in and ask for a sister."

She sat in the hospital waiting room as I arrived, drawing pictures and mentally setting aside which of her belongings she would designate as my gifts. She made room for me in the corner of her bedroom, carefully planning where my bassinet could fit.

Kait waited patiently with our grandpa while our grandmother darted in and out of the hospital room, showing her polaroid photographs of the stretched pink skin of my newborn head.

"That's your little sister," Grandma told her.

Kait's thumbs left small imprints on the edges of the picture from gripping it too tightly.

Later, when we returned home from the hospital, she played under my crib, hiding beneath the silk pink lining, vowing to protect me. Sitting on the blue and yellow patterned couch of our living room, my parents placed me lightly in her arms, reminding her to be gentle. Though by the time we were older, she would never hesitate to tease me about how pale and wrinkled my newborn body was, in those first moments she looked upon my scrunched face in awe.

I have a theory that Kait depleted every drop of color from our shared gene pool. She had tanner skin, darker hair, blue-green eyes the color of fresh seaweed, freckles that dotted her nose. She arrived sudden and fast. Our mom had planned for anesthesia, but there was no time. Kait couldn't wait. Kait never waited. She emerged as a presence, a dramatic burst, a violent entry. There was blood on the walls of the hospital room. She made herself known immediately.

Where others walk in life, Kait marched. Head held high, arms rigid. She bulldozed through each developmental milestone. She was walking at ten months, potty-trained by eighteen months. Kait was uniquely determined, excessively stubborn, charming during the most unexpected moments, with a kind of mature, sardonic humor, as if she had arrived in this world professionally trained in comedic timing. Every action was performed with an inherent confidence, a reckless unfurling.

By the time of my birth, it seemed the reservoir for such vivacity and saturation was running low. I was born a shadow of my sister — paler, blonder, wispier, and more hesitant. I took my time, emerged quietly. My skin was cloudy thin, nearly translucent, like parchment paper. Through it you could see the blue of my veins and a purplish bruise nestled between my eyes where my head had rested on our mom's pelvic bone in the womb. "An angel's kiss," she called it, to be kind. Everything about my existence screamed fragile. Where Kait's birthstone was a diamond — sparkles and flair — mine was a garnet, the color of a scab.

My sister used to tell me fairytales, so now I'll tell you one about a girl so loved she didn't speak. *No, really.* She said "ma" for *mom*, and "da" for *dad*, and even "bee" for *blanket*, but beyond that, there was no need for language.

If I needed my blanket, Kait laid the soft fabric over my body and swaddled me warm. When we had babysitters, she told them what foods I liked and when I needed to go to bed. Everything was taken care of, and communication renders itself unnecessary when you are understood on a molecular level.

A pediatrician once wondered if my quietness was a result of a hearing deficiency. He recommended my parents test his theory by playing a game of whispers. During a long car ride, when I was around four, my sister, mom, and father spoke only in hushed tones.

Sitting in the backseat of the car, I listened silently until their conversation turned to me.

"Do you think she can hear us?" Kait whispered.

"I don't know . . . She isn't saying anything," one of my parents murmured back.

Fed up with their odd behavior, I finally yelled: "Hey, I can hear you! Stop whispering!"

The story went down as a family epic. A tale repeated at dinner parties and holiday gatherings in that jilted, memorized tone — how everyone erupted in laughter and relief when I spoke up. I think back to that sometimes: My early years were so peaceful, I was so doted upon, so understood, that I had no *reason* to speak. No need to ask for anything at all. Kait gave me everything.

The fairytale involved two other key characters as well.

There was a tall father with a tangled mess of dark, wavy hair. Darker than brown, but not quite black. He helped us with our homework, teaching us to *feel* math instead of just memorize it — wind our way to the answer through trials and tricks. We watched shows on the Discovery Channel, took long walks through cavernous museum halls. When I asked typical kid questions like "Why is the sky blue?" he answered honestly. He told me blue light is scattered more than other colors because it has shorter wavelengths. He didn't provide a childish, simplistic version or fabricate a magical reason like the "Fairies painted it blue." He was frank and truthful, entrusting me to decipher the science for myself.

Instead, magic was our mom's domain. If my father's role was in teaching us to ask questions, to ponder more deeply, to seek the truth, our mom's was in letting us linger in the unknown, in the imagination, in the magic and inexplicable.

My mom is classically beautiful: golden-blond hair, eyes the shade children color the sky, and the facial symmetry you see in magazines. She was and still is the kind of pretty that is impossible to deny. It is as sure as the sun, almost not worth mentioning.

She is also accommodating to the point of nearing excess. When I was a freshman in college, I casually remarked that I found a new brand of gum I liked, different from the one we habitually purchased together for years. A few days later, she mailed me a box of twenty packets. The mint-colored boxes sat on the corner of my desk for months.

"You're going to spoil those girls," our grandmother cautioned her periodically.

She does, but she also doesn't. She spoils us with love, with unconditional regard, with the unequivocal, precious knowledge we are valued in this world. Our words matter, someone is listening. She lets us sit in the passenger seat of her car for hours after she picks us up from school, listening to every detail of our little worlds, never bored, always captivated by what Rebecca said or who Sam thought was pretty.

She is empathetic and thoughtful, providing rides to men with special needs who work at the grocery store and dedicating the same rapturous attention to their stories as our own. She is kind because she is kind, not because she is trying to prove something.

Mom was always working to *better* everything, searching for an outlet to improve our lives, if only in subtle ways — a home project, a new color for the walls. She was one of the first female stockbrokers in her class, competing with overconfident men and ignoring how they bragged about their performance after class, unaware they answered the question incorrectly. She navigated an era before the "Me Too" movement, a lawless land without consequences. Later, she would sacrifice her hard-earned career to take care of us, learn to wear many other hats, and exceed at them all — mother, wife, real estate agent, interior designer, charity organizer, sober coach, domestic abuse hotline responder.

While the parenting norm at the time involved "helicopter parents" with sharp, unrealistic expectations of their children, our mom taught us that it didn't matter if we were pretty, smart, popular, successful, as much as it mattered that we were kind. This was the baseline. We could be anything, but we were nothing if we were not kind.

I remember watching her once, checking out at a store register, rows of fabric samples behind her, dusty and bright. She laughed with one of the employees, smiling easily as she pulled a credit card from her purse. It was an ordinary moment, but I kept returning to it over the years, trying to find an explanation for the quality that struck me in the moment — a natural ability to make others feel at ease. A smile that felt like a pat on the back. She had a way of making everyone feel special, of making my sister and me feel equally important. She responded with the same amazed "Wow!" at every scribbled art project or orchestrated dance performance — never tiring in her encouragement of us.

She was always somewhere between the two of our vastly different personalities: not quite as quiet and reserved as myself but not as wild and unconventional as my sister. There's a soft, generous calm about her, but she can also be wickedly funny, bluntly sarcastic. She completed us, brought our opposites to a happy medium.

Mom tells me that as a baby I had the same deep blue eyes I have now, but they were too big on my small face. They made me look perpetually serious as I stared at the chaos following my big sister everywhere she went. There were dance recitals, soccer practices, piano lessons. Our parents indulging Kait's changing passions with patience and humor. Life was a continuous carpool ride filled with endless amazement at the talents my older sister accrued. She was just like me, I thought, but bigger, stronger, and tirelessly bold.

Our age gap varied depending on the season—in the months between my birthday in January and hers in April, she was five years older. From April to the following January, the difference grew to six years. I cherished those precious three months when my age was one year closer to hers. One less year of division, one step closer.

She was my very own parallel line—on the same plane, changing alongside me, but always staying the same distance apart. I wanted to grow older, taller, just to catch up. If I could only run faster, leap farther, then *this* time I would bridge the gap. *This* time, we would intersect.

And yet, for as out of reach as she so often seemed, the truth was, Kait had wished for me. When my parents asked me if I wanted another sibling a few years after I was born, I paused, thought about it for a moment, smiled with mischief, and said: "No. *I'm* the baby."

And thus, as family legend goes, they didn't try. How easily my life could've been up to the same selfish whim of a preschooler. But Kait chose me, and for that reason she was all I ever wanted to be. The only person whose approval I needed.

We moved around a lot in these early years: The names and locations of streets and zip codes pile on top of one another until they are indistinguishable. Our father worked as a network engineer in the early days of the internet. The market was expanding, growing and changing, requiring us to change and move with it. While most of these homes have since merged together in memory, one stands distinct: Marblehead, Massachusetts, where we spent several years together as a family.

The place we actually lived the longest is the suburbs of Philadelphia, but Philly is green. Philly is landlocked. Philly is psychiatric facilities with lights that flare and flicker. Philly is turmoil and unraveling endings.

Comparatively, Marblehead is blue. It is beaches and family dinners and the happiest I can recall any of us being. In the face of loss, certain images persist, becoming personal myths, religious symbols we return to. Marblehead became our touchpoint, our foundation. When everything went wrong, it was the memory of this town that Kait was drawn to as moths circle porch lights on summer nights. *Marblehead was where things were right and okay,* she whispered to me one night, years later. *How do we get back to Marblehead?*

The town is approximately half an hour outside of Boston. Its streets are dotted with wooden New England homes of all colors and shapes. It is a quintessential Massachusetts fishing village — a storybook blanket.

Its name came to be in the 1600s when early residents mistook its rocky, granite ledges for marble. The story made us laugh. We rolled the town's name in our mouths, inventing a space between the two words and twisting it into an insult: "Marble head."

"Your head is full of marbles," we taunted one another.

We had a Marble Fairy, along the lines of the Tooth Fairy, invented by my parents.

On special occasions, I would wake, rolling over in bed to find a marble under my pillow. Like the Princess and the Pea, each morning I felt for the round shape under the feathers, grasping the cool globe and bringing it to my eyes, mesmerized: Even the mass-manufactured marbles had distinct swirls of colored glass stretched and pulled together, creating webs of life.

In Marblehead, we lived in a grayish-blue house. This always struck me as important. The *blue* house. A little home on the corner, the shade of a robin's egg. Next to us was a yellow house. I was once the kind of girl who lived in a blue house next to a yellow house.

Our home was located on what is known as "the Neck," a peninsula that extends into Massachusetts Bay. To get there, you have to drive on a narrow strip of road, water hugging either side. Old lampposts cast a glow over the smooth asphalt and the sliver of beach and waves. It is in this house that Kait and I shared a room, blue like the rest. The posts of our beds were stained a denim color, and we had hooked rugs with images of mermaids. While living here we also adopted my first dog: a lovable bichon frise named Sailor. As the rest of his litter was playing with my parents and sister, he quietly climbed under my sweater where I sat in the corner and remained there until it was time to make our selection. From then on, he was always by my side.

Later, when we moved to Philadelphia for my father's job, my greatest claim to first-grade fame would be that the movie *Hocus Pocus* was filmed in my old town.

"And if you look closely when they fly over the village, you can see my house!" I told girls at Halloween sleepovers. I slowed down the scene, pointing to a small dot of color in the distance, "That's it!"

But the real witches weren't in Marblehead. For us, the monsters and frights would come in Philly. Marblehead was peaceful. Marblehead was good.

I look back on my childhood the way you remember a restaurant you visited in a foreign city in winter, escaping the chill of the air and ducking into a random café, warm and cozy. It's the first bite, the warmth, the feeling of safety, the best meal you've ever had. You return years later, older, changed, and try to find it again but can't. The streets are unfamiliar, unwelcoming, and when you finally do return, the lights are brighter than you remembered, the food colder, less flavorful. You never quite recreate it again.

Of course, there were problems, but any serious ones — money, health issues, marital discord — were kept from my sister and me. Kait and I were protected, swaddled in a world of soft, fluffy, inconsequential dramas: My father stepped on a nail in the garage and had to go to the hospital. Kait and I interviewed for a prestigious charter school and one of us didn't get in — we never discovered which. (Mom requested not to be told, wanting to eliminate any impetus for jealousy or comparison.) In the process of moving, we had a squatter take possession of our home, an ugly lawsuit following. And once, a car crashed into our kitchen while we were away on a weekend trip. Mom received the call from the police late one evening.

"A car is in our kitchen," she repeated to herself incredulously.

A car is *in* our kitchen, in our blue home.

But the walls could be repaired, no one was seriously hurt, and everything was as perfect as anything ever was.

In future years, I would come to understand the strength behind our mom's kindness; that she was no stranger to grief and had already lost several loved ones by the time of her marriage, including a childhood classmate and her high school sweetheart. The effusive warmth and charm that appeared so natural to me was born of this loss, and it took energy, sacrifice, and, most importantly, strength to sustain. I would ultimately realize that the rational mind that made my father so gifted at helping me with my math homework was also the reason why he was so frequently absent from our lives: away on business trips and occupied late into the night with long hours at work. It is why he stands out like a cardboard cutout in these childhood memories — somewhere between an ambivalent witness and a stark absence.

Yet in those early years of innocence, I was naïve to all of this. When I heard the story of my assumed deafness, I did not think of the terror that underlined it or that the tale was only funny in retrospect because the fear of a serious lifelong disability had faded. I did not think of the time my parents spent lying awake at night worrying, or the long hours in doctor's office waiting rooms, wondering if their child was going to be okay. I did not guess at the quiet resolve in our mom's gentle compassion, nor did I realize that her urge to spoil and protect us was derived from a sincere understanding of the hardest edges of life. I did not wonder why it was so often just my mom, sister, and me. All I knew was that I was happy.

Perhaps all childhoods are mirrors we hold up, finding our identities in the reflection. Over time, these images fissure and crack, become foggy and confused. We become foggy and confused in turn. We crack in turn, too.

There's a beach nearby our old home, and if you walk the winding, narrow sidewalk down to the water, you can collect the best sea glass you'll ever find. Kait used to hold my hand as we made our way down the crooked weave of the walkway, guiding me across the uneven stone. Her hands were always so rough, callused seemingly since she was a little girl like she had years of experience from another lifetime already behind her. I would hold her hand and marvel at the difference between us — the contrast of my pale skin next to her tan.

The beach swelled with jellyfish, and we ran from their squishy clear bellies as they washed ashore. I spent hours with my parents and Kait sorting through the rough sand to find pieces of glass in every shade of blue you can imagine. The edges were worn and soft, grainy like sand itself, smooth to rub under your thumb.

Sometimes, if we dug deep enough, we would come across the cavernous shape of a seashell — our fingernails scratching the hard surface. Holding it against my ear, I thought I could hear the giving and taking of waves, crashing and receding on a beach. As a little girl, my sister told me several theories of why and how this phenomenon occurs. Some were silly and fantastical: conch shells are mermaid cell phones. The rushing roar is the scratch of a walkie-talkie jumping on a radio channel. And when you use it, you receive direct communication to the ocean — no matter where in the world you are, a long-distance call.

Other theories prophesized that the sounds were trapped in the very molecules of the shells, the native environment of their past memorized by their being. I like this idea best: Even shells are impacted by their origins, unable to shake the ocean. They were formed in an environment of noise, and now they are never without it. Like how after a concert, your ears continue to ring; shells are still reeling from their past.

The truth is less mystical but more haunting. It was once thought the echo was of your own blood rushing and throbbing in your ear — the whirl of your body's internal rhythm. This has now been debunked — in a soundproof room, a music studio, the noise stops. There's only silence. The echo is nothing more than a reflection of your surroundings.

How tricky perception is. You believe you're listening to waves but really you're hearing the normal give and take of everyday life. Nature plays many tricks on our minds. It was, I suppose, the first evidence of a hard-learned lesson — one that I would have to approach again and again in varying intensities — the simple truth that our senses can fail us. Betray us. Lead us down crooked paths and hanging ledges. Drop us off in unfamiliar landscapes and scatter the breadcrumbs in the wind.

When I remember these years, I think of the taste of the salty air, alive with possibility. I think of the tiny, cramped kitchen before and after the car is inside of it. I think of the beautiful blue and yellow dollhouses our maternal grandfather, whom we called Poppy, spent weeks hand-crafting in his garage, filled with blue putty and refined furniture, as small as a fingernail. Every tiny detail further proof of his love and care.

I think of being pushed by Kait down the hill of our street in a pink Barbie Jeep, and the dress-up games she made me play, slipping into pink plastic baby-heeled princess shoes and Hawaiian-themed coconut bras, turning me into her very own life-size doll. Perhaps some kids would find this process objectifying, limiting, but I only took it as flattery — grateful to be by her side in whatever capacity she wanted me around.

I think of the feeling of sand, how it creeps in everywhere. Weeks later, you find it in your running sneakers, in your bag, in the forgotten corners of your drawers. The impermanence of waves, the ocean's destructive quality: water consumes houses, beaches, constantly reinventing the mounds of the shore into new designs. Everything that goes in comes out transformed: eternal but evolving. I see the sailboats in the harbor, their long-necked masses like strange birds from a distance, congregating in flecks of white. I think of our life there, and I think of home, even now.

And above all else, I cannot help but look back on my childhood and be reminded of how lucky we were. Our family was not excessively wealthy, never entirely without worry or care. My parents worked their entire lives, from teenagers to adulthood, paying off student loans well into their marriage. At many points, they were living paycheck to paycheck, squeezing every dime to support two young kids. My father's parents had come here from Ireland, our mom's parents from Sweden. Neither came from money, but they had carved out a life for my sister and me that was more than comfortable. We never wondered if there would be food on our plates, we never went without.

There are entire fields of psychology rooted in the idea that all mental trauma is derived from our childhoods and subconscious needs never met. But that can't be said for Kait and me — we were fortunate. We were privileged: We had a good life, a blessed life. Yet mental illness can be as unpredictable and indiscriminate as a natural disaster. It doesn't happen to you until it does. You're safe until you're not. If you had peeked into that little blue house on the corner, you would have seen two children spilling over with love and two parents trying, and trying, and *trying* their best no matter the circumstance.

Our childhood was as idyllic as a Norman Rockwell painting. It was truly a fairytale. We had everything, and yet everything would still collapse. It wasn't enough. And if our foundation couldn't save us, then whose can?

Who stands a chance against mental illness?

Two

When I was six and Kait was eleven, we were forced to confront the reality of one of our superstitions.

There was a large hanging mirror looming between the stairs' landings, reflecting the deep blue of the ocean. Kait and I would teasingly chase each other around the house, our socks sliding against the hardwood floor, propelling ourselves across the polished wood like professional curlers, as smooth as ice.

Mom worried after us as we ran up and down the staircase, rattling the frame with our frantic footsteps. *You're going to break the mirror and get hurt!*

We never did hit it, but it fell one night for other, mysterious reasons. My family awoke to a sound like the screeching roar of a train grinding to a stop as the thin wire that held the mirror gave way. There had been no hit, no catalyst — the wire simply gave up, gave in after a valiant, silent journey; every day, dragged down bit by bit, its fibers frayed and raw. The glass broke into hundreds of tiny shards, some the very size of the grains of sand.

We knew this particular consequence well: Breaking a mirror condones you to seven years of bad luck.

Looking back, I wonder if the superstitions were true. Was this the reason for everything, seven years of bad luck? *Was this what our rituals had been trying to evade all along?*

Seven years later, Kait would be eighteen, and I would be thirteen — another unlucky number. She would soon embark on a journey of hospitals, rehabs, and psychiatric units. She would soon suffer a fall of her own — crack open the way the mirror shattered and spilled across the floor.

Seven years later, it would be 2010. A memory from this year bubbles up here: unprompted, fully intact, impossible to shake.

We are standing in the living room of our Philadelphia suburban home — a far cry from our childhood by the ocean. I have just recently turned thirteen, while Kait is a few months away from her high school graduation. I can see the light yellow walls, creamy and smooth like the last lick of sunshine before it fades. The French-printed, deep sofa, with curved arms. The white crown molding. The hardwood floors.

Mom asks me if I'd like to "run an errand with her," and I always say yes, because I like the quiet of driving together. The calm. The peace.

"Remember this color in your head, okay?" she tells me.

I trace small squares of fabric and paint samples, flipping through the tiny booklets she borrows from stores, relishing in the minute difference of one shade versus another.

Though our mom loves to decorate, to fix up each new home, that isn't my strength. Imagining where certain pieces should go and how a room should all come together is an impossible task for me. It defies comprehension. But color — color I can memorize, color I can carry in my mind to paint stores, find the nearest match, and coordinate how each would flow into the next. Color stuck. Color was simple.

I choose the shade of the living room wall. I choose the color of almost every wall in the house. I predicted how it will look next to the plates hanging on the white built-in cabinet. I know how it will complement the grain of the wood bar in the corner and the marble of the kitchen counter.

In my memory, we are standing there, I am leaning against the arm of the sofa, Kait is by the door, our mom by the white bookshelf on the wall, filled with pottery. My sister has just teased me, made fun of my appearance or my outfit or the way my hair has fallen on that particular day.

"You should be nicer to your sister," our mom tells Kait. "She worships you, you know."

I roll my eyes, tuck hair behind my ears. My sister is a woman now, mature and unattainable in my eyes and a seemingly different person from the doting companion I knew in my childhood. We are no longer little girls, bound together by dress-up games and shared rituals. In the trials of adolescence, we have grown more competitive, combative, and my sister's behavior has transformed from amusingly rebellious to something scarier, more out of control.

When she hears our mom's rebuke, Kait scoffs. Her hip juts out from her tall frame. She runs her elegant hands in the air in a gesture of exasperation.

"She does not! She's a jerk to me, too!"

"All she does is talk about how much she looks up to you, how beautiful you are. How she wishes she could look like you," Mom tries to plead with her.

I look away, indignant. I imagine what they see when they look at me: pale skin dotted with red bumps I have tried and failed to cover with makeup a shade too orange for my complexion.

"Look, I can count the constellations!" Kait has frequently said to me, drawing a line with her pointer finger from one blemish to the next. I whack her hand away in frustration.

My nose with the bump on the bridge — a trait passed down from our Irish side.

It's so spooky living with a witch, Kait teases me, flicking the angry red ridge.

The comments become so infuriating, so seductively poisonous, I spend hours in front of our bathroom mirror, twisting until I can see my profile and hiding the bump with my thumb — inventing a new, clean slope. In the right light, I think I almost look like Kait.

"But who cares if I'm pretty?" Kait shouts. "Can't she say something else? That I'm smart, funny, interesting?"

The memory cuts off there, ends prematurely. The tape goes blank.

I feel a blanket of shame then and now. The horror of inexpression. Words left unsaid.

"Who cares if I'm pretty?"

Had I been objectifying Kait? Am I still doing it now, when she's gone?

Why hadn't I been clearer how much I loved all those other qualities, too — her imagination, her whim, her adventurous nature, her humor, her uncanny, almost supernatural instincts? That time she stood up in a concert hall and pretended to play the violin, mimicking the slow sway of the bow up and down while we whisper-shouted, *"Kait!" "Kait, stop!"* unable to conceal our muffled laughter. How she could glance at the back of a car and arrange our luggage with supernatural ease, arranging them efficiently like the levels of Tetris she conquered on long car rides. Us in the backseat, me leaning my head toward hers so I could watch the rectangles fall into position, the explosive reward of witnessing the game end, the pieces satisfyingly clicking into place.

A girl from her high school tracked me down on Facebook years after their graduation just to tell me that when the other girls were mean to her, my sister was always kind. "She was nothing but great energy," the girl shared with me. "Good soul." That was Kait. She was hilarious, beautiful, fun, but she was so much more than that. She was so much more.

Our age gap meant my sister was often more a parental figure than a peer. She knew everything before I did — the secret of the Easter Bunny, Santa Claus, the Tooth Fairy — but she continued the myth for me, continued to wait up, put out the milk and cookies, scatter half-bitten carrots in our grandparents' backyard for the reindeer. She acted as surprised as I did when she found Santa's ripped button in the fireplace, or a postcard from the Tooth Fairy by my bedside table.

In 2002, right before Christmas, Kait confessed to our parents that she no longer believed in Santa. She was ten, she knew better. Yet, just as we were leaving for our grandparents' home, my father realized he forgot something and ran back into the house. On the table, he discovered a letter addressed to Santa.

"Dear Santa," it read. "Since you see me when I'm sleeping & know when I'm awake. And you know if I've been bad or good. So, then you know for goodness sake, that I have tried but did not succeed in being good."

Kait drew bells in the four corners of the page with confident, crisp lines. Her script was round and plump — her *d*'s curling inward as they always did, as I tried and failed to imitate in my own writing.

"Sorry about my grades, didn't mean to let you or my parents down. So what I want for Christmas is some pills that make you smarter + some magical dust to make me nicer."

"No coal, please (If I do, my sis should have some too!) Just Kidding! ½ way," Kait wrote, bargaining her presents for my own.

"Love + lots of it!" she signed it, and then: "P.S. And yes I am a believer!"

In the word "believer" the *e* is missing, making it read "beliver."

Two years later, on a different Christmas Eve, Kait and I, twelve and seven, respectively, were lying on the pull-out couch in my grandparents' guest room, once our mom's childhood bedroom, unable to sleep. The warm, soft glow of a nightlight in the corner cast over our features like a buttercup held below a chin.

"Do you think Santa's going to come?" I asked in a small whisper.

I worried I hadn't been good enough. How embarrassing it would be to arrive next to the tree in the morning and find no presents, like being stood up for a date.

"I think I just saw him!" Kait turned to me in the darkness of the room, laying her head on her pillow and facing my body. Her eyes glowed with mischief.

I bolted out of bed, letting the thin cotton sheet fall from my shoulders and squinting from the window at the stars that dusted the sky and the white snow that gleamed with the moon's reflection.

"I saw Rudolph's nose peeking in our window. He winked at me!"

"Wow," I sighed in awe.

I ran to the windowsill, craning my neck and searching for the red blink of a sled in the open air. I barely slept that night. It was the best Christmas ever.

The lies were so convincing, at times Mom questioned if Kait believed them herself. Was she simply a good sister, or was there something more confusing at play? Some twisting of reality? Had she deluded herself in her act of persuading me?

Our mom shared a series of photos with me recently. In them, Kait is three or four, her little feet in cozy pink pajamas and a big oversize sweatshirt, sitting on the carpeted stairs surrounded by rows of stuffed animals. She has set them in orderly lines, carefully placing herself between a bear and a lion. She wraps a blanket over her legs in one, sits politely in the next, tiny hands neatly nestled in her lap. In the last picture, with typical Kait sass, she has one leg laid flat, her face crumpled in a giggle.

"Can you see me?" she had asked Mom the moment the camera clicked. "Can you tell which is me?"

I laughed so hard when I heard the story that I cried. I was twenty-two years old, the age my sister was when she disappeared from us, and still learning about her in flashes of retrospect. The laughs became a steady flow of tears. It was her little voice, her little legs. The innocence of the question. The idea that she could blend in. She has never blended in.

But I hadn't told her this. Instead, I called her pretty.

And now, dear reader, I am doing the same to you. I am describing the precise color of her eyes, the color I could carry with me and paint the walls with. I am failing her still, all over again. I am viewing her through the hero-worship lens of a little sister — the way I always have. I'm telling you of our childhood by the beach, of mirrors breaking and superstitions and a sacred fairytale world that is more folklore than memory by this point. I am failing to remember what needs to be remembered. Failing to capture what needs to be captured.

Three

There's an old sailing hymn I learned from living near the ocean:
"Red sky at night, sailors' delight.
Red sky at morning, sailors' warning."
The rhyme was used for two millennia to predict weather patterns. When the morning holds an orange glow, there's a high air pressure trapping dust and scattering the blue light of the sun. High pressure indicates good weather, so when the sunrise is red, good weather has already passed and is moving east. This means rain is on its way.

As I try to piece together the past, make some meaning from it, I see my sister in the light of a red morning sky: the beauty and vibrancy of her childhood a harbinger of the storm that was to come, as if light that bright is destined to bring rain eventually.

The line is thin and narrow — the signs so hidden in normality, they're impossible to detect until you take a step back. That's the problem: Life only begins to make sense retroactively. Like any good narrative, the foreshadowing is there, hidden in plain sight but inaccessible when you need it the most.

While I used to believe my sister's erratic behavior emerged dramatic and sudden — inexplicable and without reason or cause, our mom explained signs of a burgeoning behavioral issue I never saw myself.

According to her, Kait was six when she fired her first babysitter.

Mom arrived home to find the babysitter sitting outside on the stoop of our porch — the children she was responsible for nowhere in sight.

When asked what happened, the babysitter replied simply: "Kait fired me."

My sister knew which details to tell, or invent, to eventually get her way: stories of babysitters rummaging through the fridge, dirtying up the sofa, inviting boyfriends over. Over the course of the next few years, other babysitters would be dismissed with a wave of Kait's little hand, until eventually, our mom gave up on hiring anyone at all, choosing instead to stay home with us. She suspected this kind of tyranny was unusual behavior from a small child, but Kait was her first kid, and she didn't know what signs to look out for yet — which ones pointed to something truly wrong.

When Kait was in kindergarten, a boy in her class bit her. In retaliation, she pushed him down at recess. She pleaded self-defense, but by the time she was called into the principal's office, her bite mark had dissolved into a light indent. Always a problem solver, Kait excused herself to the bathroom, biting her young skin hard enough to leave a bruise before returning, tears glistening. Mom looked at the strange double set of teeth marks with horror, realizing for the first time that her daughter's word may not be as ironclad as she once thought.

Even in Marblehead, my idealized, perfect Marblehead, the peak of our family's function, our mom had a flower service on speed dial. When Kait's friends' parents called, as they often would to complain about her most recent fight with their children, Mom had the solution ready, the apology notes sent in a matter of minutes.

For Kait, boundaries and rules were soft, subtle guidelines that demanded pushing. For me, they were walls — ten-foot-tall concrete barriers requiring a two-foot radius before approaching. She used to compare our relationship to the movie *Uptown Girls*.

The 2003 comedic drama features the late Brittany Murphy as a carefree party girl, living in New York City on a trust fund from her rock star father, and Dakota Fanning as a perfectionistic eight-year-old coming to terms with her own distant father's terminal illness. Murphy's character tries to shake some fun into Fanning's life, while the little girl persuades the older to grow up. The dynamic, the clash, the role reversal is fun to watch, but it's also heartbreaking. Their worlds are spinning out of control like the teacup ride they frequent at Coney Island. One leans in to the whirl, the other seeks to control it.

"Obviously, I'm Brittany Murphy and you're the uptight little girl," Kait said.

The first time I watched the movie, I cried because it was good and sad in its own right. The second time I watched it, I cried because of how right Kait was.

As far as I know, my sister's childhood was not fraught with trauma. As far as I know, it was as peaceful as my own. Although there may be elements of mental illness in the complicated branches of our family tree, they were not immediately clear or half as severe as the issues Kait would develop in later years. This seems to be the path mental illness takes: zigzagging and inconclusive. The scratchy line of an Etch A Sketch, disappearing when you shake it.

As I write this, I wonder sometimes if others will see the early instances of rebellion as proof of my sister's genetic predisposition to mental illness. Will it seem obvious, inevitable? Will it separate her from the rest of the "normal" world — *other* her? That wasn't me, they may think, that won't be my kids. We use any deceptive logic to convince ourselves we're safe from grief.

"Protective factors" is one of those vague, blanket psychology terms that conveys everything and nothing at once. It means to distinguish the qualities that cushion against developing a mental health crisis: self-esteem, cognitive ability, familial support, social capacity, supportive parenting. Every box is checked for Kait: You couldn't find a smarter, more confident, beloved child. Sometimes the red morning sky, the perfect storm, comes out of nowhere, sometimes the signs reveal themselves too late.

Since we lost my sister, my mom and I have talked a lot more about my childhood. She tells me that from the day Kait was born, she worried about her constantly in a way she never did about me. Disastrous scenarios flooded her brain: turning around in a department store to discover Kait missing, searching beneath racks of clothing only to come up empty-handed, panic ballooning higher and higher in her chest. The concerns were always external fears — some tragic freak accident befalling my sister — but she never had to worry about my sister as a person. Kait had "it," that internal spark that would always propel her forward: tenaciousness, determination, individuality. If anyone could tackle the difficulties of life, it was Kait.

Mom wondered if there was something more to her fears than the usual anxieties of a new mother, if there was something more, some intuition warning her about unforeseen danger. Now it's clear that perhaps we should have been more worried about what was happening internally to Kait — what mix of neurochemicals was being concocted in her brain, what that determination and impulsivity would develop into later.

I suppose that if I chose to I could look back on my sister as a girl and see the signs and symptoms peek through the veil of time. I could look back and see illness, the dawning of madness. I could see what was to come — hospitals, the ugly dim of a psychiatric unit, the cracked kitchen floors of a group home, the sun rising in soft oranges, pinks, reds — still light, but with the ache of a warning on the horizon.

But ultimately, I see the audacity of Kait's spirit instead — how our mom tells me that the first time my sister saw another child her age, she stood in her stroller with wide eyes, her binky falling from her mouth in shock. *He's little like me*, she said. How girls and boys flocked behind her, following her around playgrounds and teams, attracted to that indelible quality of self-assurance. She refused to wear dresses most of the time, because she wanted more flexibility to run and play and jump, but when she went to the grocery store, she insisted on wearing her best princess dress, all ruffles and glitz. She was always trying to give her toys away, wanting to share with anyone and everyone she knew. She changed her name in kindergarten. Kaitlyn became Kait — a simple chopping of letters, a reordering of identity. An assertion of self.

My sister was exuberantly bright. Children immediately liked her. People were drawn to her. I was drawn to her. At her best, she was pure light. Many laugh from the head with an airy puff, but Kait's laugh began in the core of her stomach, or maybe even from the ground itself, the earth's molten middle. It erupted from her, loud and fearless and unapologetic.

She was funny in a way that suggests a complete detachment from social care. She used different voices for different characters, made songs out of phrases, stuck her head out of a car window to yell, "Hey, Big-head!" at a friend. Kait was confident and hilarious and at least five years ahead of every trend. She wore fringed purses, cropped tie-dye T-shirts, pink or purple shoes, and colored sunglasses before they came back in trend, and then as soon as they did, she dropped them for something more radical. Once a style made its way into the glossy pages of a magazine spread, Kait was already above it, beyond it.

At restaurants, she rarely ventured beyond the kids' menu, even at twenty-one, but she had no qualms ordering a beer to wash the discounted burger down. I tried mussels and clams when I was old enough to swallow, because I liked the shock and attention it garnered from the adults around me. Kait continued eating her mozzarella sticks in the corner, indifferent to the show, above the public display. She liked what she liked, and even the approval of others was not enough to change this.

In every way beyond her appetite, she was curious and adventurous, nearly to a fault. One winter when she was twelve, Kait stuck her tongue to a frozen flagpole. We had just watched *A Christmas Story*, as we did every Christmas, and she wanted to make everyone laugh by pretending to recreate the scene — that was her role in our extended family, to make us laugh. But when she tried to pull away from the pole, she realized that her tongue really *was* stuck. Our parents panicked, pouring steaming hot chocolate where her tongue met the metal, leaving splashes of brown in the white snow. When she finally wiggled it free, her taste buds were numb and useless for days.

Every time I saw a snowy flagpole that year, I considered copying Kait. Not because I hadn't learned from her experience, but because I so acutely wanted to replicate it for myself — taste the cold metal and frozen buds, feel her exact feeling, relate to her on every level.

She radiated joy, even in the silliest of ways. Sometimes she wanted ridiculous, impractical items like a pair of rainbow moon boots — not because everyone else was wearing them but precisely because no one was. It seems an obvious, simple trait, but how rare such a quality really is: to want something simply to want it. Not to imitate, not to fit in, but to start something all your own.

Some nights Kait's hair was perfectly curled or straightened, the blond locks flowing down her shoulders. Other nights, her hair was wild and curly, pulled back carelessly into a ponytail. The event didn't matter, only her mood.

When our parents bought us ski jackets one winter, I stood in the aisle for several minutes, considering the practicality of the white versus black down. White was a better color for the ski pants I already owned, but black would stay clean longer.

Kait grabbed a puffy Hawaiian jacket from the corner shelf. Modeling it between the wood-paneled aisles, putting on the careful gait of a fashion walk. It had a bright orange neck that flowed into the pink image of a star surrounded by turquoise flowers like a giant bull's-eye.

"It's perfect!" she decided upon seeing her reflection.

"How about I get the white, you get the black, and we can share?" Mom suggested to me kindly.

As a small child, my sister would sit in our mom's car in the front seat, buckled into her carseat (before there were safety regulations prohibiting this), and babble until the babbling transformed to words and the words transformed to full sentences. She was into everything, eager to learn, absorbing the world like a sponge. Driving around town, she and our mom would chat about different topics, and sometimes, in certain moments

—listening to Kait's uncanny observations—Mom almost forgot she was with a child.

When our mom was pregnant with me and Kait was around five years old, our family went to Disney World. Mom wanted Kait to experience the park before she had a baby sister in the way, or she was too old and the magic was lost—they wanted to catch that last afternoon summer light before the autumn of innocence arrived. Kait sat on my father's shoulders, calling after the cast members parading as her favorite characters.

"Minnie!" she shouted hysterically, like a teenager at a boy-band concert. "Minnie, look at me! Minnie, look. At. ME." Kait always wanted to be seen.

But a few moments later, when the character turned around, my sister's face drained of color, contorting and pasty white. "Mom," she whispered in horror. "There are *zippers*."

Is it strange such a thought had not occurred to our mom before—that Kait would not automatically understand that the costumed characters were merely pretending, masquerading? My sister was so precocious, sharp, mature, Mom assumed such an innocent thought was beyond her. This was Kait in a nutshell: ahead of her times, quick, and then suddenly, ingenuous—disarmingly childlike.

I think of a picture of Kait I saved on my computer's desktop. It was taken two years before my birth, "before my time," as our mom would put it. Kait is four. She's giggling, and her delicate shoulders in her pink fleece are scrunched to her neck. Her green eyes are squinted and mischievous.

I remember her like this. Joyful, alive. Achingly *alive*.

Phase II, Acute

Green

Four

We moved to the city of Philadelphia in 2003, when I was entering first grade and my sister was going into the seventh grade.

Our father was frequently away on business trips, designing and implementing fiber-optic networks in new countries and regions. It was the age of the dot-com bubble, between the late '90s and early 2000s. People were using the internet with increasing frequency, and the stocks boomed with the flux. The opportunities came fast and didn't stay long. If you blinked, you could miss it, so — as we'd done a few times before, and would do again later — when my father received a new job offer that he couldn't resist, he and my mom seized the opportunity, packing us up and leaving Marblehead behind.

My father began working in the tech industry back when it was called the World Wide Web and filled with blocky text and glitchy web pages. I could never quite determine what exactly he did at work. All I understood was that he was someone behind the ideas of the internet, the very concept. While the rest of us only used technology, applied it, he understood it. Every television in our home was self-rigged by his own design, so when one broke or lost the signal, we were helpless without him. No manual was of use. He wore the standard tech uniform: a graphic T-shirt under blazers and blue jeans. As a toddler, my sister stuck her favorite Barbie stickers all over the white bulky base of the computer in his office, and they remained there for as long as he had it. Something in him (What was it? Sentimentality? Nostalgia?) prevented him from removing them.

Our new home in Philly was a brick townhouse in a residential neighborhood of the bustling, winding downtown Center City. I was six, and I learned to do cartwheels on the rough sidewalks, avoiding the rubbery gray spots of melted gum, first with two arms, then with one. Kait or Mom would spot me, guiding my legs over my head and planting them firmly on the ground.

We attended the same Quaker school that year, near the Benjamin Franklin Parkway and within walking distance from our home. Every Wednesday and Thursday, we had "Meetings for Worship," similar in some ways to a Christian church service. Much of the details of this time escape me, but I will never forget that building: its historic tilt, brick with white detailing, a sense of slipping out of time and back to America's roots — if you listened closely, it was almost as if you could hear the ring of the Liberty Bell, the creak of its fracture.

When we walked from our classrooms to the house, I searched for Kait's face in the crowd. I stared at the back of bobbing heads, looking for her telltale wavy hair, listening for her laugh. The moment I spotted her, my chest surged with pride. That was my sister, I thought. That tall, beautiful girl, that's my sister. When she or her friends waved at me, I felt I had done everything in the universe right.

I loved that school. There was a plastic treehouse in my classroom with books hidden in the alcove, and a field on top of the building's roof for gym class. There were long, winding staircases and a pool two floors deep in the ground. I liked life in the city, but Kait didn't. We had moved four or so times before Marblehead, and for Kait, each new school was growing harder to keep up with. I was too young for any change to matter, too innocent for it to make an impression. My life was a tiny universe consisting of my immediate family, but Kait was older, more aware. She had to redefine herself in a sea of new faces with each move.

After all, how many times did my sister stand in front of a classroom and introduce herself to a room of strangers? How many times did she size up the students before her, decide who were the bullies and the victims, the mean girls and the boys who stuck pencils up their noses?

How many recesses did she stare at the asphalt and quickly scout out which of her classmates was the easiest to approach? Did it matter? At one school, was she one version of herself, and at the next, another? When the present unfolds like a slap, these are the questions you return to as prayer. *What went wrong? Could we have stopped it?*

In seventh grade, groups were already formed, lines drawn and protected. Kait was no wallflower — she was bold, and reckless, and brave — but the move was hard. It was always hard. And the change was drastic: from the ocean to a concrete arena. The rules were different.

My sister was reaching an age I could no longer relate to. She was gradually shutting me out more. We were growing apart in small and then large ways. In Marblehead, I had been permitted to tag along, never pushed away — she always seemed proud to have her little sister around.

There's a polaroid of us from her tenth birthday party, taken just two years prior to our move to Philly. Kait stands in front of a white car with her friends — nineties fashion in full effect: baggy overalls, oversize sweatshirts, headbands that match the exact shade of the jacket. An idyllic wooden suburban home watches over in the background with black shutters and white clapboards. My carseat is large and bulky. It requires two spots in the car. In order to fit it, Kait has to invite one fewer friend.

She does so willingly, eagerly. *Of course* I am invited. *Of course* she wants her little sister there. The party is held at a nail salon, and there are more pictures here. Me, five years old, my tiny leg resting a foot above the pedicure basin. I look at the big girls around me, with their trendy outfits and long hair. I understand, even then, even as a preschooler, how lucky I am.

By the time we moved to Philly, though, this status quo was changing, shifting the way all relationships do in early adolescence. She was shedding me, outgrowing me. I couldn't accompany her to middle school dances. I couldn't enter her room when her friends were over. I couldn't fathom what bras were and what it meant when she told me I would someday need one too. There were so many objects and ideas I would need or understand "someday." I liked Build-A-Bear and Webkinz and the Disney Channel. Kait was turning thirteen. Girls in her grade were getting their periods, swapping stories in the hallway of first kisses and comparing bases like in a sports game. I took to carrying candy in my dress pockets, handing them out in trade for friendship — a barter system of socialization. The calculus of making new friends in adolescence was so much less simple for Kait.

That year my sister dressed as "Mom's Worst Nightmare" for Halloween.

She adorned her girlish, preteen features with black lipstick and dark eyeliner. Her dirty-blond hair was tied in a loose ponytail with tendrils framing her face. She wore a black graphic tank-top over a baby blue short-sleeved shirt. A green tie extended from her neck to her navel. She had on three layers of pants — long gray socks, cheetah-print pajamas, one of my pink dresses worn as a skirt — and a flowered apron over them. She slipped into our mom's black-heeled booties.

The costume was an act of defiance. Kait was prohibited from roaming the streets of Philly without parental supervision. Instead, she was stuck with us for the holiday, left to walk her baby sister around the city, holding an empty pillowcase before us as an offering. She responded to the news with typical teenage grumpiness: long sighs and exaggerated eye rolls. The decision thrilled me, of course: As usual, nothing made me prouder than being seen in public with Kait.

I was Dorothy from *The Wizard of Oz*. My blond hair was pulled into short braids and my checkered blue picnic dress sparkled against the red of my heels. I carried a stuffed dog in a woven basket. My socks were the same brand I wore every day: white and ankle height with frilly ruffles. I wasn't aware of it at the time, but looking back I can only imagine what a strikingly awkward pair we must have been, the difference between our ages ever more apparent as she grew further out of reach.

In some ways, you can see the childlike mischief, the charm, the hilarity of Kait's stunts growing into something more during these years, something dangerous, taking on a life of its own. But in my parents' minds, in all of our minds, Kait was a *good* kid. Sure, she was in occasional trouble, but it was just normal kid stuff. It was getting into petty disagreements with girls in her classes, not hallucinations and paranoia. It was not *disease*, not *illness*. Just teenage rebelliousness. Besides, everything about mental illness was, and largely remains, a hushed whisper. A label that terrifies more often than it liberates.

Our family moved to Philadelphia for my father's tech job the same year MySpace was created, and my sister immediately jumped on board. She used social media with a reckless abandon indicative of an era before college admittance scandals and Edward Snowden: before ad-tech and government surveillance and the word "influencer" was added to résumés. Because of this, there's a certain raw authenticity to her online presence that's lacking in today's overtly curated culture. Looking at it now feels almost invasive: I'm walking into an inner world that was denied to me at the time.

On the profile, she's frozen in time, posing for a selfie with friends, lips jutted in a pout. Straighteners appear from one frame to the next until her curls are pin straight. You can almost smell the rubber burn of melted hair.

There are jean skirts and lip-gloss and oversize tank-tops that flow just a little too much. There are long necklaces looped twice, and over-plucked eyebrows. And above all else, an almost palpable feeling of *wanting* emanates from the photos. A need to be known and understood. A simultaneous desire to fit in and be recognized for your own distinct brand of individuality. Like everyone else but *just* different enough to be interesting.

When I was thirteen, I stood in front of similar mirrors and used similar cameras — the kind with flashes that take up half of the frame, largely obscuring your face. I too burnt my hair with a straightener in my friend's bedroom, getting ready for a bar mitzvah. I tried on different personalities and wardrobes like a makeover montage in a nineties tween movie. Decided to be a skater girl one day, bought a skateboard, fell once, skinned my knees raw, abandoned it the next day. Went to the mall with friends, wandered around Juicy Couture until an employee kicked us out. I sprayed myself with free samples of Sephora perfume until my mom complained I was giving her a headache. Like Kait, I experimented with bands of dark eyeliner — coating my waterline until I accidentally poked my eye, watching the black bleed into the white of my cornea.

I had gone through this very same phase, itchy with anticipation to grow into who you believe society wants you to be. We squeezed our innards to fit the same mold that every teenage girl in America at some point tries on. Like Cinderella's stepsisters shoving their swollen feet into the glass slipper, we made all of the same blunders, only years apart. When Kait was thirteen, she was impossibly cool to me: terribly old and mature and unique and perfect, but in reality she had been as lost as I would be at her age — as anyone and everyone is at thirteen. We had both dealt with mean girls, bad hair decisions, precocious boys, and demanding teachers. We had both been searching for meaning, for definition and identity. I can't help but search the past for signs, but it all looks so normal: the everyday growing pains that we all experience at this age.

I wish I could hug a younger version of myself and tell her that any perceived slight by Kait is unintentional: She was only trying to discover who she is. She was walking the first walk of adulthood with shaky legs, and she couldn't have her little sister trailing after her wherever she went. I wish I could hug this younger version of Kait and tell her it's all going to be okay, too. Tell her she'll figure it out, grow into herself, become the person she's meant to be, but then, wouldn't that be a lie?

At thirteen, the cusp of adolescence, something was beginning to transform in my sister; a barely detectable ignition that sparked in the core of her being and snaked its way into every aspect of our lives. Even so, my big sister, the one who had so carefully cared for me throughout my childhood, was still there, at least sometimes. She still let me sleep in her bed, crawling up beside her and listening to the sound of the traffic outside her bedroom window. She still let me watch television shows with her in our converted attic. I was exposed to every MTV reality show that aired in the early 2000s: *Next, Parental Control, Room Raiders.* We watched *Cribs* and *Entourage* and music videos explicitly too old for me. "This is what it is to be cool" was the hidden thread in Kait's education of me.

Sitting on fluffy chairs, flipping through channels, we played a game called "Next One's You." We took turns scrolling through shows and commercials before abruptly stopping and announcing, "The next thing on the screen is you." A zoomed-in image of a cartoon character's goofy expression. A small dog barking at the screen. A commercial for adult diapers or herpes cream.

We laughed so hard we cried, our stomachs sore from the effort, leaving us cramped and exhausted. At the time, the idea of being anyone other than ourselves was still absurdly hilarious.

Realizing that so many of our superstitions were common childhood games, I've tried Googling this TV game since, typing variations in Reddit forums.

First, "Next one's you, television game."

And then, "Television game where you wait for a person to appear on screen."

Even, "Scrolling through channels game."

I have never found a trace of it anywhere. Only now do I realize that we invented it: one of those sibling rituals as irreplaceable as every aspect of growing up together under one roof, one experience of coming to know the world. A bond impossible to replicate.

When I broke my arm that year, Kait eagerly filled the role of caregiver.

A windstorm hit the city without advance warning. The window of Kait's seventh grade classroom was shattered. The students hid under their desks to escape the shards of glass blowing across the room. My class was outside during the storm, playing on the jungle gym. I liked to do flips on the highest bars I could find, bend myself in the crevices of the monkey bars or hang upside down by the slide. I wore pink slip-on shoes, and they were tucked into the cramped spaces of a tall, corkscrew-shaped metal climber. When the wind hit, it blew me out of the bubble-gum shoes and swept me to the ground. I landed on my left elbow, shattering the bone.

I remember very little of the moments preceding it, but I can recollect the fall itself; looking up at the sky, seeing a flash of color still tucked into the metal bars and thinking, *I'm falling*. It makes me wonder now about the falls that were to come: Was there space then, too? Time to make peace or regret?

I knew immediately upon impact that something was broken. My sister was summoned to sit with me in the school nurse's office, and as soon as she saw me there, tears streaming down my face, cradling my arm, she rushed to my side. She spent the next hour comforting me as we drove to the emergency room. She sat in the backseat, forgoing her usual passenger seat. She brushed my hair, patted my shoulders. Despite the pain, I was thrilled to have her attention again, be her little doll, her baby sister. In the moment, it didn't matter that I would never again in my life do cartwheels on the street, or round-offs, or front walk-overs. All that mattered was that Kait was acting like Kait again.

And yet, these flickers of my sister's return never lasted forever.

That year, when my sister was thirteen, our mom was called in to the principal's office on more than one occasion to discuss her most recent spectacle. It was a miracle in itself, how expertly she managed to entangle herself in the pivotal drama of the day. Though being the new girl at thirteen is no easy task, Kait weaved her way into the focal point of her new social scene, for better or worse. That was her way — audacious, gutsy, a dash of trouble.

The nature of these fights was at least partially influenced by Kait's embrace of confrontation: her desire and ability to control those around her. The fights were a product of her general disposition, but they were also within the confines of everyday drama — the kind of arguments a thirteen-year-old gets into, about boys, clothes, cliques. They were not yet reason for concern. Not yet what they would become. Perhaps if I, the uptight rule follower, had been born first, my parents might have considered her behavior more worrisome, but she was the first teenager they had ever raised. How were they to know?

After a few months, we were ultimately asked to leave the school. Kait was fighting with the daughter of a powerful Philadelphia family, associated with an equally powerful and beloved Philadelphia sports team. It soon became a matter of them versus us. One had to go, and we were the obvious answer. My parents were already planning to eventually move to the suburbs, so that's exactly what we did.

It's one of those moments you look upon in retrospect and see as a milestone in the story, a sudden break, the earth's crust unsettling from its shelf. But at the time, my parents weren't sure how seriously to take it. My father didn't believe in therapy; still, they took my sister to a doctor just in case. The child psychologist evaluated her under careful scrutiny before proclaiming Kait a healthy and well-adjusted preteen. And like that, the question was resolved and we moved on. Any conversation around a diagnosis was dismissed.

This was also the year that I invented my first superstition independent of Kait.

On my seventh birthday, blowing out candles on a cake with frosting doled out in thick white waves before me, I made a wish that I would come to repeat every birthday until my seventeenth.

"I wish my dreams come true, my family is healthy, and *my sister gets better.*"

I remember the wish, though not exactly what prompted it. While we were still in a state of relative wellness, in my seven-year-old mind, there was already an issue to "get better" from. Despite my parents' efforts to shield me, I had detected something amiss in our family dynamic, processed the trouble Kait was getting into, the ways she had withdrawn from me already.

Helpless to make a change, I resorted to the only solution I knew: superstitions. I vowed to repeat this same wish whenever I saw the clock strike 11:11, when I blew out a candle or broke the brittle snap of a wishbone.

"I wish my sister gets better."

It became a mantra, a reflex.

Twice a day I closed my eyes tight, squeezing them shut to block out distraction. I let my fingers press into my palms, crossed my middle finger over my pointer.

I wish my sister gets better.

Five

I think about the concept of inevitability a lot.

Our mom's favorite subject has always been history, and her favorite books historical fiction. Once, while struggling with an elementary school assignment, I told her that I didn't see the point in history. "Why look back?" I asked.

We were sitting on her bed after school, the four carved wooden posters looming over us, watchful gods. I'll never forget the way that she looked at me, carefully evaluating something in my features. "We look back so we can learn from our mistakes," Mom told me then, emphasizing the phrase, lodging the lesson in my brain. *We look back on the past to learn from our mistakes.*

And here I still am so many years later, doing just that — looking out for a red sky.

Many of America's Founding Fathers, including Benjamin Franklin — whom our Quaker school was inspired by and who inhabits every corner of Philly — believed in an understanding of the world known as deism. The belief supposes an existence of a supreme being, a creator who invented the universe but does not interact or interfere with humankind directly: a kind of indifferent, impersonal God, often compared to a watchmaker. The way a watch requires a watchmaker to run correctly and independently, the universe requires a creator. The physical world — its rules, its molecular design — is so exact, unfolds at such a succinct rate, that it is like the mechanical perfection of a watch. Once it's set, it goes on and on without interruption. All unfolds exactly as planned.

I try to imagine a timer set at the exact moment of the Big Bang. A slender hand moving swiftly in and out of frame with the slightest twist of a knob. The universe erupting from a singularity and then expanding indefinitely. The littlest moments leading to infinite consequences. I imagine this clock as a timer, ticking away as space continues to grow: around and around and then unwinding. Every minuscule change, every penny on the ground you did or didn't pick up, every text you did or didn't send, predestined.

It's a nice idea: comforting. It lightens the blame, and when it comes to my sister, I am attracted, innately, to anything that takes away blame (even if I know nothing will ever truly eradicate it).

In Kait's early preteen years, we were on a cusp, unknown to us. Two paths were diverging before us — the one we took, filled with dissolution, and another, alternative one. Maybe if the child psychiatrist who dismissed Kait as "just fine" had a different day — if she hadn't met with a cranky patient before our session or woken up too late, missing the beep of her alarm clock, spilling coffee on her new blouse — she would've seen a sign, given us something to treat. Maybe if Kait hadn't gotten into a fight with that girl from her class, we would've stayed in the Philly school district. Maybe if I had read one sentence of one textbook sooner, I would've recognized the symptoms before it was too late. Maybe one *singular* difference could've shifted the whole narrative. After all, sometimes a watch malfunctions. Sometimes the maker needs to intervene.

In Kurt Vonnegut's *Slaughterhouse-Five*, we are introduced to the time-traveling Tralfamadorians. For them, one moment does not precede another. All is laid before as a "stretch of the Rocky Mountains." Every instant is permanent, but they're able to move between points, focus on whatever interests them, live in any moment they choose. Death is but another "state," unavoidable but temporary, like a papercut. Life is an endless recycling of old material.

So perhaps the past is fixed, unchangeable, inevitable. Perhaps if you were to return, you'd repeat all of the same mistakes. Perhaps there never was anything we could do to fix the situation. We were destined, designed to fall apart.

Even so, if you gave me the chance to go back and try to fix things, knowing change may well be impossible — knowing I could end up continuously reliving the worst moments of my life and undoing the best — I know I'd take it. I'd still try.

Six

After Kait was asked to leave the Quaker school, we moved to what's commonly referred to as the Main Line: the western outskirts of Philadelphia named after the four-track railroad that divides the area. Kait began eighth grade at yet another new school, while I entered the second grade. Our new street was near Villanova University and had old, looming trees dotting the backyards.

We moved from our tiny blue house by the water of Marblehead to the crowded, brimming brownstones of Philly, and now to a suburban oasis of green. Like an artist moving through his stylistic periods, we were in our green phase. *Everything* green. The carefully manicured lawns that led to old stone houses. The pine needles that fell over everything like confetti. Moss on tree trunks, and signs that read DEER CROSSING.

Near the water, vegetation doesn't grow like this. The wind blows the smaller plants, brushing them with sand, and curls the branches of the more resilient ones, rendering them horizontal. Living by the water, everything is blue. Living in the city, everything was brick and concrete. But here, in the suburbs, our world was distinctly green.

I had never before seen so many trees, so many long, sprawling lawns with built-in sprinklers, walking trails, and pristine college campuses. I was amazed by the vibrancy of it all, the strength of the hue, the variety of life hidden in the bushes. I loved how rooted everything was — solid and permanent.

The rest of my family preferred the openness of rocky beaches and sand dunes to the richness of dirt and the bark of trees. They wished to go back into the blue, back to the sand, back to before.

The move to the Main Line was, in retrospect, one of the hardest moves we made as kids. In the new public school district, both of us fell behind, slightly and in divergent ways. Kids in this town grew up faster than we were accustomed to. The game was different, the stakes higher. We overcompensated in our own ways.

I reacted to being behind in the curriculum by pulling the biggest books from the shelf during quiet reading time, liking the thick weight on my lap. I flipped through pages, jumping from one passage to the next, barely comprehending the text but finding thrill in the rustle of paper, the satisfaction of watching the bookmark's steady progression, chunk by chunk. I hung the arbitrary "reading awards" in my room, plastic gold medals banging against each other like a wind chime — the closest I ever came to earning a sports trophy.

Slowly, I began to form an identity distinct from my sister. I discovered that the shy, quiet girl so loved she didn't have to speak had a few things to say. I fell in love with stories and storytelling, finding an openness and vulnerability on the page that was harder to come by in real life. There was magic there — in the worlds captured by the shape of letters, in the human connection of bridged years and shared souls. In life, I could never live up to the exuberance of Kait's personality, but with writing, I found myself part of something universal and yet also all my own.

I began crafting miniature books out of construction paper, binding them with yarn. There are drawers and boxes filled with these creations. Sometimes, if I was lucky enough, my mom would laminate the covers, and it felt so official — I could almost imagine my words resting on a bookcase. The thought made me dizzy with joy.

Kait in turn handled the transition differently, partying more, harder than everyone else — her mischief taking on a new edge, a self-destructive quality only those close to her could recognize.

◆ ◆ ◆

There's a condition called synesthesia in which one sense is blurred into another. You see colors in musical notes. Numbers become sounds. You can taste color, or feel the heat of red. The first known case was described by John Locke about a blind man who reported he could see the color scarlet when he heard a trumpet playing.

I will never experience synesthesia itself, but I wonder if it feels a bit like these memories, which are in and of themselves a series of strung-together associations, lined before us as a narrative, and clumped together in sections of time. Kait and I had been raised by the sea, and now we were landlocked — the change seemed significant somehow, suffocating.

By the water, you can see for miles. The horizon opens up to you, allows you to imagine the world is knowable. Nothing is hidden or obscured in the openness above the flat blue waves. You can watch the water meet the line of the horizon, the universe dropping into the blue. As a child, I never worried too much about what was beneath the ocean, the world of mystery.

Blue feels like freedom to me, while green makes me think of the Amazon rainforest, where two and a half million species of insects crawl in nooks and crannies, their numbers and variety growing faster than scientists' ability to identify and name them.

Looking back on those ten years we spent in Philly, I picture Kait's mental illness as growing green, rising and twisting, morphing into something uncontrollable, dangerous. Changing faster than our ability to find the name or words for it, too. Tangled roots of a forest, confusion, branches crossing and breaking, tripping you at every turn.

Seven

As a high school freshman in our new school district, Kait fell out of her bedroom window while sneaking out to an upperclassman's party. Our home on the Main Line was Spanish style: white stucco exterior, red tiled roof. Black framing accentuated the windows like a picture frame. A sloped emerald hill and steep, cracked driveway. Occasionally, a bird or a storm would dislodge one of the terra-cotta tiles and it would land on the gray asphalt, split open like an ancient clay ruin, crumpled like crayon.

As always, Kait's bedroom shared a wall with mine, but we had long outgrown our Morse code of knocks. The older sibling, Kait laid claim to the larger of the two spaces. When my sister ran to her bedroom, whooping in victory, our mom, ever the gentle mediator, whispered in my ear with a soft smile and a wink: "Don't worry, yours has more windows, better lighting."

Even as I tried my best to make my new space my own, Kait's bedroom was the pinnacle of everything cool and teenaged. Simply to be invited in was an honor. There was a hodgepodge of collected posters, antique furniture, and vintage decorations. Marilyn Monroe winked down upon me from the wall. A band poster with its loose edges curled in one corner with poorly placed tape. Carved wood and metal crosses hung beside her bed like a morose temple — the senseless order almost sacrilegious. Anarchist. Chaotic unity. While I never bothered to change a single aspect of my room for the ten years I occupied it, Kait reordered hers constantly. It was alive, evolving and growing with her.

My sister sometimes let me in to sit on her bed and confided in me about the trouble she was in, twisting my hand until I pinky-promised not to tell our parents. Keeping her confidence was my own form of rebellion — a way of partnering with her, us against the world.

When she wanted a fake ID, she pulled me into the bathroom with her to shoot the photo. I took my job seriously, straining to hold the camera steady. I balanced on the porcelain toilet seat, stretching for the perfect angle: just the right mix of unflattering shadows and flash to properly imitate a DMV's unforgiving florescence. She believed she could make a business out of it with a little beginner-at-PhotoShop luck. (Our parents eventually discovered the scanner and laminator she purchased on eBay — and just like that, the jig was up.)

She told me about sneaking out of school to buy a lizard at PetCo and sticking it in a friend's backpack as a prank. She told me about skipping class, going into the city — an act so out of the realm of my normal, I could only envision Ferris Bueller and his parade. Kait's class was the last year in our high school with the privilege of leaving campus during free periods. By the time I entered, you were required to have a pass — from a nurse, a parent — just to exit the building at unscheduled hours. I suspected my sister's escapades had something to do with that.

Kait's bedroom had a small window that opened up to the back of the house, above the driveway, facing our garage. The room was located directly above the kitchen — the window jutted out onto the small strip of roof above our kitchen pantry's ceiling.

The night Kait snuck out, she crawled onto this peaked roof and tried to jump onto the bushes below, trusting the pile of leaves to break her fall. Her friends waited in a car by the street at the end of our long driveway. In the process of wiggling out of the window, Kait slipped. She lost her traction on the uneven tiles and tumbled to the ground.

In the years since I have learned about the relationship between concussions and mental health, this moment has taken on more significance in my mind. New research has shown that chronic traumatic encephalitis (CTE) from repeated head trauma can result in behavioral changes, including aggression, suicidal thinking, and reduced impulse control.

A 2017 piece published in the *New York Times* reported on 111 NFL players' brains examined by Dr. Anne McKee, a neuropathologist and director of the CTE Center at Boston University. Of those 111 autopsies, 110 former players had neurodegeneration associated with CTE.

How many concussions did Kait suffer from after (and including) this night? How many times did she fall off a chair or a couch or a table at a party, hitting her head and laughing off the pain? Not as many head injuries as a professional athlete might have, but maybe not a great deal less, either.

But at the time, we didn't know to ask these questions, so when Kait dusted herself off, shushing her friend to keep quiet so not to wake our sleeping parents, there were no CT scans, no warning alarms sounding.

Her bottom lip was cut, and dripping blood. The gash needed stitches and left a rough, tiny scar, but one of her friends captured the moment, and the picture remains on her Facebook page: Kait's hair wet, eyes wide and unfocused, the scarlet red weaving down her chin like a river. She's wearing a gray sweatshirt and minimal makeup. Her tan skin is fresh and dewy. Of course she didn't think to dress up for the party. Of course.

As my sister became increasingly more turbulent and temperamental, it should follow that her social life would fall into disarray too, but many of Kait's public antics were the kind praised by high school students: the type of legends that heighten rather than destroy one's popularity. She pulled off a senior prank by gluing a wooden phallus to the statue of our school mascot. She talked back to teachers, walked out of classes, wrote A-S-S-H-O-L-E on her choir teacher's chalkboard when he reprimanded her. She went to summer school to make up for her absences from class, and when our vice principal confronted Kait in the school parking lot for leaving early, grabbing her by the backpack, the zipper ripped further open, spilling bong water all over the woman's neatly pressed jacket.

Another Kait legend (cultivated by her, propagated by her) goes like this: As a senior in high school, my sister snuck into a dive bar in the small downtown area of Martha's Vineyard where we were vacationing and randomly happened to meet a celebrity several years her senior.

Amid the uneven brick sidewalks, swollen with age and heat, lush summer trees, and clapboard-covered shops, my sister recognized him immediately. His face was plastered everywhere at the time, on movie posters, magazine spreads, gossip websites. I wasn't surprised when he continued to text her for weeks. Kait was meant to brush shoulders with fame. She looked to the Marilyn Monroe poster hanging on the wall of her bedroom not as art, but as a manual for success — a guide to the future.

After her own phone was confiscated by our parents, Kait transferred the celebrity's number into my pink Razor flip phone so she could continue the conversation. Occasionally, I flipped to the screen displaying his name and number to my sixth-grade friends.

When we watched a movie with him in it, I teased, "Should I text him?"

Being related to Kait made me someone.

My sister fell in love frequently and dramatically with boys and clothes and ideas. Where I liked to weigh the pros and cons, make careful mental checklists, and wind my way to a conclusion, Kait rarely thought twice. She moved on pure instinct, and when she loved something, she loved it deeply. She *had* to have it. Those lace flare pants, that multicolored beaded purse, the boy from her calculus class. The practicality wasn't a question. She loved it, and so she wanted it. Although sometimes, once she had the object of her desire, she lost interest in it altogether — as was the case with our new puppy.

We found the dog, a small, frightful Maltese who we later nicknamed Lilly from Philly, at one of those horrific mall pet stores, shaking in her cage. She had crooked teeth and was deemed unsuitable for breeding or competing in any kind of dog show. For that terrible, superficial reason alone, the puppy was in the process of being continually marked down, the sticker price falling lower and lower — the number crossed out with a red marker and then recalculated in the corner. My sister cried when she saw her defenseless, nervous body, and the sight stoked some primal instinct in her. The store's next step was to euthanize the poor dog — Kait decided that we had to take her home.

My sister pulled me aside outside the store and said, "You have to beg Mom or she won't agree. It has to be a team effort." I nodded obediently.

Together, we whined and pleaded, and pretty soon our mom, so doting and loving and perhaps secretly wanting a puppy of her own, caved.

In the car a few minutes later, as the puppy sat on my lap chattering with displacement, Kait frowned. "She has no personality," she complained. "She can be your dog. Sailor's mine."

I was shocked by how quickly my sister changed her mind after spending an afternoon begging for a puppy, but I was also used to her fluctuating interests and how suddenly she bounced from one idea to another with such speed and violent passion, it often left me with whiplash.

This reclaiming of the dogs happened periodically throughout the years: Kait changing her mind and wanting to formally declare one dog as "hers" depending on her mood. I was happy with either: Lilly was reserved and obedient, kind of like me, where Sailor was wild and playful, like Kait. He had deep brown, soulful eyes — surprisingly humanlike — and he'd stare at the stars on our porch or rest one paw on the car's armrest to look out the window, as if lost in thought. Despite what Kait said, both dogs felt like mine from that day on. Sailor had always been tied to me, since that day when he hid under my sweater as a puppy, and all three of us were in the same boat — enchanted by Kait's attention, captive to her whimsy, desperate to make her stay.

When I needed glasses in the fifth grade, Kait wanted a pair too.

At the ophthalmology chain For Eyes — the punny name a little too on the nose for me — the fluorescent lights beamed down on the rows of frames, backlit like museum artifacts. I tried glasses on in the narrow, slightly warped mirrors between shelves, trying to find a pair that looked most like "me." The problem was that looking like "me" was not something I aspired to. Adolescence had stretched me in strange and unwelcome ways — the softness of childhood replaced by bumpy knobs and sharp edges.

Every time I saw my reflection, little condensation clouds appeared behind the glass as my eyes filled with tears. The glasses looked grotesque, disfiguring. They felt heavy on my nose.

"Look over here! Look how smart I look!" Kait announced, holding a pair of light-brown tortoiseshell frames.

She pushed the glasses further down her nose like a caricature of a scornful librarian. She ruffled her hair, smiled in the mirror. Kait was here because I valued her opinion above all others. Anything she touched turned to gold in my mind.

The frames themselves weren't too expensive, so our mom bought them for her, with clear glass instead of a prescription. Kait wore them in most of her classes, pretending to squint at the board and refusing every request by her classmates to try them on. My sister picked out a similar pair for me, the interior of the frames lined with pink, a color meant to draw attention in a way I otherwise never would.

From the time Kait entered eighth grade until her high school graduation, my sister and I were in the same school district. For the first time in our lives, we had teachers in common. Five years after her, I would emerge in their classrooms a familiar stranger.

"Leddy?" I heard during roll calls — the teachers' voices rising subtly.

For the first few weeks of school, my instructors waited for my calm, quiet demeanor to implode, as if I were hiding behind a veil of pretend innocence.

Eventually, they always realized their mistake.

"You're nothing like your sister," I heard time and time again.

What a compliment they must have thought it was — an assertion of my good behavior, my soft voice, my dedicated work ethic. While many of Kait's teachers loved her personality, her flair, many were also frustrated by her inability to follow the rules.

What they didn't realize was just how badly I *wanted* to be like Kait. I didn't want to cause trouble, I didn't want to cross barriers, push lines, but I wanted to be the kind of girl who wanted to. I wanted to wear those glasses Kait picked out for me, because they looked like my sister — because I wanted my pale Irish skin to tan like hers. I wanted to wear her clothing, the random assortments of trends and colors clashing and yet meshing in a way only Kait could make them come together. She was colorful and unique and everything in the universe wrapped up in one. She wasn't the best nor the worst of it. To me, she simply *was* it.

Once we were roughly the same size in clothing, my sister would often creep into my bedroom and steal my sweatshirts. I'd come home, dig through my drawers for some sports jacket or another, and discover it missing.

"Mom!" I shouted downstairs in the voice all teenage girls use, as if everyday inconvenience is further proof of life's great conspiracy against them. "Kait stole my sweatshirt again!"

What would ensue is what I assume ensues in the homes of all sisters: bickering, with our mom acting as the middleman, the careful tallying-up of who has what of whose belongings, and then finally, the begrudging return of whichever item sparked the debate. A shirt tossed into the hallway with a "Fine! Have it!"

My clothes always returned to me smelling like cigarettes. This was my major complaint. Even after I washed them, the fumes of tobacco were embedded and braided in the fiber. Outwardly, I acted as if it were the greatest inconvenience, but internally, I was reveling.

Despite my refusals, nothing elated me more than knowing something of mine was of value to Kait. I would say I wanted whatever item she stole back, but what I wouldn't say was that I only cared about it because Kait's interest in it had made it something of importance to me. What she had stolen became the most precious object I owned. If she wanted it, then that meant it had her approval. If I wore it, maybe I would, too.

In the years since Kait has been gone, I have now lost track of which sweatshirt is whose, but I wear them both, slipping my thumb into the worn holes of the sleeves, rubbing the fabric between my fingers and pretending I can still smell the ghost of tobacco.

My sister was the kind of girl people write books about. I was the kind of girl who read such books, who listened to such songs and wondered how a spark in one person could light a flame in so many others.

• • •

When Kait was eighteen, she bought a life-size Barbie while she, my mom, and I were shopping for a younger cousin's gift.

We were at one of those chaotic party stores that sells everything from massive foil balloons to gardening supplies to snow shovels for winter — somewhere between a convenience shop and a Party City. Amid the overflowing aisles, Kait saw the doll resting on a high shelf.

"Oh my god! I need it," she squealed, more certain of a lifesize Barbie doll than I have ever been about any decision I have ever made. And her enthusiasm, her uninhibited happiness, was impossible to resist. Despite the impracticality of the purchase, our mom bought the doll for her and Kait left the store delighted.

That was the thing about my sister — her joy was contagious. She who experienced such lows — the fights, the trouble, the drama — also reached unimaginable highs, and something as insignificant and ridiculous as a Barbie doll could change the course of the entire day for all of us. I spent most of my life riding the waves of her moods, learning to read the movements that would set her off in either direction.

Risk-taking, aggression: symptoms of head trauma but also traits inherent in my sister since she first learned to speak. Is it over-pathologizing to draw a connection between CTE and this increased impulsivity? Or is it all connected? Because in the years that followed, Kait's mood swings would take on a new sense of urgency. Where is the line between acknowledging a person's human faults and uncovering the edge of a mental health disorder?

My sister was a force: funny and wild and unpredictable and as fickle as a summer storm. Wouldn't it be easier if the qualities that were her downfall weren't the same ones that made her so easy to love? Wouldn't it be easier if the source of her darkness was not also her light?

For years, the Barbie, soon forgotten, continued to sit in the corner of her room, smiling brilliantly, its neon-pink lips collecting sprinkles of dust.

Eight

Before I turned nine, Kait made me watch practically every horror movie released. I watched *The Ring* when I was six. *The Hills Have Eyes* when I was nine. I saw *The Blair Witch Project* in a small cabin in the New Hampshire woods when I was seven. Sometimes the movies were proposed with a consequence for refusing them.

"If you don't watch this with me," Kait said, "I won't talk to you for a month."

Other times, there were no strings attached, no ultimatums, except for the simple fact that it was an opportunity to join my sister.

So more often than not, I chose to watch, though I did so behind the veil of a pillow half concealing the screen. I watched the little girl from *The Ring* crawl from the television screen, watched the disfigured men in the mountains look over the smooth desert landscape in *The Hills Have Eyes*. The jumps and frights became so ingrained in my consciousness that to this day if there's a static signal on the television screen, I will sprint first and ask questions second.

When I grew up, I gradually learned to say no. No more horror movies. No more ultimatums. At eleven, I vowed never to watch one again, and I haven't for more than twelve years. Still, the images are trapped in my mind, as readily accessible and innate as language.

Horror movies were tied to my relationship with Kait, woven into our lives together. They were why I often asked to sleep in her room or my parents' and why I hated being home alone. Our house was old and creaking, built in 1925. Compared to the quaint, cedar-shingled New

England homes of our childhood, it felt hollow. The thick cement walls were always chilly — they sucked the heat out of a room like the draining of a life force. The rooms were less cozy and cramped, more cavernous and grand. Originally purchased as a fixer-upper in a nice neighborhood, the house seemed to be in perpetual progression. A give and take: While my parents fought to drag it into the modern age, it fought to fall apart. Just keeping it running, sustaining stasis, required constant maintenance.

The floorboards creaked with age, and you could imagine you heard footsteps in the middle of the night, pattering above your head, in the hallway beside you, and even, if you felt especially paranoid, alongside your bed.

The last sleepover I had at my house was three years after we moved to the suburbs of Philadelphia. It was a July night in 2007. I was in the fifth grade. It felt very much like a scene from a horror movie.

My friend and I crept down the stairs to investigate the sound of shouting. Fights between my parents and Kait had become increasingly common since I turned eight years old (since that first year we moved to the Main Line, since my sister suffered her first head trauma), instigated by her erratic moods and explosive temper. In the last few years, I witnessed my sister becoming more and more unstable. I knew that she could be violent when reprimanded. The first incident I can remember occurred when I was around eight — I watched my sister rip out a fistful of Mom's pretty blond hair. But typically such an explosion would never occur with a guest over. Kait knew better, and we all knew to avoid any situation that may trigger her.

When I came downstairs, my mom was clutching her face.

Go upstairs, go back! she gestured with her free hand.

I wanted to ask her what was wrong, to demand answers, but I knew that this was beyond me. I knew I would, as always, do what I was told.

Before retreating, I peaked at my sister once more. She was still the person as familiar to me as my own reflection — but she had the look of a stranger, a mask turning her lovely features vicious and strange. This was not a face I knew, not someone I could reason with.

My friend and I went back upstairs, pressing our heads to the door, attempting to hear the commotion. "Does stuff like this happen a lot?" she asked.

I shrugged in response.

The answer was a secret I couldn't betray — a silent oath I believed all children took not to discuss the intimate dramas of their households. I approached every peer with this sacred belief that we were each protecting some horror behind closed doors. None of us was truly alone, because we all were.

It is important to note here that mental health issues do not lead to violence — individuals diagnosed with psychotic episodes are no more likely to be violent than anyone else. Nor is there any excuse for violent behavior — not in this instance, and not ever. When so few narratives of severe mental illness exist in popular culture, each one holds a responsibility to stand as a collective example. But the truth of our story is that Kait *was* increasingly violent in the years before and especially following her diagnosis. Whether it was her loosening control over her thoughts and feelings, frustration at her inability to function at the level she previously experienced, or simply her own underlying temperament, Kait was at times aggressive. It would be an injustice not to acknowledge how hard it is to care for someone when they are both suffering and inflicting suffering onto you.

That night, our mom drove herself and Kait to the hospital so my father could stay home with me and my friend. Mom suffered a hematoma on her left cheekbone; her eye was bruised and swollen for weeks to come. Kait was sent to a psychiatric hospital, for the first evaluation of many. They released her undiagnosed.

From then on, it was no longer safe to have friends over. We couldn't guarantee their safety any more than we could our own. Kait was seventeen. I was eleven.

When my sister and I were growing up, she'd pin me to the ground and tickle me. She'd wrestle me and say something like, "I'm going to get you!" There was the revving of her feet, like a bull before marching, sand kicked beneath her heels: "Watch out!" I'd run away, giggling, tripping over my feet, jumping over couches and ottomans. When Kait declared, "The ground is lava!" I switched to leaping from cushion to cushion instead. The excitement was always in the burnt edge of danger. The adrenaline spike, an air of urgency. Always, she inevitably caught up to me. Kait seized my body in the air and brought me to the couch, pinning my arms behind my head and tickling me: tiny fireworks pricking my rib cage the more I laughed.

I've always found tickling kind of odd — how it's both painful and pleasant at once. You're laughing, and at first the burn feels good. It aches like your limbs after a long day at the beach, jumping over waves: an exhausted high. But then your muscles contract. You have the distinct feeling of being out of control: a carnival ride that was supposed to be fun but on a dime has grown terrifying.

Some theories claim that tickling may have evolved as an evolutionary defense mechanism. The most vulnerable parts of our bodies are ticklish — our feet, our armpits, our stomach, sides, and neck — because we're most sensitive in these spots. If true, this idea purports an innate sense of faith in the person tickling you — like how a dog will roll over and expose his belly if he trusts his owner. We only reveal our most unguarded selves when we believe them safe.

For years, Kait's aggressive behavior still felt like this to me: a game of pretend. I still carried a vague belief in some invisible, impenetrable line, confident that there still existed a safe word that would make it all go away. And yet the night of my last sleepover was different. I knew something innocent had been lost deep within my body. I would never again be free to fully let my guard down before my sister. The next time she jokingly chased me, there'd be a tinge of real terror to the encounter. My heart would quicken. Her weight on my wrists would squeeze binding and punitive: too tight. I no longer knew what those hands were capable of. That evening was the first time I heard my mom scream, helpless to make it stop. It wouldn't be the last. We had crossed into unprecedented territory. In the time it takes to read this page, everything had changed.

I started to tell my friends that my home was haunted like in the scary movies Kait and I watched. I told them stories of books flying off bookshelves, doors slamming without a hand to close them. Kait egged on this fear, this growing paranoia.

"They don't like you, you know," she said one day.

"Who?" I asked, wary of the coming insult.

"The ghosts. They think you're weird."

Kait laughed as my face went from red to white to red again.

Maybe it was a childhood prank, maybe it was the beginning of her hallucinations, or maybe she really knew something I didn't. Either way, the sentiment clung to me like wet fabric. I began looking at every archway with narrowed suspicion. I stopped dancing in my room to the latest Taylor Swift song. There were eyes on me now, and for years afterward, the sensation of omnipresence was constant—a shadow in the background of my days.

In general discourse, we tend to separate hallucination from everyday life. Hallucinations are errors that occur in times of intense emotional stress, from oxygen deprivation, in life-and-death moments, out-of-body experiences, or psychedelics. We brush off these aberrant encounters as beyond the fray, but hallucinations actually make up far more of our foundation than is commonly acknowledged. They're implicated in our religions: the prophet handed a message from a holy figure; the widow who grabs at a fragment of her husband as he passes, a younger version of him gently pressing her hand. Even the spiritual rendering of early cave drawings, the shapes and figures of horses in motion from Lascaux, overlapping like a double exposed image, are reminiscent of an apparition of sorts. The largest religion in the world is based on a man dying, resurrecting, and appearing to his followers once again. Would you not consider this outside the realm of normal? We are a society founded on a deviance from accepted ideas of consciousness, and yet we are simultaneously terrified by them.

Perceptual quirks also emerge in less consequential corners of the human mind. The brain is constantly processing the signals and stimuli it has access to, and when information is limited, it fills in the best it can. Our minds are sensitive to a stirring out of our visual range, because this movement represents a potential threat. In such a moment, the brain must work quickly to interpret what it has seen, and when it rushes to do so, it's prone to error. We assign anthropomorphic motivations to inanimate objects, see faces in the clouds — a nose here, a smile there — we imprint our understanding onto the world. To be alive is to constantly make sense of senseless stimuli. Sometimes we see what we believe should be there rather than what actually is.

While I was worried about the paranormal, I avoided all gray areas — dimly lit corridors, turning a corner too quickly, blurry mirrors, dust settling in my blind spot, dogs barking at thin air, the wind creaking the cupboards, the pipes aching.

When we were younger, Kait persuaded me to play Bloody Mary with her and a friend. We went into a bathroom and said the chant thirteen times, flashing the lights on and off. The image we were terrified to see was all the more present, because we held it at the forefront of our minds. When our senses were disturbed by the flashing light, the rush of the faucet, it was all too easy to envision our terror.

I sought to circumvent such disruption. I learned to wait until the bathroom door was closed to look at myself in the mirror so that I couldn't imagine I saw a face there in the distant corner behind my back. I slept every night with a small chair blocking my bedroom door. At first, I put it there to prevent the tilt of the old floorboards propelling the door open. Later, I leaned the chair as a barricade to prevent my sister from getting inside.

Ultimately my friends believed my haunted house stories, and I began to believe them too, with a certainty of terror, looking over my shoulders like a heroine in a gothic novel, growing madder by the day, running from the wrong source. I created such fear around our home, a growing contempt, an insatiable hatred. Perhaps it was easier to explain this than it was to explain the real reason why I couldn't host the weekend sleepovers or have friends over after school anymore. Because it was a terror closer to home that really stained the place — the energy of our struggle and heartbreak, the knowledge that at any point, Kait could light a fuse and set it all on fire.

Nine

It was sometime in these early teenage years that my sister discovered she had polycystic ovarian syndrome: a hormonal disorder linked to the development of small cysts and prolonged or missed menstrual periods.

Mom tells me that as Kait's hormones surged, her mood swings peaked, and a pimple would explode on the middle of her forehead: a physical indication of the internal battle in her body.

Was this disorder a reason behind her explosive temper? As a child, Kait had always been stubborn and single-minded, but the violence was new. It was out of control, with sudden and dramatic outbursts unlike anything we could explain.

After the incident at my last sleepover, Kait was becoming more and more "dysregulated." I hate the slant of this word, how it suggests someone's emotions have spilled over a prescribed daily limit, as if emotions are stagnant, never to go beyond a threshold. Glasses topped to the brim. The word glows cold and metallic, with the stainless-steel glint of all clinical terms, like an operating table or an untouched showroom kitchen. A line drawn in the sand: This is normal, this is not. But how else to describe the irrational absurdity of the volatility? A world with no regulation.

The same year that Kait was diagnosed with PCOS, I began experiencing pain toward the tip of my pelvis in the form of a small, sharp pinch. Sometimes this pain would be debilitating, leaving me crouched before the toilet in the bathroom, groaning until someone came and found me. Other times, the feeling would come in a wave: a precise stabbing, and then a sudden release.

When the pain caused me to miss days of school, my mom took me to see a doctor. In a hospital room attached to my pediatrician's office, I lay back on an examination table while a woman spread a cool gel over my lower abdomen and performed an ultrasound. It was a sensation I had seen mimicked in movies or television shows — an experience I expected to have in some distant, imagined future when I was pregnant. The device pressed into my skin, forming little hills as it searched. A small, circular bump appeared on the screen, looking like a grainy image of the moon filled with craters and shadows. It was, as we had suspected, an ovarian cyst.

All I remember is an uncanny sense of relief — finally, I was receiving medical evidence for what I feared might only be imagined. If I couldn't see it, how could I know? What a comfort it was to have my pain corroborated. Even our own suffering doesn't seem real until someone else confirms it — with a thermometer, a test, a psychiatrist. *Can you see it too?* we want to ask.

I was prescribed hormonal birth control that day and with it never experienced a serious symptom again. While I wasn't diagnosed with PCOS like my sister, I can't help but wonder about every dot left unconnected during that time. Like a child abandoning a connect-the-dots drawing, we left certain ideas and diagnoses untraced in the chaos of living.

PCOS is attributed to abnormally high levels of the hormone androgen, and has been said to affect one in ten women of childbearing age. Mom had ovarian cysts too. She discovered them when trying to conceive Kait and me. They are among the reasons why there is such a big age gap between the two of us.

Here's the real kicker: PCOS has been linked to severe psychiatric disorders, including bipolar disorder and schizophrenia — two of the diagnoses doctors floated around Kait.

According to Psych Central, as many as 60 percent of women diagnosed with PCOS have at least one mental illness. Androgens and insulin resistance (the leading cause of PCOS) are also implicated in the development of psychiatric disorders such as schizophrenia.

The brain is complex: a walnut of grooves and curves, neurochemical reactions flitting in the crevices. Because it's so complicated, scientists are still largely uncertain why and how psychosis develops. There are certain verities: a clear genetic predisposition, environmental factors like trauma, stress, malnourishment, or a preexisting condition like PCOS. And as my mom desperately researched Kait's changing temperament, searching through books, websites, and any burgeoning research for an answer, she also stumbled upon a possible linkage between marijuana use and psychosis.

A report from March 2011 in Harvard Health recounted a study that followed two thousand teenagers throughout their young adult lives. Those that smoked marijuana at least five times were twice as likely to have developed psychosis than those who didn't smoke at all. Five times. Twice as likely. According to the study, smoking just *five* times doubled their risk. And early use could hasten the onset of your symptoms by three years.

Another finding in the same report states this:

> Young people with a parent or sibling affected by psychosis have a roughly one in 10 chance of developing the condition themselves — even if they never smoke pot. Regular marijuana use, however, doubles their risk — to a one in five chance of becoming psychotic.

A sibling already has a one in ten chance of developing schizophrenia. *I* already have a one in ten chance of developing schizophrenia. This statistic stalks me, my own personal boogeyman: the shadow in my closet, the hand beneath my bed that grabs my ankle, pulls me under. But this risk could potentially *double* to one in five when marijuana is introduced. In other words, I could have as high as a twenty percent chance of developing a psychotic disorder if I decided to smoke regularly.

There's a picture on Kait's Facebook of her eyes wide and alert above a plume of smoke, a Cheshire cat smile hidden beneath the fog. After the fact, I learned my sister was high the night of my last sleepover as well. I know she smoked frequently in her high school years, but so did many of her friends and they were just fine.

Investigators from the University of Oxford analyzed data from a Swedish registry of hospital admissions and criminal convictions in two separate studies and found that rates of violence increased when someone was diagnosed with schizophrenia (or bipolar disorder) *and* a substance abuse disorder. This data was significantly higher compared to the general population and those who only had a psychiatric disorder and no substance abuse.

Of course this research is still being conducted, and many scientists in the field are divided on the matter. While it's possible that frequent marijuana or alcohol use could bring about psychosis, so too can the overuse of other stimulants and hallucinogens. Causation is not correlation, and, for now, to draw any hard conclusions would be a vast oversimplification of the issue. Besides, there are also many health benefits to cannabis use for people who suffer from chronic pain or anxiety. Everyone has a unique brain anatomy and what is a lifesaver for one person could spell out disaster for another or vice versa.

New data into the subject is developing, and many of the studies weren't available for us at the time, but our mom was constantly on the lookout for the latest insight — always waiting for some miraculous solution or explanation for my sister's behavior. She warned me about this possible correlation when I was still a preteen, when it was only a whisper in the science community.

The point is that there are many, many brain–body connections left to be explored. Like the pimple that sprouted evergreen on my sister's forehead in the midst of a meltdown, or the precious pocket of cyst on my ultrasound screen, I wished desperately for a physical manifestation to explain the emotional volatility slithering beneath our lives.

◆　◆　◆

Other ailments in my own body popped up soon — little roadblocks, demanding to be seen and felt: bumps under my armpits discovered to be swollen lymph nodes, stomach-aches, piercing migraines. All of which are associated with chronic stress but seemed to me to be of an entirely different origin: an insidious underlying illness.

I convinced myself I had everything from cancer to a rare infectious tropical disease. I became obsessed with finding problems with my body: a midway point between anxious dread and hopeful expectancy. Something was wrong with me — there had to be something, and soon, finally, we would uncover exactly what it was.

What was I so desperately searching for? Why had I become so fixated on the physical?

Stress, a figment of the "mental," affects the body. This is a fact. We lose hair, gain weight, develop acne and stomach ulcers. Stress can even kill you — it can trigger a heart attack or stroke, burst a blood vessel. Anxiety, too, can make our hands shake and our hearts race, sending muscle twitches and tremors, sweating and shallow breathing, migraines and stomach pains, bile.

People die from "broken heart syndrome": intense grief alters the heart muscle so profoundly that it can mimic a heart attack. New research suggests that depression increases a women's risk of developing osteoporosis as much as other factors such as smoking or leading a sedentary lifestyle.

So *why* with this indisputable research is it so hard to accept, intuitively, the connection between the mind and the body? Why did we carve out a distinction in the first place?

The mind–body complex has challenged philosophers since ancient Greece. Aristotle wrote in his treatise *De Anima*: "It is not necessary to ask whether soul and body are one, just as it is not necessary to ask whether the wax and its shape are one, nor generally whether the matter of each thing and that of which it is the matter are one."

While I acknowledge that there is something more than matter and biochemistry at play in the human mind, to deny or ignore its effect on the body, and conversely the body's effect on it, is to deny limitless human suffering. When we segregate the principles of medicine from the neurochemistry of psychology, we let so many cases fall into the void. When we implicate mental illness as a condition of the soul, we ignore the benefits of medicine, the strides of science. We get lazy. We grow ignorant.

There's an ailment known as Morgellons disease in which individuals report sores, a pervasive feeling of itchiness, and, most curiously, the appearance of little fibers emerging from their skin like worms peeking out from the earth. It's a rare condition — according to the CDC, 3.65 cases were reported out of 100,000 participants in their 2012 study — but there is a high commonality of experience. I first read about it in Leslie Jamison's essay "The Devil's Bait." Jamison tilts the ailment in the light, examining it on all sides — exploring the possibility of a physiological disease versus a mass delusion.

In the essay, Jamison attends a conference at a Baptist church in Austin, Texas. The patients she meets have variations of where and how they acquired the illness: exposure to an addict's sores, swimming goggles, ingrown hairs, sand flies, a fishing trip. But each expresses a similar sinister unease — they're finding something inside their bodies that doesn't belong. Stinging, writhing, itching ensues. They scratch, dig, tear, rub, freeze, douse with insecticides, and laser these areas. Their faces and bodies are covered in the scabby aftermath. Then, in the unhealed lesions bloom the threads. Fibrous material of all colors: stringy and *other*. Some pluck them out and bring their doctors Tupperware containers of their findings, an offering of sorts.

The baseline presumed by the essay is that Morgellons is an illness of the mind. Many therapists believe it resembles a diagnosis they already have: delusional parasitosis, or the belief that there are parasites under your skin. It follows logically why such a condition would exist: Parasites are essentially a human fear, rooted in an evolutionary necessity. We are naturally repulsed by what poses the greatest threat to us in the wild: spoiled food, infected bodies, loose fluids. It's deeply unsettling to think we are not alone in our bodies — that something has made a home of us. When fibers in 115 patients were examined, researchers found them to be of cottonlike material, likely from fabric. Others have even suggested that Morgellons is a product of the internet — as more and more people share their experiences online, the cases grow.

This follows too. When I was on the verge of hypochondria, I was spending hours on WebMD. Every symptom I heard about, I manifested. Even reading this — the fibrous filaments, the dry skin, the gaping, festering wounds, the creatures burrowing beneath skin — may make you want to itch.

Still, the thesis of Jamison's essay boils down to a need for empathy. The suffering, no matter the origin, is real, and we must respect this. It is isolating to have an invisible illness. It is maddening. It is lonely.

The misleading dichotomy of "physical or psychological" isn't that different, perhaps, from "real versus imagined." After all, why should one supersede the other? Suffering is never imagined. The brain *is* the body, the brain *is* physical. We accept that our bodies can be injured — a broken bone, an infectious disease — but we ignore the injuries endured by our brains, because we assume a sense of control over our psychological hurt. This control is often an illusion.

I had been looking during those early years of Kait's behavior to find physical symptoms. I wanted a box of my suffering. I wanted to get it "fixed." I was obsessed with treatment of any kind — my own, Kait's — craving the perceived openness of diagnosis, the straightforwardness of having a label to what plagued us.

I was looking because no one had been able to tell my family what was wrong. The system of mental healthcare was almost lackadaisical in its acceptance of our fate. Why had no doctors thought to connect Kait's cysts with her changes in mood? Why had no one thought to examine the hormonal dysregulation as a factor in her sudden violent temper? My

parents were left to sort out this irrationality themselves:
change before our eyes, with no real hold on how to stop it.

When Mom looks back on this time in our lives, she returns with two
key takeaways:

"First, that mental illness is very much real," she tells me. "Second, that
the families need support and education. You can't save someone when
you're drowning yourself."

If the answer isn't intervention from the medical system, then perhaps it exists in the need for more family services, wraparound systems
that teach psycho-education and coping mechanisms. Unfortunately, my
parents and I couldn't afford to go to a psychologist during these years
— paying for the therapy bills my sister was now rapidly accruing was
too much of a financial burden, let alone adding sessions for the rest of
the family.

And yet so much of the tragedy of my sister's condition was our inability to understand why it was happening. Perhaps if we had only known,
only understood, then we could have supported her better, rallied around
her, lifted her off the ground and up to the girl she was supposed to be
all along. Perhaps we could've seen the signs before they manifested into
full-blown symptoms.

My mom regrets that it happened so subtly that she couldn't really
step back and notice until the situation was too far gone. You think you
can get ahead of it, fix it. She's a little girl walking ahead of you, spilling
paint from a bucket. You crawl behind her, trying to mop up every spot
before it soaks into the fibers of the carpet. You can spend a whole life
cleaning up after these mini messes, never managing the bigger problem
at hand. You're trying so hard to survive, there's no time to think. No
time to sleep. *She'll grow out of it*, you say. *This is normal*, you hope.

How do you explain that the signs and symptoms are so difficult to
recognize because they're rarely publicly advertised? There's no annual
exam to test whether your daughter is losing her mind. No sign in the

doctor's waiting room, listing the symptoms like a multiple-choice question. Besides, medical professionals often disagree with diagnoses. They jostle them around, throw clinical terms in the air, and expect you to catch them.

Or, if the subject is brought up, we talk about mental *health* — the art of maintaining a steady, positive internal life. No one tells you that it is a spectrum like anything else. No one tells you what to do when that ship has sailed — when you begin to lose your mind. No one tells you what a precious, fragile gift your mind is in the first place. No one tells you it can be lost.

The heartbreak, too, is that some days my sister held on. Kait was beautiful and fun, charming when she wanted to be. This masked her degeneration, let it rot inside of her because the outside was so *normal,* so shiny.

Mom tells me that one day Kait was agitated before school: depressed, lethargic, angry. The worst cases flooded our mom's mind, clinging like static: imagining my sister's head sloped across her desk, falling asleep in class, or yelling at another girl in the hallway. Partway through the day she finally caved in to the anxiety, calling the high school front desk to check in on my sister.

"Kait?" the faculty woman answered in surprise. "Kait's doing great! I can see her right now — she's laughing with a group of friends."

The girl on the Facebook page: cool, carefree, colorful, funny, smart.

And then, gone.

Ten

My sister's sanity slipped slowly and quietly — the way you lose a train of thought or slide into a dream at night: there and then not. She lost her edge little by little. An avalanche that picks up one rock and then another: a steady progression, and then, in a flash, a tragedy. Uncontrollable. Too late.

Even now, I struggle to put a timeline to it. Clearly, events were escalating, but still, we had no diagnosis. We remained in the waiting room where mood swings and irregularity could still be chalked up to growing pains.

There was also a great deal of beauty in our lives that poked through the struggle, but an unfortunate aspect of the human mind is this: More than the everyday calm, we remember the panic, the fear.

Still, when I think of the good, the moments of peace, I recall one story in particular.

There are deer crossing signs that dot our neighborhood, peeking out from behind overgrown trees and tilted in the lopsided ground near stoplights. Again and again the same image meets you at every corner: the black outline of a stag springing to action against a neon yellow background.

One December when I was in middle school, my mom, sister, and I bought little red dot stickers from Staples, the kind originally intended for office inventories. I forget who had the idea first — Mom or Kait, because it could never have been me (such a wild, spontaneous thought would not have occurred to me, and even if it had, I would never have the guts to speak it into existence) — but somehow we decided our town needed a little holiday spirit before Christmas. In the dead of night, long after I should have been in bed for school, we dressed in all black: black sweatpants, black jackets, black hats. Kait dug up an old black ski mask from a duffle bag in our basement storage.

We giggled as we piled into our mom's car, already high on adventure, covertly hushing each other and then falling right back into hysterics. The night had an anticipatory glitter to it, making everything prettier in its glow — like the evening before some big event when your legs ache with excitement and you can't help but smile in your bed. Our town was quieter, softer in the blanket of midnight sky, and it felt like a place where anything could happen. I could hear the rushing sound of the creeks in the woods as water slid across dark rocks, and the green of everything turned silver and mysterious in the moonlight.

At the four-way intersection near our local high school, I left the leather seat of the back row while my sister ran ahead of me.

"Jump on my back!" Kait said, bending over as if we were playing a game of leapfrog.

I climbed onto her shoulders like I had as a young girl, and she held on to my legs to steady me. Reaching as high as I could, I took the red sticker and touched it precisely, lovingly onto the very tip of the sign, sticking it firmly on the image of the deer's nose.

"Woohoo!" my sister cheered wildly. "It's Rudolph the Red-Nosed Reindeer, baby!"

"Shhh!" I laughed. "We're going to get caught!"

All across town we went, vandals in the thick of night, as we stuck and smoothed over the stickers, transforming our sleepy neighborhood into something different, more special: a Christmas miracle, Santa's very own village.

My face ached from smiling, and my mom swears she laughed so hard she thought she was going to pee herself at one point. The next morning, it felt like a dream — the antics, the festivity, how we ran and hollered and climbed, as wild as stray animals. The enchantment of the night was faded, already a memory, but as we drove to school the next morning, we passed our creations and giggled once more.

Before now, I never told anyone about that night. I carried the secret in my pocket like some illicit crime, but the glint of the sticker was a wink all year. Even as the rain and snow peeled our work, disintegrated the coating and washed away the color, the little red dots were a reminder that magic still existed in the world. A reminder that despite everything, we were still a family, different but bound together, and Kait brought that spirit out of me — something rebellious and eternal as earth and time itself, as strong as morning brew and ancient dirt. She made me someone I wanted to be around. When she was well, healthy and herself, she sprinkled her dust on all of us and we were better for it.

I keep thinking of those little red dots and all they were. I suppose it was the last time we would ever be that way again: united, silly, a team. Our father as usual off somewhere traveling for work, always absent in these memories, leaving us alone as a pack of three women.

In the end, I suppose it happened like this: There were good days among the bad until there weren't. There was hope until there wasn't.

Phase II, Active

Red

Eleven

Until only a few days before my sister's graduation, our parents didn't know if Kait would be allowed to attend. Her grades were dismal, and had been getting progressively worse all throughout high school: a spiral in the wrong direction, like so much else. It had been a happy, last-minute decision not to make her repeat her senior year. When we received the green light that Kait would receive her high school diploma after all, it felt like a new beginning.

Our school colors were red and white, so boys in red caps and robes and girls in white caps and robes took up the first rows of seats every year. (In 2017 the administrators finally realized the tradition was gender binary and graduates switched to wearing only red.)

On the day of her graduation, we struggled to find seating in the crowded, cramped outdoor arena, craning our necks to catch a glimpse of the huddles of graduates. It was one of those sweaty May days when the air conditioner cranks on in the middle of the night, turning the floors and walls slippery with the sudden chill. The sunsets grow a touch pinker, the clouds a touch fluffier, and the air holds the humming promise of summer, the world suddenly feeling open to possibility.

Kait was wearing a white dress with embroidered roses, almost violent in their vividness. The leaves were outlined in thick green stitching, popping out of the white as if trying to escape from it. Her blond hair lay in loose curls.

I had chosen to wear an embroidered top, keeping in theme. My shirt was an off-white halter-top with a mix of purple and blue flower designs. I tried it on first without an undershirt, attempting to make the look older, more chic. I stared at my twelve-year-old body in the white arched mirror of my bedroom before I chickened out and abruptly threw a ribbed neon-pink tank underneath. Who was I fooling anyway? The light blond ringlets of my childhood had transformed into a muddied, hesitant mix somewhere between blond and brown.

"You look pretty," Kait said when I walked down the winding stairs of our entranceway: a rare comment of such generous overstatement, it made my heart squeeze. Even as my sister drifted further and further away from the girl she used to be — even as she morphed from protector to someone needing protection from — I was still chasing after her footsteps in the sand. Even when I suspected that her path was one I shouldn't follow, I wanted to fit into her mold, to make myself in her likeness.

I was reminded in that moment of when she had descended the same staircase a few years before on her way to junior prom. She had taken photos in this very space in a short navy blue dress, and I watched from above, admiring the scene like a glimpse into the teen movies I watched. Her date placed a corsage on her hand. They smiled uncomfortably while our mom grabbed a camera.

Kait truly did look beautiful today. She looked like a girl with her whole future ahead of her, a bright light with nothing to lose and so much to gain. She *was* a girl with her whole future ahead of her.

As she made her way up the graduation stage, my sister made her excited face — the slightly dorky one, with a wide smile and her nose scrunched up. I wondered why for a moment, then, suddenly, I saw Kait's hand dig into a pocket and toss on a pair of strawberry-red heart-shaped glasses. She paused and waved at us, and we all laughed because it was such a Kait move. Something only she would do: proof that despite the turmoil of the last few years, she was still herself.

A girl with her whole future ahead of her.

Twelve

Every story has its tipping point: a leveling-off, a final shove, a fragmentation. In an ideal world, I would lean in to this moment gracefully. We'd see the movie montage before the dramatic climax. There'd be a musical score to signify a tonal shift, the sharp chords of danger as our protagonist approaches the corner around which the monster lurks. A studio audience screaming "*Run! Run!*"

But no, this is real life, and there was no one to warn us.

It's said that people with anxiety watch the same movies and television shows, or read the same books, over and over again. This reconsumption of media can be explained by the "mere exposure effect," or the idea that we prefer what we've previously seen. It can also be examined as "experiential control" — the payoff of knowing what is to come has a calming effect equivalent to a meditative chant. It reaffirms that there is order in the world.

I am the kind of person who reads the last page first. The type of girl who searches the plot summary on Wikipedia before the movie ends.

The moral here is that when you know what happens next, you can relax. The punch line is that life rarely grants you a warning.

In the midst of life, we are in death. "Life changes in the instant," said Joan Didion.

This was our instant. One of them, anyway.

◆　◆　◆

After graduation, my sister began taking classes at Drexel University, a half-hour drive from our home. She had just moved into an apartment in the city with a few roommates.

She was not officially matriculated as a full-time student; her poor performance in high school made this impossible. Instead, Kait was taking a handful of courses with the hope of eventually becoming a full-time student.

It was around this time, on the bluff of early adulthood, where everything is supposed to *start*, that Kait's life took an irreversible turn.

Standing atop a brownstone's stoop in the early October air of a Philadelphia night, just one month into her first semester of college, another student engulfed her in a hug. I don't know who he was or how she knew him. All I know is that they tipped, and she fell.

I imagine her stomach dropped like all those times you leaned too far back in your chair in elementary school. The tightening of muscles, the sudden panic, the laughter sputtering as you rode that edge, that careful precipice, that loss of gravity.

Except Kait wasn't so lucky. She didn't right herself in time; no one caught her. Her head hit the concrete.

She cracked.

I waited in the hallway of the intensive care unit of Philadelphia's Children's Hospital on a plastic chair, remembering the last time we were here together, when I broke my arm and my sister spent hours comforting me. I wished I could do the same for her now.

I tucked my backpack underneath my seat to avoid the hurried feet of the doctors, the wheels of the patient's stretcher, and the vacant stares of the family members absentmindedly trailing behind like lost children in a shopping mall. I was twelve years old, in seventh grade. My life was preoccupied with exams, bar and bat mitzvahs, and the mini chasms of my social networks. I sat with a textbook in my lap, balancing the hard cover as I flipped through page after page, reading without processing the words.

The smell of a hospital is a distinct poison: antiseptic wash and the sweaty, rancid odor of the sick. The two smells compete against each other, fighting to overpower, but in the battle, something worse is created — the smell of struggle. Fights simultaneously lost and won.

I remained outside in the hallway for hours, both listening and trying not to listen as my mom spoke to doctors and my sister lay several feet away from us, unconscious. My father was away on a business trip in Denver, and a storm had snowed him in at his hotel, so our mom struggled to manage the crisis alone.

I overheard that the ambulance had arrived not long after my sister fell.

There was dirt on her clothes, Mom says. She couldn't figure out how the dirt got there. Was it the way my sister fell? Or did the paramedics lay her on the ground before she was brought to the ambulance? How long did it take for them to realize that something was truly, deeply wrong? When exactly did her friends' laughter cease, swallowed by dread? Who was it that called 9-1-1? What stranger or acquaintance was there in the moment my sister fell from us?

When the emergency response team arrived, they carefully placed my sister's body on a stretcher, cradling her gently, lifting her above the crowd. In the privacy of the ambulance, they tore through her clothes with scissors to access her airways, performing emergency care. They cut through her favorite bra in order to do so — later, this would be a detail that stuck with Kait.

She had traumatic subarachnoid hemorrhaging, bleeding in the sensitive space between the surface of the brain. I remember her needing surgical staples — the skin of her scalp ripped open — because she complained about the small patch of hair the doctors shaved in order to do so. I wonder now, was this focus on the shallow — the hair, the bra — a way for my sister to avoid confronting the bigger changes that were to come, the same way I found myself focusing on the physical, tangible things I could see and grasp among all the bigger, intangible worries swirling around us?

My sister was sedated for three days so as to not disturb her healing. I spent this time staying with a friend while my mom sat at the hospital alone. The doctor warned us that Kait wouldn't be the same when she woke up. For a moment, my mom and I wondered aloud to one another if perhaps this could incite a positive change. There was no denying that before Kait fell, she was struggling, losing grip on something. You know the term "knock some sense into you"? Secretly, in the depths of our subconscious, all evidence to the contrary notwithstanding, we hoped that maybe this would do just that.

When Kait regained consciousness and we were permitted to see her, I noticed that her bright hair was matted like an animal's fur. Her eyes were tired and puffy, her freckles stood out brilliantly on her now pallid skin, but her delicate features, the small slope of her nose, the wide shape of her blue-green eyes, and the childish pout of her full lips were still familiar. The white of the bed illuminated her face like a halo in the dim beat of the lights. She looked like an angel — one from Gabriel Garcia Marquez's short story "A Very Old Man with Enormous Wings." Like an angel, forgotten and fallen, torn and battered by wind and rain.

Our mom led me into the room. She reminded me to be gentle, speak softly, tread lightly, and her tone reminded me of how she must have advised Kait when I was brought home from the hospital as a newborn: Be soft, delicate. Our positions were reversed now, and yet it still felt as if I was meeting my sister for the first time. In some ways, in retrospect, I suppose I was.

"Your hair looks disgusting" were the first words out of my sister's mouth as she appraised me, somehow making the bundle of itchy sheets look more like a throne than a hospital bed.

I was trying a new shampoo, attempting to give my hair the glossy glow my sister's had. In the hours without a shower, it had fallen limp instead.

"You've looked better yourself," I shot back, flushed with frustration.

The tension broke. I blinked away tears, and we both coughed, a soft, hesitant chuckle.

The superficiality of the moment, the sister bickering, the teasing, felt almost normal for a moment, but the doctor was right in predicting Kait would never again be Kait.

In the days following, it soon became clear that my sister's thoughts were no longer her own. Suddenly, there were new voices, and they demanded to be heard. Had they been hiding there all along? Was everything prior to this moment the "genetic predisposition" psychology textbooks mention in ominous sidebars and highlighted definitions — and this, the flip side: the environmental influence? The event that set the rest of the narrative in place, unraveling to its inevitable end: the fall, the crack, a kindling.

Thirteen

Just a few days after her head injury, there was a moment when my mom looked at Kait and thought: *She is going to kill me.*

After her fall — what I will always remember now as *the* fall — Kait's condition worsened dramatically. She returned home for a few days to recover. She had just suffered a traumatic brain injury, was prescribed anti-seizure medication (Dilantin, Percocet, Phenergan, a senna tablet), and told to stay still and rest. But Kait didn't want to rest, she wanted to return to her apartment, she wanted her freedom. Most of all, she wanted cigarettes.

(Later, once I was in college and studying behavioral psychology, I learned that nicotine may help suppress some symptoms of schizophrenia by increasing the neurotransmitter dopamine. According to a 2001 study in *Psychiatric Times*, "Nicotine and Schizophrenia," between 72 and 90 percent of patients with the disorder smoke regularly. It's widely believed that cigarettes are one of the many self-medication tools individuals diagnosed with schizophrenia use. This knowledge applied to the past makes so much sense now — no wonder the need for cigarettes felt so urgent to Kait, no wonder they were something she would kill for. *And how cruel to fill in the pieces of the puzzle retroactively, to discover it fit together all along.*)

My sister was still tall and lean. She still had that same tan skin, those same freckles of her youth, and the same piercing green eyes marked as blue on her license. She continued to go to tanning beds, even bought a membership. Freshly fried and covered in tanning lotion, smelling of summer and candles, she would stand outside on the twilight streets of our college town and light a cigarette. The shadows of the lamppost and traffic lights curved before her, slithering like a bed of snakes.

My parents were well aware of these bad habits. Tanning beds and smoking: a deadly combination. Cigarette packs were confiscated. Lectures given. Fights fought and lost. My parents showed her what lung cancer looked like — the black, spongy decay like mold on the rim of a kitchen sink. They warned her of my mom's skin cancer, but in the end, these weren't the worst of her bad habits, nor were they the deadliest, and there were bigger fights to be had. I think a part of us knew, even then, that Kait's life was unlikely to last long enough to be shortened by cancer.

Mom was trying to persuade Kait back into bed, repeating the doctor's instructions, explaining how she could cause further damage if she moved too suddenly. Kait wasn't listening — she wanted cigarettes and she wanted them *now*. She looked at Mom like she was willing to do anything to get her goal, threatening her, crowding her, cornering her and screaming.

I'm going to die, my mom thought. *I'm going to die over a pack of cigarettes.*

Finally, our mom stepped aside and my sister shoved past her and ran to the car.

The violence, the sudden turn, the two versions of Kait, were dizzying. My sister's eyes would gloss over and then narrow — she changed personalities frequently and feverishly. She turned wild in her anger, a ravenous animal locked in a cage, willing to do anything, destroy anything to get what she wanted.

My sister wasn't allowed to drive at the time. She had been arrested a few weeks prior for underage drinking. When Kait stole the car, she floored the gas pedal, leaving dark, angry skid marks on our steep, cracked driveway. This would ultimately become our greatest fear — Kait, in a manic state, driving aggressively, hitting someone else, hurting herself or others. These were the thoughts that pounded in the back of our heads as Kait's pounded with voices of her own. What if she hurts herself? What if she kills us? Worse even, what if she kills someone *else*? An innocent party, an outsider, victim to her illness and our inability to control it. It was one tragedy for the chaos to be contained in our own nuclear family, quite another to have it leak toxins onto someone else.

I emerged from the house hesitantly in her absence, the way birds emerge from trees after a storm, surveying the damage. Outside on the driveway, I smelled burnt rubber and exhaust.

After some time, Kait returned to our house, both she and the car intact, and I don't recall exactly what happened next: what was said, how she looked when she pulled back into the driveway, or how we received her. I only remember the stirring — the inciting movement — and then the lightest feeling of dust settling. The softness of adrenaline fading from my fingertips.

It's a cycle my twelve-year-old body would come to memorize. A reprogramming of my system: the spark, hyperattention to detail, the sense that this is *it*. I would see red: not metaphorically as I once thought the phrase to mean, but genuine red. Blood rushed to my eyes and an increase in adrenal hormones flowed through my body: stay or go, fight or flight, a sense that I was going to pass out, my vision fading to black pinpricks as if lint were clogging my vision. And then, a cliff, a dropping, numbness. I learned that violence is one thing, but fear of violence is something else entirely. This anxiety peeled me back, layer by layer until I was an exposed nerve on the world, sensitive to the slightest ruffling.

What we mostly know about the effect of traumatic brain injuries on personality and thought has been surmised by trial and error: biopsies and case studies. Most famous of these unfortunate, illuminating accidents is perhaps Phineas Gage: a mid-nineteenth century American railroad worker who suffered a terrible accident when a premature explosion sent a three-foot iron rod through his skull. Miraculously, he survived, but lost his left eye and much of his left frontal lobe in the process. The famous quote pulled from friends and family and cited in textbooks and online forums alike is "Gage was no longer Gage."

The reports vary in their dramatics, from his becoming aggressive and listless to becoming childlike and disturbed. The sentiment strikes a chord with me. I know what it's like to watch someone you love "no longer be." I know how this unbecoming can unravel before your very eyes.

In the ways Kait changed after her traumatic brain injury, it's all too easy to conceive how a brain injury much more severe could result in drastic personality shifts. However, new evidence (supporting the idea of neuroplasticity) has suggested that Gage, unlike Kait, may have adjusted better than previously thought. There's a photograph of him, one eye missing, still handsome and healthy, his shiny hair slicked back. He's holding the iron rod in his left hand as if to reclaim it. It's believed he may have begun a second career as a stagecoach driver in Chile.

Other famous cases include a twenty-seven-year-old man known only by his initials, H. M., who, while seeking treatment for his epileptic seizures, had his hippocampus suctioned out of both brain hemispheres by a neuroscientist. His seizures largely disappeared, but with them so did his ability to form new memories. This is how psychology discovered the hippocampus was implicated in memory.

All of this is to point out the indeterminate, almost juvenile leaps and assessments the field of neuroscience has had to make in the absence of concrete data. All of this is to say that when the doctor told us Kait may change, he couldn't specify how because he didn't know.

All of this is to say how unprepared we were.

Fourteen

Weeks later, on Valentine's Day, Kait returned to her apartment, but soon began fighting with her roommates. When she was in the hospital, they had visited her. Now, they asked her to leave. Kait was scaring them with her odd behaviors. My sister packed up her belongings and moved out.

Kait was granted medical leave for the next semester, so when she returned to Drexel University in the fall, she was permitted to begin over again. She found another roommate, another lease, another deposit. Shortly after, this new roommate requested she move out too. She was afraid of my sister too.

Finally, Mom decided to get my sister an apartment by herself. Making this financial decision was a sacrifice, one that required penny-pinching and careful planning and even the possible forfeit of my own college fund (something that frightened me but seemed an obvious sacrifice in the face of my sister's more dire needs), but Kait had proven incapable of living with others, and this was the last straw of hope that my sister could lead a normal life.

In a page from September 2012 of Mom's thick, leatherbound datebook, she laid out a timeline of this process:

> Kicked out of apartment freshman year. Threatened with restraining order.
>
> Come home.
>
> Kicked out of apartment with roommate.

Moved to single.

Kicked out for strange behavior.

Come home.

Summer → Hired college consultant.

Philadelphia Community College (apartment, single, kicked out —
she threatened managers)

Come home.

On the page is a series of perpetual beginnings with the same tireless conclusion. She wrote "Come home" repeatedly, as I spell it here. Not *comes* home, not a retelling of events, but rather a directive. *Come home*, she seems to say to Kait even now.

Our mom has always been gifted with a single-minded determination to *keep going*. In another time, we might've called this quality grit, or perseverance, or even character, but to me, it's most accurately summarized as a selfless form of survival: never allowing herself the *luxury* to quit. To take a breath, give up. Throw in the towel and have a pity party. Instead, Mom keeps living, keeps trying, keeps doing her best.

When she talks about this time now, she tells me that she couldn't complete a thought. There had, quite literally, been no time to think. There was only a circus of catastrophes, senseless and tangled.

"If I had just one hour to myself," she says. "Just one hour to sit still and rest, I could've done something. I could've helped."

Comparatively, my father wanted little to do with the roller coaster.

When they had first gotten married, my mom had an impulsive premonition, the kind that startles you with its urgency — if any of her future children ever got sick, my father, brilliant and savvy, would be able to find a cure, even if there technically was none. This was a comfort for her as she walked down the aisle. My father was the type of man who would protect us from unseen forces, who could reinvent the wheel, discover a new way forward.

She wasn't wrong, necessarily, but the crux, or maybe rather the irony, was that my father did not believe in mental illness. He didn't search for a "cure" because he did not believe there was one. He saw Kait's behavior as a result of too much partying, a poor temperament. He threw himself into his work and his own vices, believing the chaos was a bubble he could pop if only the tension built enough. It'll get worse, he reasoned, and then it'll get better, like a wound that festers before it heals or a fever that rises before it breaks.

He wasn't alone in this sentiment. None of us could fully comprehend what was happening. Why couldn't Kait stop? Why couldn't she pull it together? She must have some control over her thoughts and actions — surely she must still have free will?

It's impossible in such moments to see the truth clearly, to understand that someone who appears to "have it all" on the outside can be so fragile inside. We couldn't begin to imagine the interiority of my sister's brain: the voices and hallucinations, the paranoia, the whispers. If you've never experienced it yourself, how foreign the concept is. A voice in your head? Not the voice you hear when you read these words, one that's a faint echo of your own. No, this is a different voice entirely: dislocated from self. It's more akin to the boom of a newscaster, deep and rough, when the television is left on in the room over. Except it's inside your brain — bouncing in your skull, telling you to do things, telling you to feel things. You listen.

Kait reported to my mom that there was a swastika in the tiled floor of her apartment's entryway. She couldn't live there, she said, because the building was owned by Nazis. A pit grew in our mom's stomach. Like the nursery rhymes that warn if you swallow a seed it'll grow vines, it grew bigger and bigger.

This is not okay. Something is wrong.

When Mom checked the apartment herself, the patterned tile did faintly resemble a swastika. There was a small truth to the delusion, but not enough to warrant the response it evoked in my sister.

When we were little girls, Kait had told me she saw Santa Claus through the window of our grandparents' home, keeping the magic alive for me.

After the fall, Kait saw Santa Claus again. She called Mom to tell her he was riding in the sky. She wanted to fly with him.

Terrified for her safety, our mom convinced Kait to contact 9-1-1. At the campus hospital, she underwent a drug test. There were none in her system.

Soon after, there was a man in her living room, fixing her television late at night.

Then, a woman cutting her hair in her sleep.

New characters emerged every day, waltzing into my sister's consciousness, demanding a place in her head. Paranoia: an insistence that people could read her mind. She yelled at a woman on the train because the woman's "thoughts were evil."

And in the time it takes to move from freshman to sophomore year of college, when my sister should've been burning microwavable noodles in a cramped dorm kitchen or exploring a newfound passion for art history or dancing in poorly lit fraternity house basements, her heels sticking to the floor slick with beer, my sister had become *that* person. The one you hide from on the subway. Look away from, avoid eye contact. My *sister*, my hilarious, charming, perfect sister: now other. The irate madwoman on the train.

Fifteen

Around this time in 2011, our mom read about a nationwide trend of Adderall addiction in teenagers and young students. The symptoms included mood swings to the extent of mimicking bipolar disorder, an increase in hostility, insomnia, paranoia, incomplete thoughts, risk-taking.

It has to be that, she thought.

She had Kait report to the university nurse. Again, there were no drugs in her system.

After leaving the nurse, Kait marched into the Dean's Office. She yelled at him, accused the man of horrific thoughts. He walked her to a security car, and they admitted her to University of Pennsylvania's psychiatric ward.

When it proved not to be an addiction to Adderall, my mom also wondered about Lyme disease. Our childhood in New England came to mind.

We spent most summers on the beaches of Nantucket, where the incidence of tick-borne illnesses is among the highest in the country. I can picture us now scurrying around sand dunes and running through overgrown paths to the beach, but as far as we know none of us ever contracted it.

Finally, Kait was admitted into the hospital for more tests. And here, at last, over Kait's six-day stay, we finally got a diagnosis. The hospital conducted multiple tests — neurological scans, bloodwork, a Lyme panel — until eventually, they returned with a label: schizophrenia. This is how such diagnoses come to be: in the absence of any positive results, a process of elimination.

It took me a few tries to spell the term correctly. I imagined there would be "p" in front of it like in *psychology*. I typed "pschitzo-fren-ia" first and then "schitzo-frenia" next. What did it mean to be schizophrenic? Did it go away? It had a funny ring to it — foreign, and exotic — an illness to be found in a history textbook, a rare disease from long ago.

I discovered the etymology of the word had Greek roots: *schizo* (split) and *phrene* (mind). My sister, my other half, had a split mind: a split self.

Mental illness is tricky to wrangle, near impossible to nail down.

Diagnosis evades and varies from one doctor to the next. The terms and jargon grow locked in themselves like a snake eating its own tail — the subsets and overlaps are an indecipherable code. There's schizoaffective disorder and schizophreniform disorder, not to be confused with schizotypal personality disorder. There's bipolar I and bipolar II: not twins, not even siblings, but diagnoses with separate standards. Manic. Hypomanic. One and two. The psychology world is a web of pig Latin, as maddening as the conditions it attempts to name.

There's paranoid schizophrenia, catatonic schizophrenia (movement inhibited, rigid, and frenzied), and undifferentiated schizophrenia. When I try to Google a clearer definition of "undifferentiated schizophrenia" beyond "vague symptoms of schizophrenia," the fifth most popular suggested question is "Can schizophrenics love?"

And like that, I'm undone. I put definitions aside.

When someone you love is exhibiting signs of a psychotic disorder, you are not thinking about the minute differences of the thorny, knotted terms of the DSM-5. You're just thinking, *What can I do?* You're thinking, *Help*. You're thinking, *Please*.

Before ObamaCare, the Patient Protection and Affordable Care Act, took effect, Kait had no insurance. She wasn't a full-time student, and our parents were unable to keep her on their plan, so my family had to pay for her treatments out of pocket. A social worker suggested a free research program at UPenn for brain behavior studies.

The doctor was researching new medication and therapeutic techniques to treat schizophrenia, using fMRI, EEG, and ERP scans. Mom was initially resistant to the idea of psychiatric medication, but the doctor promised that he'd once cured a woman who believed she had spiders crawling all over her body — up her legs, arms, hair, in her nose, burrowing in her eyes. He believed he could help Kait, too. It's difficult to disagree with such logic.

Because my sister was too noncompliant to consistently ingest a pill orally (this impulse was hardly new — the stubbornness, the rebellious strong will — but the stakes were higher now), Kait began taking the anti-psychotic risperidone as an injection.

During one of these visits to receive the medication, Kait grew suddenly unnerved, adrift from the world — her grasp on material surroundings looser and looser. She shouted in the waiting room, yelled at the hospital workers who tried to calm her. My sister was taken into an examining room resembling a cold jail cell. Her eyes were wide, her pupils dilated, lost somewhere in their waves of blue and green. She was raving and ranting, and it was as if a spark had been lit — the madness creeping over her, overtaking her. She accused my mom of being an undercover assassin. Kait was gone, lost somewhere between a dream and a memory.

Our mom managed to soothe her, talk her down and placate her until finally, Kait seemed almost normal again. Yet as Mom turned to leave, my sister lost it once more. Security was forced to restrain her so Mom could escape unharmed.

Kait was admitted to the psych ward after that, this time for a longer period. Her medication was adjusted, her behavior observed.

This was the moment, our mom says, when she first understood what it meant to be the physical manifestation of the word *crazy*. Not the colloquial phrase, not the "The weather is crazy today," but really, truly, authentically insane. The origin of the word — madness, disturbance, unhinged. A detachment from reality, a severing of some invisible string grounding you in the here and now. Where did Kait go? *How do we get her back?*

Sixteen

While writing this account, the very pages you miraculously hold now between your fingers, I leaned on notes and fragments of documents my mom kept over the years. She would discover stuff periodically, cleaning out a closet or sorting through boxes under her bed. At the time, she felt some urgent impulse to collect the hard facts that surrounded our increasingly porous reality. In a world of the impossible, the unlikely, these shreds of police reports, hospital records, prescription labels, proved something infallible: the simple truth that it was all really happening. Those days, we could never be too sure.

Inside these documents, the past continues to return in surprising ways, shocking me with its vitality, hot to touch.

There is a printout from the U.S. Department of Health & Human Services on PCOS. Underneath the orange section titled "Does polycystic ovary syndrome (PCOS) put women at risk for other health problems?" there's no mention of mental illness.

On the interior fold, our mom has listed our student ID numbers, one digit apart. There's a thin blue note the doctor at Penn Medicine wrote to Drexel University after Kait's head injury, suggesting she be excused from the semester of classes. The date reads 11/5/10, a month after her fall.

There's a draft of a note our mom personally sent the dean on the back of an envelope with TIME-SENSITIVE MATERIAL stamped on the front. In it, she asks for his understanding, explaining:

Due to circumstances out of her control, Kait has been unable to complete this term. She is currently under the care of Psychiatry and Neurology at University of Pennsylvania, as well as in therapy. We hope that Kait will be able to attend school again in January. She is doing much better and looking forward to it.

The "in therapy" clause was added atop the line as an afterthought. Did mentioning therapy run the risk of rendering Kait's condition away from the neurological and into the behavioral? Would this make it less "real," less valid in the eyes of the dean? In the world of stigma, these are the questions a struggling mother must ask herself to protect her child. These are the concerns that must be addressed while fighting for your daughter's life.

In an envelope addressed with my name on it, likely an old report card, I find a business card for the Brain Behavior Laboratory at Penn Medicine, soliciting volunteers for the research study, and another patient sheet with the date 11/10/10. On it, "brief psychotic disorder" is circled in an uneven loop.

I'm surprised by these dates. Just a month after her traumatic brain injury, Kait has already dropped out of school, enrolled in a research study, and been diagnosed with a psychotic disorder. When I look back on this time, I remember the sensation of being unable to see more than three feet in front of my face. Like a rainstorm blocking our visions and blurring the windshield, there was no use imagining the next day, because every day was as unpredictable as the last. True chaos creates a vortex, makes time drip and puddle, *but did it really all come apart so fast?*

A letter from Drexel University on March 24, 2010, officially dismisses Kait from enrollment. Next, out of order, a sheet lists her hospital care instructions. On it, Kait has marked that she's allergic to penicillin. She's not, but I am. For some reason, this tiny detail makes my eyes sting.

At the very end of the papers, there's the academic calendar for Kait's missed semester. Behind it, her original acceptance letter to college. Time is a shifting tide, and you never know what shore you'll wash up on.

I'm struck by the sheer density of pain, confusion, hope, and heartbreak contained in this sterile assortment of pages. Mom's crowded, frantic notes beat alive my sister's lingering hope for recovery. The doctor's words ring hollow, a sentencing we didn't yet understand. I want to cry out when I imagine my mom collecting these documents together, trying to impose logic onto heartache. The past seems inevitable. How did we not see it?

I put the papers as neatly back together as I can. The photo that happens to land on top is of Kait and me as little girls on a ferry — her arm wrapped around my shoulders. The ink is disrupted, the colors lightened by the sun.

Seventeen

A 2015 paper from Northwestern University published in *Science Daily* about the memory blockage associated with post-traumatic stress disorder reads: "Some stressful experiences — such as chronic childhood abuse — are so traumatic, the memories hide like a shadow in the brain and can't be consciously accessed."

The memories hide like a shadow in the brain.

I note here the word *shadow*. A shadow can be larger than the figure itself, elongated, looming, darker. It's ominous and foreboding, mysterious and ever-present. It shifts in your peripheral. Traumatic memories are not *gone*, they're just obscured. They take on a life of their own — sometimes bigger than the event itself. Almost always more difficult to grasp.

Sometimes I wonder if somewhere in the cosmos there's an alternative universe, playing back an endless loop of our escapes — our past selves still stuck in a constant fight for our survival. Sometimes, it seems inconceivable that we escaped at all.

The memories of these encounters hide in my brain. They're there, but they're fleeting: shifting, intangible. I forget whole years, trip over moments, stumble through my middle and high school years. Kait suffered from a traumatic brain injury and was diagnosed with schizophrenia when I was only twelve years old. The chaos, the violence, the heartache of that time slipped through my developing, adolescent brain. (Recently my mom tried to convince me of a fourteenth birthday party she threw that I had no recollection of. We went around in circles as she described the venue, the guests, how it was the first boy-girl party I ever held, while I vehemently denied its existence. Only after I saw the photographs did I believe her — still, for as long as I stared at the images, no memories arrived.)

My body has protected me, concealed the very worst of it, but in doing so, it has also made me an unreliable narrator with silhouettes for memories.

Here's what I can recall:

We pack bags. Mom and I shove emergency pajamas and overnight cosmetics — contact lenses for the morning, face wash, toothpaste — into hidden suitcases, tucked behind curtains, readily accessible in a rush. We memorize the closest exits, the quickest way out: Everywhere is a fire drill. When Kait is in between apartments, she stays at our family house and Mom prefers that I sleep in my parents' room. There's a balcony there. We could jump into the bushes if we needed to, if it got to that point. There's comfort in this knowledge. When I sleep alone, I barricade my door with furniture; a chair or the bench at the end of my bed where my old American Girl Dolls are stored. The childhood objects weigh it down.

There's a scene in the memoir *Brain on Fire* by Susannah Cahalan, when, beginning to undergo the symptoms of a rare autoimmune disease, Cahalan exhibits schizophrenic symptoms and hallucinations.

In the car on the way to the hospital, she hears her mom's new husband call her a "whore" in the front seat.

"What did you say?" she demands.

Her stepfather is bewildered. The car is silent. He didn't say anything, but she *heard* it. She really heard it. More than a whisper, more than the chime of the wind. She heard a real, physical voice. *His* voice.

"*What the fuck did you say to me?*" Kait will snap at us.

Again and again, I haven't said anything. Again and again, she claims she can hear my thoughts. Again and again, she lashes out — physically or emotionally, often both.

This period of symptom-rich psychotic break is often referred to as the "active phase" or sometimes even as "florid" psychosis. The word choice here implies flowering: the end result of schizophrenia, a bud that has bloomed. The denotation reminds me of a sped-up video of a flower unfurling in a single breath: the soft petals exhaling open.

The active phase of schizophrenia is none of this. If it is a flower, then it is one that has been crushed and crumpled, bleeding color into the earth. It is no more a beginning than the onset of Alzheimer's is. Schizophrenia is many ends, countless ends, piled atop one another.

In psychotic bursts, Kait makes threats. She'll burn the house down in our sleep, she says. We believe her. She knows where the knives are, and she'll whip them out. We take to hiding them. She thinks we're trying to kill her, keep her captive. We're out to get her. She'll get to us first. All we can do is run.

My sister chases us with an iron poker in the backyard. She throws a heavy, bronze full-length mirror at Mom. (I recently found images of the broken shards scattered across the upstairs balcony and downstairs in the foyer. Just like the mirror that broke when we were children; more than seven years later we found ourselves with another seven years of bad luck, this time self-induced.)

My sister hits my father in his sleep with a weight (there's another photo of the bruise behind his ear, yellow and purple with inflammation). Kait throws pottery at us — expensive Italian Deruta our mom has been collecting piece by piece for years. There's a photo of the trail of shattered pottery leading into our living room. In the background, you can see the teal of my rain boots. I thought Kait would appreciate the bright color, but she was too far gone by that point to ever notice.

When I was younger, twelve, thirteen, even fourteen, my mom would tell me to run into my bedroom and lock the door when Kait entered into a delusional breakdown, and I would listen. I used to grab our two dogs and usher them upstairs with me, locking the door behind us and leaning against the wooden frame for good measure. I held their shaking bodies as they sat in my lap. "Shush," I tried to comfort them while petting their soft fur. "Everything is going to be okay." *Shush*, I tried to tell myself, too, *everything is going to be okay.*

For a while, this worked. There seemed to be some limit Kait had drawn with me, holding me captive, making physical threats, throwing objects in my direction but never actually seriously harming me. Something stopped her every time from following through; some part of the older sister who once shielded me from the world now was shielding me from herself, from the battle being waged inside her brain.

But as I grew older, I could no longer bear being away from my family in these moments of crisis. I needed to be there to protect my mom (in reality, there was little I could do to help, but it's impossible to surrender even the falsest sense of control in these moments). I continued to hide the dogs, to keep them away from any danger, but hiding was no longer an option for myself, and the more I challenged my sister, the more in danger I became.

Once she tried to push me off a balcony at a rental beach house we were staying at. Earlier that same day, she comforted me over my pubescent breakouts, letting me borrow some face wash and concealer.

Now her hands reach toward me. She wraps her full hand around my wrists, squeezing them tight, holding me there as a prisoner with handcuffs of her own design. I try to fight back, but it's useless. As much as I writhe and wiggle, I am trapped, powerless. I have never felt so impossibly small in this world. Mom distracts Kait by calling attention to herself long enough for me to escape. This is how we survive: taking turns in sacrifice, a game of diversion.

We keep lacrosse sticks hidden behind curtains although we know we'd never have the guts, the brutality, to actually defend ourselves with them. When my father is home, we mostly stay put and attempt to deescalate the situation, but when he's away, as he often is, Mom and I flee instead. Kait is stronger than us. Not only is she physically larger, taller and more muscular — but she seems to be fueled by a rage that never dims. There is no other option. Leaving is the only way to stay safe, to stay alive.

We escape in the middle of the night — in the morning, after school, before sports practice, at noon on an otherwise peaceful, quiet Sunday. The chaos has no bounds, no time frame, no workday hours. It's eerie how quickly the shift can occur — supernatural or even dystopian, like a robot whose commands have changed in the midst of an action. Kait will laugh one moment, and then the next take the wheel of the car out of Mom's hands, careening us into traffic.

After fearing for your life enough times, you learn that the shaking doesn't come on gradually anymore. It doesn't start small and grow large. It sparks at once. Your body is ready for it, for the fear, because it's used to it by now: a well-practiced race, a seasoned athlete with muscle memory. Your tremors begin loud and violent. They take over your body before a thought can solidify into coherency. You think, *Surely I must break this time. Surely my body cannot withstand this any longer. My bolts and screws are falling out of place. I am coming undone.*

I grab my backpack, and I complete my homework in hotel rooms, in the public library, in the passenger seat of our car as we wait in a random empty parking lot. We eat a dinner of Chipotle in the front seat, but our stomachs never rest long enough to enjoy it. Mostly, we go to a small, unexciting hotel chain near our home and I study for my exams by the dingy light of the room's meager desk. When we walk into the front entranceway, I wonder if the employees can see the truth smeared on our faces. Our clothes are randomly, haphazardly thrown on; we wear no makeup. Our eyes are alert and distrustful; animals backed into a cage. We used to be a band of three, but now I hunker down with Mom and our dogs alone.

I worry sometimes about seeing someone I know. What would I tell them? How could I make them understand? I love my sister, and it's not her fault — she's ill, tortured by her own mind — but I'm still terrified. It's still not okay. I show up to my morning classes, and I put on my brightest smile. I start wearing as many colors as I can find: bright shirts, bright backpacks. Black and gray and muted tones are in, a minimalist style, but I don't care. So much of my life is out of my hands now, but *this* I have control over, so it has to be bright. It has to be happy.

I paint myself my own flag, and I think of my sister and how before her illness, she used to do the same: her colorful Hawaiian ski jacket and rainbow moon boots, creativity splashing out of every choice. That girl is fading, so I try to carry a piece of her with me: an act of defiance against the person she is becoming. A protest against the disease bleaching her day by day.

The only person I reveal an inkling of Kait's condition to is a childhood friend who I know can be trusted. We have no classes together, share very few close friends. Our friendship exists in a vacuum, so I don't have to worry about her seeing the look on my face when I arrive late to school one morning, or stress about her gossiping to anyone else we know. After all, this isn't my story to reveal, and I can't risk violating Kait's privacy. News of tragedy spreads like flames on dried leaves, consuming and fascinating in a horrifying, dangerous way.

I don't say it to my friend in person — that would be too difficult — I text her instead. I tell her I spent the night before in a hotel. We called the cops — for the what, the fourth? fifth? sixth time that month? — our familial drama spewed onto the front lawn, an open-air show for our quiet neighborhood. There was a restraining order left unfilled on the counter of my kitchen. Our mom was too heartbroken to ever follow through with it, but the appearance of its yellow, punched frame frightens me: so permanent, bureaucratic and official, an intruder in our home.

At lunch, sitting at a separate table across our crowded cafeteria, my friend recalled how the girl next to her happened to point out how happy I always looked. Like sunshine, she said: light hair, colorful clothing, a wide smile, unbridled joy. *What does a girl like that possibly have to worry about?* the girl wondered. *If only she knew,* my friend thought.

I learned long ago to zip myself up, leading two separate lives: a splintered self.

I devote myself to academics, taking as many Honors and AP courses as I can find, forcefully flinging myself into some future I can't imagine but hope is there when the smoke clears. I do everything you're supposed to do — I laugh on cue, I go to the parties and the dances, the sports practices (lacrosse, tennis, squash, and crew) and the volunteer clubs, and I present myself the picture of ease. When the whole world is upside down, sometimes the sanest place is closest to the ground.

Kait developed multiple personalities, different versions of herself, and in their presence, I created my own.

Eighteen

I found my reading habits drawn to dystopian and fantasy stories around this age: Harry Potter books, *The Hunger Games, Twilight, Uglies, The Lightning Thief*, anything with a clear enemy. I loved the transparency of it all: good and evil. My life was a constant breaching of moral code, a subversion of expectations where my sister, my first friend and protector, was now someone I needed to protect, and also someone I needed protection *from*. In every other aspect, I had always drawn careful lines and took great pride in my self-imposed tidy boxes.

In these books, I loved the commonality of a shared enemy, a cause to fight for. A person to fight against. The Harry Potter books offered the greatest escape — even the color of the Death Eaters' magic was divisive, a clear signal of who was to be trusted and who was not. The villain, Voldemort, was *"born bad."* Other characters were more complicated: Snape, Dumbledore, Harry, even J. K. Rowling herself, who has since become a polarizing political figure, but the main villain was really, in the end, quite simple. He hurt people, and he had to go. I craved such certainty of conviction. When he died, you didn't feel loss: You felt cathartic relief. Finally, everyone could relax.

The villain of my life was also the victim. My villain broke me, but my heart broke for her. There was no winning, only new ways to lose on a gradient scale. I wanted to hate her, but I didn't. I wanted to fully let her in, but I couldn't. So I turned to fantasies, and in my dreams, I became my own protagonist. My sleep was consumed by narratives of good and evil: entangled, complex storylines of alien abductions or kidnappings or dark magic. I fought against evils of my creation. I triumphed, I conquered. Finally, fighting back would not mean hurting someone I loved. I would no longer have to simultaneously juggle pity and fear: There was a mission, a goal. When someone in my dreams held me back, threatened me, hit me, I could hit them back. I could escape. I could *win*.

Sometimes, late at night, after watching some cheap movie thriller, my friends and I would debate the concept of a fight-or-flight response: If the moment presented itself, we asked each other, would you fight or run for your life? The question was proposed as a distant, midnight kind of musing, the way you habitually pull back a shower curtain whenever you're in the bathroom — you know no one is there, but you check anyway. *Just in case.*

My friends giggled because they didn't know their answers — they could only guess. I didn't laugh, because I thought I knew mine.

I have this dream where I'm cornered in an alley and some hooded crook is wagging a knife at me (he is always hooded, masked like a superhero, shadows cast over his face in long misshapen waves).

There's a theory that every person in your dreams is someone you've seen before: The idea behind it is that the brain is incapable of inventing new faces, only recycling ones it has already processed in passing: the woman in the grocery aisle examining the bruised apple, the lanky boy who fills up your gas tank. When faced with an attacker, I never see a face, because to see one would be to give my attacker interiority: a mother waiting up for him, a failed dream, a sister who admires him, a complicated childhood, perhaps, that has led to this very moment — him and me in that shadowed corner.

When the man steps closer, I whack him on the side of his head with an open hand, shatter his eardrum like a former wrestler once taught me. I shove his nose until it tickles his brain. I won't let anyone hurt me again. I won't even let them try. (In real life, I do none of this. In real life, the slightest harsh grab of my wrists sends my bones rattling.)

I used to worry that Kait would hurt someone in a manic fit — some poor individual in the wrong place at the wrong time. I also worried about someone hurting her back. A stranger bumping into her in a crowded doorway entrance. Kait would shove the man against the wall, spit on his new sweater, say something terrible and unfortunately true. What if he was dangerous? What if he took out a gun? "She's sick," I'd want to tell him. "Please don't hurt her."

Ignoring the complexity of humanity makes one complicit in horrific atrocities and lapses in judgment. It's perhaps the worst kind of cognitive bias, but when your whole life is muddled, sometimes you *covet* simplicity of any form.

On the rare occasions when Mom was at a doctor's office for her own care rather than someone else's, she faced emotional land mines in even the standard medical questions.

"Are you active?"

"Do you drink? Smoke?"

"Do you have any allergies we should know about?"

Simple answers, and then, one that wasn't:

"Do you feel safe at home?"

How was she supposed to tell them that no, she didn't feel safe? What if it's your child endangering you? What if it's not her fault? What if it's not that simple? Does the vocabulary exist for such an answer? A mother is not supposed to be afraid of her daughter. It's her *child*, inseparable as her own heartbeat, familiar as the back of her hand.

I try to imagine how it felt for our mom to be asked such a question at the doctor's office, the harsh bulbs of the office flashing down like a spotlight, the whole environment too exposing, too official, too common. Mom would pause, shifting ever so slightly on the exam table, setting off a fire of crinkles as the thin paper moved beneath her.

"Yes, I'm fine." She smiled her beautiful smile, rows of white. Her bounce of wide curls curved in to her face like a frame around a picture. Again and again, she lied ever so slightly.

In the Harry Potter series, there are dementors — cloaked and billowy soulless creatures that suck the life out of the atmosphere, draining anything bright. They're preceded by a chilly fog, the surroundings crystalizing with a coat of ice — breath now visible in a puff of white. Lights flicker out. The sun is blocked. A sense of hopeless despair dawns, drop by drop as the dementor's decaying hands poke out of their long black cape. Their appearance is ghastly enough, but what makes the dementors so formidable is their ability to force you to relive the worst moments of your life, leaving you to drown in the hopeless memories, siphoning out the good. This is an important lesson: What has the power to destroy us already lives inside us. It requires no outside intervention.

J. K. Rowling, the author of the Harry Potter series, admits using her own experience with depression as a basis for the dementors' power. It's a metaphor that's acutely on the mark. When the dementors are done with you, you're filled with self-loathing.

The only way to fight these creatures is by conducting a Patronus charm — a soft, glittery light that takes the shape of an animal meant to represent your soul. To produce it, you must think of the happiest memory you have, focus all of your efforts on this one moment, pour your energy into the very best of you.

This is ultimately the recurring theme of most fantasy stories: Evil can always be defeated by the power of love.

When the fighting escalates and I hide in my room, the miniature blue and yellow chair from my childhood blocking the door, or stand there and face my sister head-on, I try this coping mechanism. I think of my happiest memories with Kait, as if by concentrating hard enough I can cast the bad away, heal her from the inside out.

I think of us as little girls on the beach, the tide washing up clumps of thick seaweed the color of her eyes, the sand blowing in the breeze, picking up a wayward rope or an ocean-battered twig. I remember how we laughed that day in soft chimes, sharp yelps, and I realize the reversal of the metaphor is true as well: Just as we already have everything inside us to hurt, so too do we have everything we need to redeem ourselves. I do my best to focus on the light.

Nineteen

As I try to explain these years in which my sister's troubles were murky water, shifting diagnoses and explosive fights, I find myself leaning on war terms.

Every moment of respite was a *ceasefire*. I *barricaded* my bedroom door. We discussed the *trajectory* of her illness as if it were a missile headed for us. We *fled*. Kait was *combative*. We had *game plans, escape routes, safe places*.

At the time, I kept returning to the idea of the soldiers I read about in my history classes. Dramatic landscapes of men on horseback, the sky behind them alive with bursts of cloud formations and ominous stormy colors. We memorized the fights, the outcomes, the historical significance, but I was left wondering about the hours between the battles. How did the soldiers sleep knowing they could be attacked at any moment? How did they fill the lapses of time that felt almost eerily normal? Did they play cards by candlelight or tell stories of their lives back home, the women, families, waiting for them? Were these moments of waiting almost worse than the actual fighting, knowing what was to come but having no ability to stop it?

I've heard that when you love someone with dementia, the brief flashes in which the person temporarily returns can be the most heartbreaking. It's the hope, I assume, that gets you; the reminder that the one you love is still in there, and then the loss you experience all over again when they disappear back into the crevices of their minds. Isn't that the cruelest way to lose someone, after all? Bearing witness to their destruction, helpless to make it stop? A fog that creeps and then clears, only to return to its steady progression as if the moment of clarity, of daybreak, never happened at all.

Although they're not the same, not by any means, there's a thread of pain that connects these distinct traumas — the windows of hope that pop up in a degenerative disease and the pauses in an existence run by violence. I was not in *battle* with my sister, but I was in battle with the person she was becoming, with the disorder that seeped into her brain like the slow crawl of liquid through a napkin or ink dispersing in water.

In the hours or days when her turmoil settled, Kait would come back to herself.

She didn't want to be like this, she told us.

She didn't want to be who she was becoming. It wasn't her.

On May 6, 2010, only a few months after her head injury when Kait's schizophrenic symptoms were skyrocketing, she sent me the following message at 2:16 a.m.

I wish your face was little still so I could squeeze it and tell you that I will be the best sister in the entire world to you! I'm not nice to you I'm not fair to you I have so much happiness that I owe you! It's all my fault, I never want to you to see me again with the capital L on my forehead haaha you're perfect and you're perfecting everything that I couldn't!!! . . .

I act like a tough guy and I'm so sorry for being embarrassing . . . I sure hope I get to laugh at myself when I'm a little bit older

Will you let me know what you want me to do to help you forgive me? I love you more than anything in this world you're my life.

. . .

If you have any questions or are confused ask me immediately because I'm just remembering who I am . . . and HATING who I've turned into! I'm promising this to you so we don't have anything but the best loving relationship that we can . . . will you do that with your LOOPY sister? <3<3

She sent me the message immediately after one of her episodes, where she had screamed and threatened me. I remember opening the notification on my Facebook page, seeing the familiar lines of my sister's name, feeling that flash of hope and love. And then, in the next moment, being unbelievably tired. Here was the vibrancy of her personality in her word choice ("loopy," she said, as if to downplay the severity of the situation). Here was the sister I knew so well, the childhood protector, the silly playmate, but by this point I also knew too well that it was only a matter of minutes before she left me again. How could I allow myself the hope that today would be different, that this time she would stay?

This was Kait's routine: After an episode, she would apologize. It was a near impossible apology to reject. Her face was a winning combination of demure regret — eyes cast down, delicate nose pointed toward the ground — and a slight tinge of mischief. Her lips turned upward ever so slightly, as if to suggest the whole argument was a colossal joke, a simple misunderstanding between loved ones. It was real, it was authentic: You believed she meant it, but you also knew that she wouldn't be able to hold herself to the promise. Your heart cracked for her, even when you couldn't trust her.

The routine would follow with my sister leaving Post-it notes in my binders or textbooks, hidden between pages.

"I'm sorry," I saw when I flipped the book open in class.

Or, "You're the prettiestttt ever!!!!"

Some days even, "You're the best little sistaaa in the world!!"

I crumpled the neon squares in anger and disbelief, throwing them in a trash can only to retrieve the paper and carefully smooth the edges, press it between heavy pages as if to preserve a dying flower.

"It takes a hundred compliments to build someone, but only one to destroy you," I scrawled on the back of bulleted class notes.

What I'm trying to say is that sometimes Kait came back to herself.

What I'm trying to say is that I wanted her to stay.

She never did.

• • •

Just as there is a vague similarity between war and mental illness, there is also a connection between schizophrenia and dementia. Even though they are two separate neurological diseases, individuals with schizophrenia are more likely to develop Alzheimer's than the average population. Is this because the cognitive dysfunction inherent in schizophrenia lends itself to the progressive degeneration of dementia? Research has not yet determined this.

With Alzheimer's, one of the first signs of deterioration is often the patient's own burgeoning sense of frustration at their inability to function at previous cognitive levels. This can include volatile reactions, feelings of lack of control, and difficulty with emotional regulation. As abnormal deposits of proteins form amyloid plaques and tau clumps throughout the brain and tissue begin to shrink, neurons cease to function.

While writing the beginnings of this book, I sat in my local library in the magazine section surrounded by glossy international fashion spreads and economic reports. A middle-aged man pulled out the chair next to mine, igniting the creaking roar of wood on wood. He saw the open Word doc on my computer and the long list of chapter ideas not yet realized.

"What are you writing about?" he asked.

The word "schizophrenia" still had a difficult journey leaving my throat. To say it aloud seemed to break some unspoken social code not to disrupt the status quo or dampen the mood. In the few times I ventured to mention it, people looked at me as if I were actively shedding the disease: the gene codes clinging to the threads of my sweater and dangling in the air like leprosy.

"It's a book about sisters." I smiled politely before returning to my keyboard — a statement no less true but vastly simplified.

Soon after, a librarian walked by and said hello to the man. As they chatted easily, I overheard him explain his mother's recent diagnosis of Alzheimer's.

It shocked me how relatively easy it appeared to be for him to say this.

While undoubtedly incredibly painful to speak about, Alzheimer's disease is immediately understood, universally sympathized. This stranger and I both had loved ones fighting an invisible neurological brain disorder characterized by cognitive deficits and a change in perception and personality expression, and yet I felt muzzled by my sister's diagnosis whereas he did not.

Every time I thought to tell someone, something stopped me: the tone in a friend's voice as they said the phrase "crazy people" with an eye roll or a grimace. At the time, it seemed every popular television series had an "escape the psych ward" episode — producers in Hollywood thinking it a novelty, a fun, lighthearted adventure or a change of scenery. This "normal," wrongly admitted outsider always seems to look at the other patients in horror as they act in strange but comical ways: playing Poker with invisible cards, wearing clothes backwards, having elaborate conversations with themselves.

When I was fourteen, a year into my sister's diagnosis of schizophrenia, I watched the characters of *Pretty Little Liars* traipse through a state psychiatric hospital, in one episode equating villainous behavior with mental illness for their impressionable viewers. My friends screeched and covered their eyes, as I was left staring at the screen, thinking about the invisible damage being done in that very moment — how without any formal mental health education in our schools, this stereotype was the default teacher of our society.

It's surprising how misrepresented schizophrenia is in our culture: The condition is either sensationalized for dramatic effect — straitjackets, muzzles, blaringly white walls of psychiatric units — or, it is somehow lightened, made a joke out of. I cannot count how many times I have witnessed otherwise intelligent, informed, and well-intentioned people misunderstand psychotic disorders.

As a junior in high school, I listened as my AP English teacher described a character in a book as "schizophrenic." What she meant to say was that the individual's actions did not meet their intentions — they were cognitively misaligned. What she said was "schizophrenic."

It is nearly impossible to explain how often these misrepresentations come up, because they are so ever-present as to be nearly invisible. It's every time the word *crazy* is used, or *madness*, or even the expression that someone is *cracked* — the implication of being mentally unsound linked inherently to head trauma.

In 2014, when I was sixteen and my sister twenty-two and in the deepest throes of her battle, the popular child star Amanda Bynes made headlines for a series of odd Twitter rants, lashing out at family, friends, and other celebrities. The media response was quick and cruel. She became a joke. Even after she admitted to being diagnosed with bipolar affective disorder and manic depression, I watched as my high school friends poked fun at her in our group chat or over our sandwiches at lunch. *What would they think of my sister?* I thought. *How can I ever make anyone understand?*

Other questions followed: Would my friends' parents let them hang out with me if they knew my sister was potentially dangerous? Would they blame our mom? *Would they be waiting for me to snap too?* Would any sign of weakness, of emotional volatility — getting in an argument, crying over a boy, fighting with another girl in our group — be used as proof that I was "unwell," "unstable," too? I remained silent.

Even though in the last few years time and advocacy work has lessened mental health stigma enormously, particularly within the diagnoses of anxiety and depression, psychotic disorders remain largely underrepresented in public discussions. And all of these tiny moments breed further silence: a thousand microaggressions eating away at any hope for empathy or change.

You can say that your loved one has dementia without worrying about the fear, the apprehension, the recoil. You can say it without worry that someone else might consider you yourself now unsafe, scary, or even villainous. Schizophrenia is different. Schizophrenia is all too often a punch line, an insult.

◆　◆　◆

After school one day during my freshman year of high school, Kait's mood was steady. We watched a television show together in our den like we used to as children. Except this time, I was nervous. Anxiety scattered the room and weighed down our conversation. I wanted to enjoy the peace with her, to find happiness in the relief, but I didn't trust it. I never knew when chaos would strike.

I was eating a bowl of soup, putting the spoon into the bowl, bringing it to my mouth —

"Why are you holding the spoon like that?"

Kait's voice held a chilly quality, disassociated from her normal warm tone. It sent shivers down my spine. There was anger, so much anger about the way I held my spoon. Why couldn't I even hold a stupid spoon right? *What is wrong with me?* I thought.

A barrage of insults arrived soon after, venomous and poignant, resonant to my deepest insecurities. I was used to these. The shock factor was gone — I could almost ignore it. Almost.

Kait hated my nose. My laugh. How my upper lip was too thin so my gums peeked through when I smiled wide. Why was I so stupid? Why was I such a loser? Everyone hated me, you know. I was a hideous witch. No one cared about what my report cards said: I was a dumbass — only "book smart." I didn't know shit about anything.

I knew the drill by now. I was numb to it. I put the spoon back into the bowl, quietly, as if not to wake a sleeping baby. I tried to steady my hands so the ceramic wouldn't rattle as I brought it to the sink, taking deliberate, slow steps. If the bowl shook, what would she do? What incentive for cruelty would that give her? In what ways would her mind twist what she was seeing?

My sister followed me from close behind, continuing the insults.

I managed to get into my room, close the door, block it with a chair, text my mom and tell her what was happening. I wrapped my arms around my knees and sank onto the floor, my back to the door. My half-eaten dinner churned weightlessly in my stomach.

This is why I could never afford to get comfortable, never relax enough to settle down. It didn't matter how hard I tried not to trigger a fault line. Just holding a spoon was enough to do it.

And, worst of all, I believed her. I knew she was unwell, but in my adolescent insecurity I still believed her. My sister came into madness in the years I was coming into myself. From age eleven to age sixteen, as I was forming my identity, my sense of self, Kait was telling me I was worthless. I hated myself. Looking back now, I can tell I had body dysmorphia: an obsession with perceived faults disproportionate to reality. When you live in violence, you absorb it — direct it either toward yourself or toward others. I chose self-hatred. I looked in the mirror and I wanted to die the way you want to crawl into bed after a long, hard day of work. I *craved* the break. I was sick of myself, sick with myself. I was tired.

I think back to the little girls on the beach, the shorter, blonder one running after her tall, tan sister, constantly chasing after her approval. I remember that time in my life when I was so safe in Kait's love and attention, I never needed to speak at all. Now I was afraid to make a noise. How could I survive this? *Why should I want to?*

Psychotic disorders are a rare breed of illness that take more than a person's life or their ability to physically function. They drain relationships. They have the power to rewrite the past, to stain everything that came before and everything that will come after. There is nothing worse. There is nothing more terrifying than losing yourself.

Kait claimed she knew what I was thinking, and what I was thinking was disgusting. What I was thinking was horrible, and God knew it, too. Everyone knew it. How could I think that? Now even my mind wasn't safe. Schizophrenia had taken me captive too. In the silence of inexpression, the locked hours of suffering, we had become a family each sick with a singular disease. Kait's illness spread in this darkness the way all creeping matter prospers only in the dampest, most hidden places.

Twenty

Mom was alone for the majority of the events of these years.

She was alone in family court when Kait tried to leave the psych ward and she had to have her involuntarily committed. She was alone when my sister walked into the courtroom wearing shackles, and she was alone when the judge ordered her back to the hospital for more tests.

She was alone with the doctors and in most of the psychiatric wards. I visited my sister a few times, but Mom shielded me from seeing the worst of it. Seeing how Kait could be sweet one moment, letting Mom lie beside her in the hospital bed or begging on her knees on the linoleum floor to be taken home, and then in a flash, Kait's hands would clasp around our mom's throat. My sister writhing in the hospital bed, spewing vitriolic nonsense, bound to the sides of the cotton sheets like a criminal.

Most of all, our mom was alone in her decisions. My father was working, trying to keep us financially afloat. While he tried his best to help us with Kait, he didn't believe in treatments and rehabilitation centers. He believed in tough love, not "new age therapy." Every decision was a battle — Mom and I on one side of the argument, my father on the other. I would try to hold meetings in our living room, gathering everyone together in one space, including Kait, whose treatment we were discussing, and putting on an authoritative, calm front to the best of my preteen abilities. I thought that I could serve as a neutral mediator, bridging the gaps between everyone's differing emotions and complicated relationships.

Mostly, Kait stayed quiet during these discussions or spontaneously combusted in frustration — I knew it must be incredibly demeaning for her to watch her baby sister try to talk about her condition as if I some-how knew what it was like, but staying uninvolved no longer seemed like an option. And yet my attempts at mediation were fruitless, because any common ground we found was quickly lost, driving a wedge between my father and me until he felt almost like a stranger.

The next two years can only be categorized as a blur of psychiatric fa-cilities, group homes, and treatment programs. Which came first?

Kait returned home after her last hospitalization at Penn Medicine. She began regularly seeing a therapist and a psychiatrist. After being kicked out of Drexel University, she tried taking courses at Delaware County Community College. I remember her coming into my room one day with a printed sheet of paper. She looked tired and defeated; her skin was pale, her hair, once lustrous and long, was growing brittle and split at the ends from straightening it too often, a compulsive tic. Yet I remem-ber how my heart leapt to see her enter my room. Even then, I looked up to her. Even then, there was still an inherent light about her, shining from beneath it all.

"Ky, can you read this essay over for me?"

I was in the ninth grade, unequipped to be editing a college essay, but I took the paper from her hand eagerly, thrilled to be of service even as I understood what humility it required for her to ask for my assistance, her junior by six years. Kait walked back to her room slowly, sadness sur-rounding her. It was enough to break me. We overuse the phrase "broken heart," but that's what it really feels like: a physical slicing.

The sheet was filled with sentences that almost made sense but didn't. Phrases that ran into each other and then butted heads. I couldn't under-stand what I was seeing. Kait was once a talented writer, naturally sharp. It was one of her best skills. She had journals filled with quotes and ac-companying doodles. She was creative, could tackle anyone in a debate. She breezed through standardized tests when she tried — although of-ten, even before she became sick with schizophrenia, she didn't try, choos-ing to circle random bubbles instead out of teenage rebellion.

But this essay was beyond neglect. It was struggle, clear as day — I could watch her thoughts move across the page and slip. Like how people say "I can hear your gears moving," I was seeing Kait's efforts to think a cohesive thought. She couldn't complete a full sentence, let alone a paragraph.

This was not her work. This was not Kait.

Another moment, another fragment of her lost, then. I was losing Kait with every passing day.

I made edits, adding sentences in the margins, expanding on ideas and correcting grammar. When I handed the paper back to her, I told her it was great. I asked if she wanted me to type it up. She shook her head slowly.

"No, but thanks, Kyle," she said, smiling softly.

I never found out if she actually made the changes or if that final step proved too difficult. I wanted to fall on my knees. I wanted to lift her up, give her a hug, and say that I understood, promise her that it was all going to be okay. I forgave her for everything. But I didn't.

Instead, I turned back to my room, hollow and rotten, helpless to prevent her from fading away from me.

Was this a quality of schizophrenia? Cognitive dysfunction is a core feature of the illness, but head injuries cause impairments of their own. Where is the line? When did we start to lose her for good? *Why does it matter so deeply to me to be able to pinpoint a moment, a reason?*

Soon after, Kait attended Michael's House Treatment Center in California. After that, she entered a different sober-living home. This was followed by yet another. She would return home to Philly, then back to California for more treatment. There was a stay at Bryn Mawr Hospital, another sober-living facility in Pennsylvania. Thirty days at Malvern Institute. She was kicked off a plane for having a psychotic episode, held by security. She was rejected from several of these sober-living homes, told she was "unfit" for treatment due to her violent outbursts. When she was away, when we were physically safe, I felt a kind of sickening relief that only made me miss how my sister used to be even more.

This is the reality of living with someone with severe mental illness

— the trauma, the tensions, the hospitalizations, and the episodes become so tangled together, so erratic, so without reason or cause, they are undecipherable from one another. They wiggle through time randomly.

The partying was a contributing factor to the chaos, but it wasn't the basis. It seemed to be an attempt at self-medication, and when we treated this self-medication, the underlying symptoms were left to rampage. Since then, there has been a surge in "dual diagnosis" treatment centers, facilities designed to manage the co-occurring disorders of substance abuse and other mental illnesses, but at the time, the concept was relatively new.

I recently found a stack of yellow domestic dispute paperwork tucked into one of my sister's old college notebooks, preserved presumably by our mom. The edges have square hole punches as if they were ripped from a booklet. The paper is thin and wispy like printer paper peeled back a layer.

Cop cars arrived at our home at least seven to eight times, their blue and red lights flashing in our windowpanes, before finally taking Kait to a state hospital. They were growing weary of showing up, I could tell, as the cycle kept repeating. I tried to imagine what they thought as each call came in from our family, draining their resources and time. Why couldn't we control ourselves? Why couldn't we control Kait?

And yet: how incredibly lucky we were, even then. To be able to trust that when our lives were threatened by my sister's psychotic delusions, calling the cops wouldn't make things worse. We had the luxury of believing we would be protected rather than further endangered. According to the Treatment Advocacy Center, people with untreated mental illness are sixteen times more likely to be killed by law enforcement than other civilians. The whiteness of our skin, the suburban zip code of our neighborhood, made it much more likely that Kait, and we, would be treated with compassion and patience rather than violence, with sedatives rather than bullets. There are far too many BIPOC families in America who cannot afford that kind of faith in law enforcement. For as hard as our battle was, it is unthinkable how much worse it is for others without our privileges.

In mental healthcare, this process of recovery, relapse, rejection from facilities, police reports, and failed medical intervention is referred to as a "revolving door." In one place, out the next. The term suggests agency, like a little kid in a hotel lobby, spinning round and round in a circle for fun. As if the individual is choosing to be rejected by facilities, electing to be spun into a cycle of disappointment and heartache. In application, this failure of our healthcare system is less a revolving door and more a tornado. Like my seven-year-old self in my Halloween costume, you are Dorothy from *The Wizard of Oz*. You find yourself in an unknown landscape again and again, and all you want is to *go home*.

In the worst cases, individuals with psychotic disorders are often left with no options but homelessness. When your condition leaves you unable to live with family or friends and incapable of abiding by the rules of group homes and subsidized housing, where else are you to go? We were, again, fortunate enough that we had the resources to keep Kait afloat. But even being "lucky," even without headwinds against us and our whole family willing, desperate to make it work, we were in a broken system. It was bad for us, and it is a thousand times worse for so many others. Something has to change.

The facility I remember most vividly was dimly lit. The carpet in the entrance was old and stained; a musty scent crawled from the closed front door behind us up to the narrow staircase. The thick air smelled like cat litter. Mom and I walked together in the same choked silence. It was a silence of camaraderie, of mutual incapacity. We knocked on the door.

The drapes on the living room windows were drawn, smothering the light of the bright blue day and creating shadows on the cracked kitchen floor. A television was playing a mindless game show while several women between the ages of eighteen and thirty stared at the screen. I remember one of their mouths hanging lightly open. I was fourteen, and the image disturbed me.

Kait was one of the women. Her mouth was closed, but she wore the same absent expression as the others.

When she saw us, she sprang from the vinyl couch, an eager smile flashing across her face. "You came!" Kait hugged us.

My sister showed us to her room. I can't remember what the bedroom looked like except that it was also dark. I can't tell you what colors the walls were or what her bedspread was. All I know is that they were unremarkable: the same dingy, depressing shades of brown, yellow, and green that clung to everything — colors meant to hide stains.

I sat on the edge of her bed, hesitantly, delicately, as my mom went through Kait's open suitcase and began to fold her clothes. They were the same shirts she always wore, the same bright colors, and the same sweet smell of Kait's perfume.

My older sister was in front of me and excited to see me. Excited in a way older sisters rarely are. She hugged me and thanked me for making the drive. She asked about my classes as Mom moved from folding to dusting: a nervous, absent-minded habitual cleaning.

The attention made me anxious. I wanted Kait to tease me. To call me her nickname for me, "Kyle," or point at the blemishes on my forehead and tell me they formed the newest constellation. I wanted her to act like my sister.

The medicine made her less of herself than she already was. The hallucinations took away her mind, but the pills stripped her identity. She wasn't angry anymore, she wasn't enraged, but she wasn't Kait.

Seeing her in the group home was my first experience in watching a person become vacant. It was seeing someone alive but fundamentally altered, with everything you know and love and hate twisted into unfamiliar patterns and foreign shapes. It was like I was wading through pond water: I knew she was in there somewhere, my sister, my first friend, if only the waters were clearer.

The building was further in-state than our home was. It was a short ride, but as we drove I always felt the growing claustrophobia; the sense that the trees were planted closer and closer together. The landscape seemed to grow greener, more condensed. The home was part of a larger collection of apartments. There was a community pool, closed for the fall season, empty and drained. I could see pine needles collecting at its bottom in indistinct piles. Brown and brittle dried leaves had blown into the entrance of the home as well, crunching into smaller fragments beneath our shoes. I stared at them a beat too long, thinking how wrong it felt for my sister to be in this unfamiliar home with a pile of leaves as her daily greeting instead of family or friends.

We took Kait out for lunch, and we talked, and we ate, and we tried to act normal — as if anything about the circumstance could ever be normal. And then we dropped her off, watching her body disappear back into the dingy staircase in the dingy hallway.

She wasn't angry, she was sad. She asked to come home. Our mom explained in a broken voice that this wasn't allowed yet. The doctors mandated she stay for a few weeks.

Mom and I were silent on the ride back, trying to block out our individual thoughts with the sound of the radio — neither of us hopeful but without the resolve to voice our fears out loud. Imagining my sister in the home, alone with the women whose mouths hung open and the lonely kitchen floor, cracked and dirty, I felt a heartbreak unlike any I have ever known. I felt my body fissure, a sense of loss beyond words, beyond death. It was more than grief: it was grief for a life that had not been permitted to live.

I had known pain before — and I had certainly known fear. I had known running for my life, and locked doors barricaded by large furniture. I had watched windows shattered by rocks. I was not unaccustomed to pain, but this wasn't just pain.

This was a long, aching creaking that shook my body the whole car ride home, a baked cracking — clay left in the light of the sun too long, fracturing in the heat.

Twenty-one

The doctor at Penn Medicine described my sister's brain as a pinball machine.

"Information goes in"—she motioned the movement of a ball entering the slot—"and then it bounces around a bit and comes out different."

I imagined a tiny metal ball banging against the edges of my sister's soft brain tissue. An idea taking flight and then twisting unrecognizably.

During one of her stays home, Kait heard the noise of a nearby party.

"They're talking about me," she told our mom, her eyes hurt and accusatory. "My friends are out there, and they're all talking about me."

Her voice became angrier, frustrated.

"That's just the sound of a party, Kait," Mom said, trying to soothe her. "It's not your friends. No one is talking about you."

Kait didn't believe her. The noise of the party had entered her brain, bounced around, and emerged again as something different—perhaps her internal worries and fears collected at the edge of the sound, changing its form.

In the mental healthcare system, such a moment is referred to as auditory complex perception, and in my research, I've found that neuroscientists believe that schizophrenia is related to changes in the central nervous system structure. People with the disorder have reduced gray matter in the superior temporal gyrus and the primary auditory cortex (where we process sound), and some studies using diffusion tensor imaging (DTI) or functional magnetic resonance imaging (fMRI) found altered neuron connectivity among temporal, prefrontal, and anterior cingulate regions.

None of these terms registers much with me. At first, all they do is sound an alarm in my brain, perhaps in my own central nervous system, that rings out: "This is *real.*" This is neurochemical. There are brain regions distinguished for their complicity in schizophrenia. My sister's brain was atrophying in areas, shrunken and screaming for help.

The barrier between her and the world was growing in many ways: The more her psychotic symptoms increased, the more walled-off she felt from the rest of society. And yet she was at the same time too vulnerable, susceptible to the slightest shifts in the wind like the direct outcome of the Butterfly Effect — the chaos theory that a butterfly flapping its wings ultimately can lead to a typhoon hundreds of miles away. My sister was the butterfly and the typhoon, cued in to some secret fabric of the universe where messages were coded just for her, revealing secrets and whispering lies.

Kait could no longer distinguish between what was in her head and what was outside of it. A voice flitted in from a street corner and became a demand reverberating in her skull or an insult rebounding in her chest. Like a linen curtain swaying in the breeze or a piece of sheer gauze, the protection between her internal world and outside intervention was flimsy and weak.

There's another region of the brain neurologists are examining in schizophrenia: the outer layer of tissue (cortex) around a fold (sulcus) in the brain, known as the paracingulate. This structure is largely responsible for our imagination — it is activated when we predict ourselves in future scenarios or when we try to imagine what other people may be thinking or feeling. By studying structural MRI brain scans, researchers found that schizophrenic patients with active hallucinations had reduced paracingulate sulcus length (Garrison et al. 2015).

Perhaps this is the metaphorical barrier come to life: a physical shortening that belied reality for my sister — taking the noise of the party and transforming it into something else entirely.

"People usually like me," I found written in Kait's girly script inside an otherwise blank notebook. She had written it after a psychotic episode as if to self-soothe; reassure herself of who she used to be. And she was right: She was once popular without thought, without effort. It used to come naturally for her.

But she was also aware of her own unsteadiness, aware she was no longer "normal." Her friends were getting jobs, graduating from college. She was in and out of rehab centers and mental hospitals. She was falling behind, left on the sidelines, watching her classmates pass her by.

As part of her treatment plan, after exploring all other options, a provider suggested that Kait take a small yellow school bus to a center where she would spend her days completing arts and crafts projects. It was viewed as "establishing a routine." A way to pass time and keep her "socialized" like a preschooler.

It hurt to watch my sister reach rock bottom, more so when she seemed to accept this fate with a defeated passivity, rather than rage against it the way she would have in the past. When she was angry, at least she was still fighting. It felt like giving up, this life of glorified day-care.

Kait didn't want to be anything other than the Kait of high school, the Kait of her youth — the one "people usually liked."

Maybe that's why she heard the voices outside talking behind her back. She was terrified that they had discovered her diagnosis, frantic they would change their opinion of her. She didn't want to be "crazy Kait," as she often called herself. She wanted to go back to before.

Our mom drove her around the neighborhood until they located the source of the noise, gesturing at the party to Kait through the car's window.

"See, it's just strangers. Not your friends. They're not talking about you."

Kait nodded, but there was no way to know if she really understood. Was the pinball machine still misfiring? Was there a lever at the bottom bouncing the idea back up again, rattling and rocketing it?

Her friends were dropping gradually, steadily. While I felt for Kait, I also understood their perspective. She was no longer a healthy friend to have.

In developmental psychology, there's something called "theory of mind." ToM, as it is often abbreviated, refers to the ability to imagine others' mental states, including their beliefs, intentions, emotions, and knowledge as different from one's own. It's a trait most of us develop around four to five years old. ToM is often exemplified by a popular puppet experiment in which one puppet moves an object from under one surface to another without the other puppet's knowledge.

"Where will the second puppet look first?" experimenters ask wide-eyed children. If you answer correctly, you'll recognize the second puppet has no way of knowing the object has been moved. You'll select the original hiding spot.

It's a trait I took for granted until I stripped the definition — *the ability to recognize another's mental state*. The ability to recognize another's *perception*.

Now, looking back, I wonder if I ever really stopped to consider Kait's perspective. Did I truly try to understand the reality she saw, so different from my own?

Perception itself is incredibly malleable, unsettled. It moves and shifts in the wind, dependent on a thousand different factors. Are you hungry? How is the light bouncing before entering your cornea? Are your neurons misfiring?

Even colors are subjective. What I label as blue perhaps you see as green. Maybe the ocean is the color of grass to you, and lawns the color of waves.

I think back to elementary school, when Kait's perspective was all I wanted to see, when her eyes, her style, meant everything. That day in the eyeglass store, after Kait helped me finally pick frames for my glasses, I tried them on during the car ride home from the mall. I stared out the backseat window — a space I had inhabited most of my life as the younger sibling — and let out a long, slow breath of shock.

"I can see *leaves*," I said aloud to my mom and sister. "I never knew people could see the individual leaves on a tree."

It seemed like magic.

I had spent years squinting, holding a fallen leaf close to my face so that I could examine the intricate patterns and shapes, the raised path of its veins. But a tree in the distance had never been anything more than a green blob.

Now, with the seemingly simple mediation of glass, I discovered that others around me could see this beauty perfectly clearly. It had been there all along. I was missing out.

The world was so alive that night: the wet gleam of the pavement, the glittering, perfect stars, the billboard signs on the highway, illuminated and crisp. It was like being given a new world.

I wonder if Kait's perception was like this too. If all she needed were the right glasses to see the world clearly again. Like the lenses the optometrist flips through until you land on your prescription, maybe her medicine was close but not quite right, the crisp focus remaining right outside her reach.

With mental illness, we treat the symptoms, not the underlying issue, like taking Sudafed for a stuffy nose, never knowing if the cause might be the flu, a cold, a sinus infection, or allergies. It's an imperfect science, and sometimes the cure is worse than the ailment. Pain medicine works differently for a headache than it does for a broken leg.

This too is a cliché of the mental health world, the idea that pharmaceuticals are the enemy: They chip away at a person. "What's so hard about swallowing a pill?" I heard students in my psychology classes ask. The answer: a lot. The answer: It's not as simple as you'd like it to be. *Yes*, Kait's emotional regulation was improved when she was on medication. *Yes*, we were certainly safer, but it wasn't a cure-all; it was a sacrifice. We gained some security, but we lost more and more of my sister every day. It might be wrong to depict this truth, but it was our truth just the same.

Mom handed me a collection of Kait's medications recently, stowed away in a bulk-size Ziploc bag. The bags must've been purchased during the holidays — perhaps intended for the sugar cookies she used to bake — because the plastic is translucent green with white ornaments imprinted on it. Inside are seventeen different medications: risperidone (an antipsychotic), hydrocodone (an opioid for her head injury), fluoxetine (a selective serotonin reuptake inhibitor), divalproex (for seizure and psychiatric disorders), olanzapine (for mental disorders, including schizophrenia and bipolar disorder), valproate (for seizures and bipolar disorder), and so forth.

We bottled our faith in these orange containers. The optometrist burned through more and more slides. The side effects coiled together. The chemicals meshed and repelled. The pinball kept misfiring.

Twenty-two

As a way to encourage my increasingly sick sister to focus on something positive and boost her sense of agency, Mom tried to highlight what had always been part of Kait's future plans: modeling and fashion.

She was discovered years before as a teenager while casually shopping at the mall with our mom, and was selected to compete in Bloomingdale's Fresh Face competition. Even strangers walking by recognized some star potential in her, something shimmery and bright and otherworldly. While she didn't win the competition, she was scouted by an agent soon after and from there came a slew of small runways, catalog campaigns, and marketing gigs.

In one spread, she is sitting atop a mahogany bar, looking away from the camera in open-mouthed wonderment. Her hair is curled in tight, messy waves, and she could be an actress stealing a drink at a Monaco hotel, or a jewel thief, or a princess on her day off, or all of the above. In another, she has her hair in an elegant updo as she leans against a mansion's spiral staircase. One leg is popped up, and she's wearing a black dress and black heels. She smiles innocently and you want to hire her, or let her sell you a house, or cast her in a rom-com about a businesswoman looking for love.

If you flip the magazine page, you'll find Mom's personal favorite. Kait sits on a winding, polished wooden staircase. Afternoon light glosses lazily from the decaled windows. She wears tailored black pants, a crisp white button-down, long pearls, and a short-sleeved tweed jacket. She is America's sweetheart.

To look at this spread is to be vacuumed into an alternative dimension, one in which Kait never got sick, a life that almost was.

In another photoshoot, she is transformed into a bride. Her hair is held up in an elegant clip, her makeup is young and fresh — smoky eyes and pink lips. She wears a long white gown and holds champagne glasses, clinking them next to her make-believe groom. Her diamond necklace and earrings gleam in the morning light.

Then, she's married. This particular campaign was in *Nantucket* magazine for a straw hat company, Peter Beaton, known for its large ribbon bows and black-and-white-striped boxes. Kait sits on a slope of manicured grass in a preppy green and black shift dress. She has a handsome husband and three children. They look every bit the image of summertime prep. Most of all, she looks happy.

If you put the photos all together, they create a narrative. The wedding my sister would never have, the children that will never be born. I look at these imaginary kids and her pretend husband, and I yearn for them. I want to wish at 11:11 and make it all come true.

From the frozen frame of the photograph, you would never guess the nervous, shaking energy simmering beneath the shoots. The confusion between life and fantasy that was present even here. Kait couldn't fathom why the other model wore a prettier dress than she did. She felt betrayed when her groom at the bridal shoot went home with one of the bridesmaids later that night.

"God awful stuff I knowww," Kait comments on a Facebook post of one of the pictures, responding to something the rest of us could neither see nor hear, and talking to herself. "You're sick in the head."

Could these all be versions of the same girl? The girl in the photos, so poised and perfect, the girl who taught me how to apply makeup, and the girl who threatened to push me off a balcony one summer, who chased me with an iron poker? *Could they all be the same person?*

My sister's life had been halted, but in the pictures everything stood still, and for a moment, it was as if we could finally breathe.

⋆ ⋆ ⋆

Our mom tried other methods of encouraging Kait. When a full-time college degree became out of reach, she motivated her to take real estate courses. Occasionally Kait would do homework with me at our living room table.

"That looks really hard," I'd say, looking over her shoulder at her notes, scattered with cross-outs and rewrites.

"It is," Kait agreed solemnly.

I nodded eagerly, my efforts to boost her self-esteem sloppy and obvious.

We kept waiting for her to wake up, to snap out of it, return to us like a broken spell. Mom bought her journals, advising Kait to write reminders to herself. "Write *I'm going to be okay,*" she told her, "whenever you feel yourself losing control." Line after line, Kait repeated the phrase in her neat, bubbly print:

I'm going to be okay.

I'm going to be okay.

Mom went so far as to suggest Kait improve the very system that was failing her. "You could be like a poster girl for mental healthcare. People look up to you. They want to be like you. You could do so much good if you were open about it all."

She too saw the stigma, the silence, the need for change, and she also saw that at her best, Kait would be the perfect person to break the barrier of shame and shed light on the reality of severe psychological disorders. Besides, my sister was well aware of her diagnosis. She was educated in it enough to help others. Mom gave her countless books about the subject, but information didn't stay still in her head — it moved and twisted.

For a moment, Kait felt up to the challenge. "I could do it, Mom," she said. "You're right. I could do it."

A bolt of confidence surged through her, a renewed purpose. She was the girl in the magazine spreads. She sold people clothes, lifestyles; surely she could sell them awareness. Surely she could sell empathy.

Then, she faltered.

The label was too strong. She didn't want to be known for schizo-phrenia; she didn't want to *have* schizophrenia. She wanted to go back to before, back to Marblehead, back to high school. She wasn't up for the challenge — it was too much of a burden. The climate wasn't right, the conversation about less severe mental health concerns just barely start-ing to emerge, peeking its head out hesitantly. What would people think about a psychotic disorder? Who could truly understand it? I lived with it, and I still didn't.

Kait used to say that people on the streets were staring at her. Like white blood cells detecting pathogens, everyone around her could sense that she wasn't like them, an outsider not cooperating with the system. I re-member learning in biology class about the Y-shaped antibodies activated during an immune response. They attack the enemy, the teacher explained, they'll try to destroy whatever they don't recognize, whatever is *other*.

Was that how Kait felt? Like the enemy? Like *the other*?

I imagine Kait walking down a Philadelphia street, her long legs, her delicate face that required no makeup. Passersby stop to glance at her, eye her up and down, and in my sister's twisted reality, she feels threatened, discovered. They know she's sick. They know she's not like them.

"They're looking at you because you're beautiful," Mom reassured her countless times. "Not because anything is wrong with you."

This was the double-edged sword — modeling as both an outlet and a vice. It concealed how out of control my sister's life was, but it also granted her confidence. When the cocktail of antipsychotics she was tak-ing for symptom management altered her appearance, causing her to bloat and swell and her hair to thin and break, even this ounce of self-esteem was reduced. As if she could afford to lose more.

I wish she had succeeded in being a pillar for others, in following through on that dream of standing as a poster child and increasing com-passion and understanding around neurological conditions — be the light she was meant to be.

Maybe she still can.

Twenty-three

When Kait's situation seems more and more hopeless — her mind less and less her own — I amend my 11:11 wish.

"I wish my dreams come true, my family is healthy, and *my sister gets better*" became simply "I wish my sister gets better."

We're taught not to ask *too* much out of life, never be too greedy. I make the tactful decision to narrow my scope, focus only on what's necessary. What can I live without? What's the desperate need here? The answer is clear, practical.

I need my sister to get better.

This is the moment when the religious might turn to prayer. Get on their knees, beg humbly before God. Express gratitude for all they have but admit, "I simply cannot live with this anymore." I have reached my wits' end.

This is the moment one may be granted a miracle.

The man who can walk again. The critical care patient who wakes up just before the plug is pulled. Have faith. Pray. Simply ask.

I do not know prayer, but I ask and ask and ask and ask anyway. I kneel as my sister once did, praying me into existence as a little girl in her best church dress. When the fighting escalates and I'm locked in my room or hurrying into a car, my sister on my heels, I close my eyes and softly chant, "Please, please, please, please." I say it aloud, just in case whoever's in charge up there can't hear my thoughts. I anticipate the hang-ups.

My cultural language is limited, so when I try to picture a "supreme ruler," I imagine the scene from the movie *Bruce Almighty* with Morgan

Freeman cast as God. He's in this blank, sterile-looking room, the prayers of lost souls neatly tucked in the corner of gray filing cabinets. God gets to them when He can, like an overworked, underappreciated bureaucrat. This is why I ask for *one* thing. I cannot risk convoluting the files.

I don't wish that the sky will erupt in a downpour and my crew practice will subsequently be canceled. I don't wish that the test will be moved back. I concentrate all of my internal focus on one thing and one thing only. I am intentional. I am diligent, resolute.

When it doesn't rain, I think: "Maybe somebody else *really* needed a sunny day today."

When the test isn't canceled, I think: "Maybe one of my classmates *really* needed an A."

You see, I make a conscious, deliberate effort not to waste my wishes.

The "I wish my dreams come true" is the first clause to be cut. What's the point of a dream if my family is permanently eradicated? I can live without it.

Since moving to Philly, I have always wanted to be a writer.

My happiest moment of second grade is when we make a book of poems. We are given a white hardback with blank pages. It's beautiful. I love how sturdy the cover is. We write haikus and decorate them with lines from a fine-pointed Sharpie marker crawling up the sides like vines. It is as if a part of my soul is encased in the pages.

The worst moment of fourth grade is when my class is assigned to create a narrative about the Three Little Pigs. A girl named Emily introduces a bush in the beginning of her story, and by the end, the pigs have used this shrubbery to hide from the big bad wolf. The teacher praises her endlessly, seizing her work as a teaching moment. "This is a wonderful example of foreshadowing," she says. I am hot with envy. I remember every detail of the story, and chastise myself for not thinking of it.

My happiest moment of seventh grade is when my English teacher passes around one of my essays for the class to read. He's the kind of middle school teacher that looks and acts just enough like a fun uncle and just enough like a peer that he's beloved by all. He calls me over to his desk after the period bell rings. "This is really something," he says. "You should consider submitting it to a publication or a contest."

My knees are shaking. "What publication?" I ask eagerly. "What contest?"

"I don't know," he says. "But maybe somewhere."

I feel so validated, I'm queasy. I cry in the bathroom, flushed and jittery, before walking to my next class. I never submit it anywhere, don't even know where or how you submit a piece of writing, but I hold his comment carefully, preserve it, tuck it somewhere between the delicate bones of my rib cage, where it'll never get lost.

One of my friends gives me a T-shirt for my sixteenth birthday that reads CAREFUL, OR YOU'LL END UP IN MY NOVEL. I don't agree with the sentiment — I believe any revenge writing is worthless and despicable, cowardly — but the idea behind the gift is that I really could do it. *I could be a writer.* The shirt becomes an enchanted object: a physical manifestation of someone's belief in me. It is in my drawer at this very moment, now shrunken several sizes too small.

This is all essentially to say that I have been consistent in my desire. I have wanted nothing else, nothing more, except for one thing: I want my sister to get better.

This wish comes first and foremost. All else is brushed aside, pushed to the back burner, sacrificed.

If I say it enough, if I focus all my energy on this one hope, I'll manifest it.

Every 11:11, every birthday candle, every wishbone snap, every lost eyelash, every fallen star, every dented four-leaf clover — every fuzzy, white dandelion, too — I devote to this simple request. It is all I ask for. *Please.* It is all I ask for.

I guess despite everything, a part of me still believed in last-ditch miracles: the game-changing fourth quarter swing, the Hail Mary pass, the second act reversal of fortune, the experimental treatment, the nearly forgotten eyes fluttering awake from a coma.

No one can say I didn't ask.

Twenty-four

On January 8, 2014, Kait was wearing a red North Face jacket when she disappeared.

That is a fact among others. None of them makes much sense to me.

A girl walks to the peak of the Benjamin Franklin Bridge during a polar vortex. A girl in a red North Face jacket and high winter boots. A girl walks, and then, *poof*, gone.

My sister walks to the peak of the Benjamin Franklin Bridge.

I never viewed the security photographs myself. Perhaps it was easier not to know, not to have the definitive proof of seeing it for myself. Is it really her? Are we sure? The image in my head is thus one of my own creation: stagnant and irreversible. It plays in a loop, never changing (no matter how hard I try to change it).

Kait walks to the peak of the Benjamin Franklin Bridge.

Kait walking.

Kait, and then, *poof, gone.*

I repeat this mantra in my head. When I say it aloud, the image freezes, rewinds, slows down, and then continues with the same feverous, relentless pace — the same sad cycle. I want to shout out, scream: *Stop.* Some-one stop her. *Why is no one stopping her?* I know how this story ends.

My sister on the Benjamin Franklin Bridge.
   On January 8, 2014, my sister walked the Benjamin Franklin Bridge.
   My sister disappeared.
   Kait keeps walking.
   Poof, gone.

Phase III, Residual

Lavender Dust

Time will make a memory of you and a forgetter out
of me.   — *The first words I wrote after.*

Twenty-five

Mom's memory of Kait's last night, like of most other nights, is better than my own.

My sister was withdrawn. Not psychotic, not angry, not ranting, but defeated, exhausted, worn. She was going to have to return home.

At the time, Kait had moved out of her place in the city and was living in an apartment in the suburbs, only a five-minute drive from our house. She was living alone, and her symptoms were becoming progressively more unmanageable.

Kait had sat in our mom's car that night. Earlier in the evening, she told Mom that if she didn't pick her up, she was going to walk to CVS alone. The danger was easy to imagine: Kait at night, walking a winding, busy, and icy road. Mom imagined my sister slipping on the sidewalk and hitting her head again. What would one more concussion do to her lingering sanity? Our mom didn't want to find out. She came immediately.

The two of them discussed a plan going forward. Kait hadn't been told yet, but our parents were preparing to file for power of attorney. My sister was going to live with us again. She would need to be put back on risperidone, the monthly injection to control her manic episodes. There would need to be an additional medication to regulate her emotions.

Kait was familiar with these side effects: weight gain, nausea, apathy. They turned her into a zombie. She hated it because she said it was like being dead already — living and interacting with the world without being able to fully feel. A scream underwater, dulled and suffocating.

Mom knew something was wrong that night but not quite what.

Kait bought three packs of cigarettes, a beach read from the checkout aisle, a notepad, pens, and lip balm. Later in the night, she returned to the store by herself to purchase bottles of Advil PM. The police hypothesize that this was her first attempt. (Although, she appeared to give up — as if counting out the pills was too much of a task to handle at the moment.)

"I could feel her pain," Mom tells me now. "I could physically feel it."

Something was in the air, something wrong and unsettling, the earth off its axis, the moon shining too bright or perhaps not at all. Something was wrong, but fate wasn't settled yet.

I wish I could take back what happened next, those moments as I dialed my mom's number, called her crying because I was panicking alone in the house. My father was still in the office, and the dogs were barking at the staircase leading to our guest bedroom. I couldn't concentrate on my homework, and I didn't want to be alone. I thought back to all the horror movies I had watched with Kait, and I was convinced somebody or something was in the house.

I was stressed over an exam I had the following day. The anxiety attack was unfortunately nothing new, I had been having more and more of them lately: not about the big problems in my life, but the smaller ones — my schoolwork, my grades, the one force in my life I believed I had some semblance of control over. But the fact of the matter is that I called, needing my mom — and so she let Kait go.

My sister returned to her apartment alone. She didn't look well. Kait, once so full of laughter and energy and charisma and eccentricity, had grown beaten and gray by the fight for her sanity. Mom watched the back of her head as she made her way inside her apartment, waiting until she could hear the click of the door as it shut behind her, hugging her safe, she hoped.

Mom came home and I continued studying for my exam. The exam — the tests, the perfect report cards — always so *important*, always *all-consuming*.

Mom says that night felt like she was in a movie. Time froze, clocks rewound.

"Is it because I've returned to it so many times in my mind?" she asks.

Had she reviewed and revisited the moment until it felt less like a lived reality and more like a film? Or was it maybe all set in fate. Were we on a path we couldn't see yet, the only conclusion unraveling to its tragic end? If we did it again, would we correct our mistakes? Or would we be like the teleological watchmaker God, left forever with the right word dangling uselessly from our lips?

Twenty-six

Kait disappeared three days before my seventeenth birthday.

A party was scheduled at a popular Asian fusion restaurant in town. Nineteen girls were attending. My sister was not. It had been a few years since I last celebrated a birthday — too afraid to risk my sister having a hallucinatory episode or a manic fit. We decided to throw a dinner in stealth — that way, I wouldn't worry about hurting my sister's feelings, but I also wouldn't have to spend the evening on pins and needles, stressed that every little action could trigger her.

We made our plans in whispers and sidelong glances. After all, it would kill Kait to know she wasn't invited.

I've heard a common theme in grief literature — a preternatural moment in which a person immediately knows that his or her loved one is dead. A man mowing his lawn, stopping halfway with a horrible suspicion that his wife is not well. A family rushing to the hospital to hear their grandfather's last words. A beating moment, a fluttering feeling, an unspoken connection.

I had none of it.

In the first few hours, I was as cold and indifferent to news of Kait's missing person as I was to the dramas of a reality television plot. I believe I may have rolled my eyes.

"She always does this," I reminded Mom as she paced in worry across a worn strip of floor in her bedroom.

And I was right. Kait did always do this: disappear on a bender, pass out drunk on a friend's couch, give us the silent treatment. She wasn't picking up her phone, but this wasn't outside the realm of normal. Yet.

"It's different this time, Kyleigh. Something is wrong," Mom snapped.

Her worry seeped into my skin, became mine. "Something is really wrong," she kept repeating, staring into space, wringing her hands. "I'm calling the police."

To file a missing person report, the police recommend waiting twenty-four to seventy-two hours. This is because, in most cases, the individual will return within forty-eight hours. The phrase "in most cases," holds the same anticipatory warning as does the word "yet." *In most cases. Yet.*

"You don't understand," Mom told the police. "She's not well. She's sick."

That day, Mom went to Kait's apartment and found the place in shambles. It was not the mess of a careless young adult, not the hurried trash of someone running out the door. It screamed urgency and unraveling.

Mom took photos of the piles of dirty laundry, the cluttered table, the broken mug. The pillows on the couch rumpled and disheveled. There's a pizza box on the table next to a bottle of laundry detergent. A hair product sits to the left, the opened containers of Advil PM with a missing lid, an empty apple juice container, a pill bottle, brightly colored flash cards with text I cannot read, a lone cherry-flavored lip balm. A loose scattering of cigarettes dot everything, like weeds sprung up through grass.

It is telling that there was a part of our mom, even knowing in the deepest caverns of her heart that Kait was gone, even wishing with every fiber of her being that she wasn't, that was still afraid of what would happen if my sister opened the door and found her there. She kept glancing at the doorway, half expecting to see the familiar silhouette. Relief would surely come first, but then so would the familiar swell of fear and the vinegar tang in her mouth that accompanied it. How badly might Kait hurt her if she was discovered?

On the kitchen stove, there are scrambled eggs, uneaten and cold. Behind them, what looks to be a scattered ashtray, crumbling with debris and soot. A bag of tortillas lies open above the microwave, dirty dishes before it. A carton of eggs and olive oil left on the gray countertop. No sense of orderliness or long-term planning. No sense of "getting your affairs in order."

Our family became a group of reluctant detectives, uncovering every passing clue with increasing dread. We were trudging along the path of discovery unwillingly, no one wanting to fill in the final blank.

After our eighth assault claim, the police had recently recommended that my parents file a restraining order against Kait, explaining that at this point a "tough love" approach would work best. Our mom was afraid that if she didn't comply, they would be done answering our desperate calls, done coming to save us. This "scare them straight" strategy might have been a good idea, if only mental illness was something that followed logic, choice, rationality, free will. It doesn't.

Kait had just gotten out of the hospital days before. She was given no medication — not even an emergency dose, only a prescription she needed to fill at the pharmacy. Later, the landlord informed my parents that my sister was in the process of being kicked out of the building because of complaints from neighbors about her odd, unsettling behavior. She was going to be homeless. We had no idea.

In the bathroom: more clutter, more disorder. Clothes in a pile on the floor with a single white towel bunched on top. On the sink, an eye cream container with two misshapen dents in the silver cap, likely thrown in a storm of frustration.

All of this is shouting louder and louder: *Something is wrong.* Something isn't right. It's been yelling this for a while, since Mom dropped Kait off the night before, or maybe if you listened close enough, even before that — after Kait hit her head, when she saw Santa in the sky. Back then it was just a whistle in the wind, and now it's a clamor, a chorus.

Then come the notebooks — blue penmanship, girly loops — silencing in their horror.

On one page, a list labeled "KAIT'S TO-DO LIST" in large block letters at the top. In it, my sister has taken inventory of her next steps: "Get a job, go back to school, get apartment, stay sober, go to AA meetings, go to gym, eat right, smoke less, keep room clean, find a guy and be friends, see psychiatrists, stop fighting, reality checks, go for more walks, write." She has drawn two hopeful hearts at the bottom of the page.

On the flip-side of the sheet, she reminds herself: "Stop thinking so much. Block out the people I used to do damage with. Realize there's other people out there." This last part is emphasized — Kait has traced every word twice. And then, a line later, one last reminder — the most important of all: "No one knows what I'm thinking about."

My sister seems to be writing her way to sanity, trying to ground herself in the here and now. She is a coach preparing a speech before the big game, pumping herself up. *I can do this.* Then, inevitably, comes the unwinding, the exhale:

> I feel like the TV is talking only to me and that it's saying things to me that they want me to know.
>
> I think the radio is talking only to me and music has a hidden message to me.
>
> Then I feel like I'm losing my mind.
>
> I have angry outbursts & want others to feel badly so I can feel any better.
>
> I don't feel any better.

In large writing at the bottom, centered on the lined page, she states: "Psych wards are hard for me to think about, because I'm scared that I've actually been to them."

A few pages later: "I'm pissed off at the world for my life being so bad. I cannot be who I want to be because I get in the way of myself. I get so upset and enraged with anger I could kill myself or fall to my feet. I don't think it's fair that this mental illness is part of me. I don't think it's fair that my life is so sucky and I can't lead a good one. I have no friends, no boyfriend, and no degree. I am stronger than I was before but so weak that I can't keep it together when I get these awful feelings."

I am stronger than I was before but so weak. I don't think it's fair that this mental illness is a part of me.

It's not fair, Kait, I want to say. It's not fair at all. None of it was ever fair. You're right. You were always right. I'm sorry.

On a series of tracing paper, Kait has written repeatedly: "Kait goes to heaven. Kait goes to heaven. Edie in heaven. Edie."

Mom believes she's referring to Edie Sedgwick: the sixties socialite, model, all-around "It girl," and Andy Warhol muse. In the moment, I don't ask her why she thinks this, because to ask would be to dredge up pain, and to dredge up pain would be to further acknowledge how little I know about my sister. How alone my mom truly was.

I can imagine why Kait would relate to the woman, however — a beautiful, delicate blonde with mental health issues, time spent in psychiatric hospitals. A party girl: artistic, fun, adventurous, troubled. She died young of a barbiturate overdose, possibly a suicide.

When Mom came back from the apartment, she brought Kait's laptop with her. Here came my phase of the investigation: I knew all of Kait's passwords. I knew them because Kait had created all of mine — letting me copy her as always.

I sat on the couch of our living room while my parents sat opposite me. We rarely used this room, except for the times we had tried to hold a "family meeting" to discuss Kait's ongoing treatment. She had smashed the television one of those days, shattered the screen in deep lines.

I checked her recent Google searches. They read as follows:

"What happens when we die?"

A Wikipedia page titled simply "Death."

That was it. This was all of the research Kait did. One vague Wikipedia entry and my sister was somehow satisfied with an idea of the afterlife — satisfied, or perhaps just too exhausted to ask further questions. I engulfed each search quickly, skimming to the end, swallowing it whole, and then I read it again with painful precision, memorizing the syllables, looking for a code, a higher meaning.

I felt it coming in these moments. The beginning of the waves that would soon crash down on me. My grief was like an earthquake — it destroyed in its aftershocks, hitting at random, just when I thought I had regained my balance.

There was one final Google search:

"How to kill yourself?" it asked simply, politely.

When I clicked on the link, I was taken to a Reddit page. Suggestions brimmed easily: anonymous, invisible users eagerly providing my sister with the tools to end her life.

"You could hang yourself with a belt," one suggested. "I saw it once in a film. Looked pretty easy."

"How about a noose?" another added.

"A shotgun to the head seems quick."

"Have you considered jumping off a bridge?"

I closed the computer, my heart thumping somewhere deep within my stomach.

Twenty-seven

The next morning my eyes were swollen. It's happened a few times since: I go to bed and wake up with damp cheeks only to realize that I've been crying in my sleep. It's a distinctly lonely sensation; your body has gone on to suffer without you — your bones and nerves and veins processing something entirely distinct from your conscious mind.

I looked in the mirror of the bathroom I once shared with my sister and poked the sore, thin skin of my under-eye in distant curiosity. I didn't bother putting on makeup.

At this point, we still didn't know with certainty what had happened to Kait, but it wasn't hard to guess. And yet it was habitual, after years of dealing with Kait's erratic episodes, those countless emergencies, to go to school the next day and carry on.

I arrived late, receiving a note from the front office with some vague excuse of "traffic" and made my way down the fluorescent corridors to the gymnasium. Everything felt numb, heavy, and cold. There was a weight on my chest, a firm hand, and with every step it pushed me back like I was walking directly into the wind.

We were playing dodgeball that morning. I dropped my backpack by the small mass of students huddling by the sidelines. I stood in front of the middle line of the squeaky floor and let a red ball slice across my body. The pain made me feel alive for a moment. I wished they would keep coming. I wished I could be buried in the red dodgeballs, submerged, suffocated by them.

The teacher blew his whistle and I took my seat. One of my closest friends was in this class with me, and I waited for her to ask me why I was late, why my face was puffy and swollen. She didn't.

Rather, she must have said something like, "I'm excited for your party this weekend!" because I remember warning her that it may not be happening anymore. I don't know why I said this. After the night before, I wasn't sure I was still entirely in control of my body. *Is this how my sister always felt?*

By lunch, all nineteen girls I invited knew my party may be canceled. My phone was flooded with texts like "It would be nice to know?" I was rude, they thought, to cancel so last minute. Presents were already purchased. Things that couldn't be returned.

The whole concept of the once-upon-a-time party made me wish I was dead. The party I hadn't invited my sister to. The fear of her reaction felt years away. I'd have given my life to have it back. I'd have given much more than my life — I'd have given everything I ever was and ever possibly could be, every culmination of thought, every motion of effort, every infinitesimally small mistake that led to this very moment.

After school ended, my mom picked me up and drove me through the same route we passed every day for the last ten years — the green stretches of lawn, the lazily hanging stoplight, the stone houses I once loved — but today, she passed the familiar hill of our driveway and parked on the street. It was one of those irrevocable moments you sense before it occurs — a shift in the air, a sour taste in the back of your throat, the soft hair of your arm raising ever so slightly. Somehow, some way, without needing to be told, you know nothing will ever be the same.

Mom told me about the Benjamin Franklin Bridge security photos the cops had uncovered. Word associations, brief and arbitrary, came through my daze:

The Benjamin Franklin Bridge.

Benjamin Franklin — the Quaker school we attended.

Deism — fate, providence, kismet, predestination.

The sprawling, unforgiving, indifferent cosmos.

The security tapes evidently show two images. In one, you can see the outline of a young girl walking with her head down. Her bright red jacket stands out like the splatter of blood. Kait in her last moments is as impractically vivid as ever.

The next image is from a minute later. The girl is gone. In the time lapse, she's disappeared. There is no one else in the photos. The foot path is on an entirely different level than the cars — there is no chance that anyone could have grabbed her. Only one option is left.

She jumped.

I watched my mom's mouth form this explanation, her bright blue eyes looking anywhere but my face. The seatbelt hugging my chest, designed for protection, meant to separate us from this very feeling — from death, disaster — constricted me now. Strangled me now. I recalled the Reddit user who asked, "Have you considered jumping off a bridge?" and the look on my parents' faces when I told them about it: the limbo of shock, the awakening of horror. I tried to imagine my only sister walking that last walk in the brisk winter night, but I couldn't. The image was too strange, too incongruent with everything I had ever known about her. It was a fact that belonged outside of my life — a fragment read elsewhere, an idea that evaporated as soon as I reached to grasp it.

There's something about our body's reaction to grief that's almost too dramatic to be genuine. We slide down walls, crumpling on hardwood floors. The gravity of loss invents its own rules of physics. We collapse into ourselves, our chest meeting our knees, bringing our heads closer to the ground, like that'll somehow make us feel more solid, more safe — to lie on the warm pavement and press our bodies into the hard earth.

Dread encircles your brain, draining the blood from your temples and leaving a fuzziness in its wake like the static of a lost television signal. You want to cover your ears like you used to when your sister teased you as a child, because the truth can't touch you if you don't allow yourself to hear it. It's as if you're a character in a movie watching the action unfold around you. Is my hand really covering my mouth? Why am I pressing my palms against my temple? Do people do that in real life?

And if you're anything like me, the nausea comes first. The wading in the depths of your stomach, and the bile that almost rises but decides to fall instead. It's the nausea that never truly fades. It returns now and again, when you drive past a bridge or look at an old photo. You think, If only I could puke. If only I could get it out, once and for all, maybe I could dispose of the bad — this feeling, this new reality. It would be cathartic, a release, an escape.

A taxi driver further corroborated the story after my mom tracked him down. He said my sister barely spoke a word the whole ride there. She was polite — but very quiet. He dropped her off at the base of the bridge and she walked up the footpath.

Her phone signal was lost around this time: the way it would have been if submerged in water or dropped from a great height.

My parents walked the bridge themselves, tracing my sister's path and looking for some sign or note she may have left behind in the graffiti mess. There was nothing. I'm told that Kait once mentioned in passing wanting to jump from the bridge. She had actually walked the path before, stared at the water, and turned around. I wonder what changed her mind that day and not this night. More urgently, I wondered how I could have been so naïve to these thoughts of hers. How little did I know my sister in the end?

There's a train track that juts out from underneath the light blue steel. The police said that most jumpers never hit the water — one must violently fling oneself from the railing in order to miss the track. Kait must have known it was there: She had likely seen it when she first visited the bridge. She was not the kind of girl to do anything halfheartedly. Even in the end, as exhausted as she must have been, she was determined.

These are all facts: incorrigible truths. For everyone else in the story — policemen, detectives, those logical, distant onlookers — the case was closed. A done deal. A sad, tragic end but an end nonetheless.

Grief is never a closed case. Grief is the crack in the window, the chilly draft that wafts in with the night. Grief is hope in the absence of hope. Grief is saying "lost" instead of "gone," and "passed away" instead of "dead," because to say the latter would be to admit a definitive stopping point — irretrievable, irreversible. The story only goes this far.

It is laughingly easy to find excuses when you're craving them, ravenous for them: why your crush didn't text you back, why you slipped up at work, why your sister never came home. You look for answers and there they are — implausible but intoxicating nonetheless.

Soon after I learned of the bridge's security photos, my mom, father, and I went to a nearby church: Villanova University's congregation. The same church we had spent the occasional Christmas Eve in. Kait and I would giggle at the choir singers, daring one another to sing louder. Our mouths curved into little dark O's like the ruddy-faced caroler figurines our grandmother put on display every Christmastime.

The outside of the steeple was old and looming, twin peaks casting shadows over a long pathway of flowering trees now barren for the winter. The stained-glass windows rippled color on the white of the floors and the white of the walls and the deep brown of the pews. The air was as cold and hollow as we were.

We walked silently, stoically, finding seats in separate pews of the empty room, staggering diagonally. Every step we took echoed loudly, reverberating against the large beams.

On our knees, we attempted to pray.

We prayed for her to be alive, or if not alive, then to find a body. We prayed for her soul. I wasn't sure what it meant to pray for someone's soul, but I hoped someone would do the same for me someday.

I settled my head over my folded arms so my forehead lay on my fist. I interlocked my fingers, letting my knees dig deeper into the hard wood until the pressure hurt. The pain brought me back to myself momentarily, grounded me in the here and now. *This is really happening*, I thought. I felt as if I had stumbled onto a movie set and was playing a role never intended for me.

I remembered, in a moment of surprise, the last words I said to my sister. She was standing in the doorway of the back exit of our home, off the kitchen. She was wearing an oversize sweatshirt that made her look years younger. She had no makeup on, and her hair was pulled back in a simple ponytail. She looked defeated, exhausted.

"Can I have a hug, Kyles?" she asked me in a small, pleading voice I rarely ever heard from her.

I was afraid that the moment would pass, that she would slip into a manic fit or a hallucination, but I came closer anyway and wrapped my arms around her. I hugged my sister for the last time.

"I love you," she said. "Do you still love me?"

"Of course I do," I replied in exasperation. "You know I love you, Kait."

We pulled away. She nodded slightly, gave me a small smile, and then walked out the door.

The last words I said to my sister were "I love you," but this realization brought less comfort than I expected. I had said it begrudgingly, even perhaps with a touch of anger. What I should have said is "I love you, Kait. I'll always love you, no matter what you do. We'll get through this together, I promise. We'll get through it." What I should have done is grab her, sit her down on the couch, ask if she needed to talk about anything. What I should have done is lock the door, never let her leave. Last words matter so little when they follow a lifetime of regrets.

Standing in that church, remembering this moment, I wished I had a formal religious background to lean on, a discourse with a deity previously established. I didn't want religion per se; I wanted ritual and I wanted to believe. I wanted to say a prayer, a recitation written by someone else, passed down through history and shared grief, and I wanted to believe that it would work. I wanted all those wishes on 11:11 to count for something, to mean something.

The title of a Judy Blume novel from my childhood, *Are You There God? It's Me, Margaret* flashed through my brain, and following in its trails like the remnants of a comet's tail, I felt carved out. Had I ever been so young as when I consumed those pages, devouring them in the bed of our Philly townhouse before I drifted into sleep? When exactly had this innocence been lost? Would it ever come back?

As hard as I prayed, as raw and ripped and ragged as I felt, I didn't feel Kait in the church. Letting my heart bleed onto the floor in front of the looming cross, I didn't feel *her*. She wasn't there in the chill of the marble or the veiled face of Mary. It didn't feel like her: so empty and sterile, the candles smelling of pine needles, lavender, and hot wax.

Maybe it was how not-present she was that made us cry in the end. The feeling of absence beyond absence. Eventually, our bodies cramped, our knees became sore, and we walked back to the car in silence once again, wrapped in individual grief. It was the last activity we would do as a family unit.

For me, the absence of final proof, the last shred of evidence, the missing body, the impossibility, the strangeness of the act itself — all contributed to a lingering, pathological anticipation.

There's a term for this sensation, "ambiguous loss," but I only learned it recently. It is loss without closure or clear understanding. It leaves you asking questions, delays your healing process. The ambiguity, the unknown, will leave you always waiting. The promise of possibility, however faint, is harsher than any certainty.

When Kait was sick, it periodically surprised me that there could be a label, a diagnosis. In the moment, it seemed unlikely that chaos of such magnitude could be contained by language. I wonder now, does it make you feel less alone or more alone to be described so neatly by a singular clinical term? Even the most immense biblical pain can be reduced quite simply.

We waited patiently for a body, past polar vortexes, snowstorms, and the thawing of spring. We waited every day, a dreadful, morbid kind of hope. Our father walked the Schuylkill River himself, wading in the long grass near the river's edge, looking for a familiar face among the weeds. He never found one. There were helicopter searches, other missing bodies discovered and identified, but it was never Kait. We never found Kait.

Twenty-eight

The commonality of the phrase "I want to kill myself" will shock you for the remainder of your life. You will flinch, automatic, at the gallows humor. You will smile or laugh along, but your innards will churn and flip — your very personhood unsettled by the reminder. The specificity of "I want to jump from a bridge" will startle you, drag you underwater by the thin skin of your ankles, kicking and screaming as you go. *My sister really did do that,* you'll think. Every time someone says it (and, yes, it will happen far more often than you ever imagined it possibly could), you will marvel at the phrase. What a far-off, horrific phrase. *Jump from a bridge.* You'll never be able to grasp that something that graphically gruesome really happened to your family.

"I swear if Coach doesn't cancel practice, I'll throw myself off a bridge."

"If my boss gives me one more spreadsheet, I'm going to jump out this window."

"Jump," "throw" . . . Do they know the brutality of their statement? Do they know that your dreams are populated by this image?

You play along, a good sport. You work tirelessly to make everyone around you comfortable: shake it off, shrug. After all, silence is habitual by now.

At the peak of your depression, when you look at a building or down a staircase, your first thought will be *If I jumped, would this kill me?* You will die a thousand of these mini deaths before you actually die — in class, at a friend's house, during a college lecture.

At first, people are careful around you. They censor their words. Don't worry, this won't last long. You'll be thrust back into the violence of living in no time.

Three days after your sister kills herself, your AP Spanish teacher gives you zero credit on a missing homework assignment. You tell her, "I'm sorry it slipped my mind; it's been a tough week." It is hard enough to say this simple explanation without bursting into tears, but you make it through. You're proud of the smallest of functional actions these days. She says she knows, the guidance office informed her, she's sorry, but it's no excuse. A year later, her sister will die. She'll take several months off from teaching. You'll feel somehow responsible, like your inner resentment propelled the universe forward.

There is so much newfound pain and rage and despair locked into the fabric of your body. Your teeth chatter. Your brain is fuzzy with the buzzing, roving energy. Loss has stripped you of any remaining protection from the world. You feel all of humankind's suffering at once. You have always been a self-composed, tidy person, but there is only so far you can expand before you erupt — a volcano ready to spill your acid onto innocent villagers.

That same week, you sit in your homeroom study hall — time at the end of the day usually set aside for homework but occasionally reserved for a forced bonding activity. The desks are arranged in a semicircle. You sit on the edge. (It is only in retrospect that you notice these subtle shifts in your new body language. You always position yourself away from others now. Your tightly wound legs tilt toward the door, not the group. Your arms are iron bars around your chest, keeping you in solitary confinement. This is not for your own safety — any hope of saving yourself is obsolete. Something has gone wrong inside you, and you know that it will never entirely realign. You look at the others who are whole and young, and you want to keep the scratching beast in your chest a secure distance away.)

Today you are asked to describe one of your siblings for the group. The cosmic joke of the random alignment of cruel timing makes you want to laugh out loud, scream at the sky, break the fourth wall like you're in *The Truman Show* and shout, *"You got me!"* Instead, you stare at the teacher, trying to communicate: *Save me, save me, save me, save me.* She doesn't understand your telepathy — probably thinks you have something in your eye — so your lot is that you must sit there listening to everyone's wonderful siblings while your own has been missing, presumed deceased, for exactly four days. When it's your turn, you say, "I'm an only child." The words taste venomous and sour in your mouth. It is the first time you tell this lie, but it certainly won't be the last.

This is an essential lesson: the indifference of the world. When your sister was sick with a mental illness, you used to envy the kids who had blatant, straightforward issues. No guidance department has ever known your heartache before, no test has ever been pushed back for you. You would sit in class after spending the night hiding from your sister, locked in a hotel room, your eyelids pulling you to sleep, wishing someone knew — anyone at all knew. Now you have this unfortunate certainty, this transparency: Your sister is gone. As far as problems go, it's a straight line. The school has been notified, your teachers know, your friends know, and yet, here we are. While your world screeched to a halt, the rest of society continued on. In all of your loneliness, you have never felt more alone than this.

Your mom says that when your sister was born, she couldn't believe that the planets didn't stop spinning. People continued on about their days, made trips to Walmart, ran errands to the post office, sat patiently in beige desk cubicles. How did they not realize that everything had changed? Kait was *here*.

When she dies, you feel the same way. The earth has come full circle, completed 22 revolutions around the sun, approximately 8,275 rotations. Kait is *gone*. How do they not realize that everything has changed?

People will say, "I can't imagine what you're going through." What they won't say is, "I don't want to." You know this is a necessary, albeit unfortunate limitation of human empathy: If society stopped to embrace the full scope of every loss, it would cease to function — no mail, no grocery delivery, no economy. We would be in a constant state of mourning, but to be grieving and watch the world continue on is the cruelest outrage.

When you are in the middle of it, you won't be able to see anything clearly. When you're suffering, all you'll think is *why, why, why, why.* When you walk the hallway at school, you want to stop and scream until your vocal chords give up, crack into a screech. You want to make a scene, let your pain finally boil over, make a mess of it — large streaks of *red, red, red, red.*

But you don't, you continue smiling sweetly, swallowing lumps of tears. You craft lovely, glossed-over email and text responses to condolences, acting as the unofficial spokesperson for your family's devastation. Even when you receive an emoji, a little yellow circle with a single sky-blue teardrop to encompass "I'm sorry" (and you will, you'll receive so many of these animated faces — your phone popped open with manufactured sympathy — that it's almost like it's your fucking birthday), you will act with grace. You won't say, "My sister's death deserves more than a goddamn emoji." You won't curse your generation and their inability to formulate honest conversation about inconvenient truths. You are the same "good girl" you always were.

(When time has mellowed your rage, you find yourself just as helpless to others' grief — no act, no letter, no monument large enough to fill the space of our losses, the unrelenting hunger of it. You will understand the fear of stringing together the wrong words — you will come to see silence not as ambivalence but as powerlessness.)

You used to envy casseroles, too — not because you ever actually wanted a casserole, but because they symbolized community support. You still won't receive any casseroles. Suicide, ambiguous suicide especially, will be a black mat at the entrance of your home. It will suspend all natural order of mourning. Without a body, there can be no funeral. Without a death certificate, none of it will feel real. On principle, you used to not believe in a hierarchy of pain, but now you do.

In class you listen vacantly to discussions about the link between madness and creativity: genius flourishing from a blurring of reality — playwrights who hear voices, Sylvia Plath's head in that oven, or Van Gogh and his gushing ear. This may be true: Original thought is linked to a troubled mind, because extraordinary thinking is often deemed deviant by society. Your perspective is one in a trillion — limited and blinding — but eccentricity is not a brain disorder, and all true madness has ever brought you is a dead sister.

When the time came, you told the girls invited to your seventeenth birthday party that it was canceled. Precisely, you said on January 10, 2014, at 4:10 p.m.: "I'm really really really sorry but I have to cancel this. My older sister, Kait, killed herself Wednesday morning and I just don't feel right celebrating anything right now." The harshness of the statement alarms you now — had you truly been that blatant? Gone was the careful editing your family relied on for years to protect your sister's privacy: the softening of edges, the cushioning words that implied meaning without explicitly saying it. In the fog of confusion, you remember your mom and you sitting on the brown leather couch of your den after school and debating how to word the statement. Was this actually what you landed on? Were your minds that fried, your skulls cracked open like eggs, yolks tumbling out?

The name of the Facebook group is "Sour Seventeen." You were joking when you made this, but it isn't funny anymore. It rings clairvoyant. After your startling text in the group chat, you apologize again for anyone who has already purchased gifts. You are transfixed by this detail. You don't want your friends to be angry at you — you don't want anyone to feel cheated out of a free meal and a party favor. Your sister is dead. You have never known a dead person — not a neighbor or a grandparent or even a pet. You lost out of order, plunged straight into the deep end.

You realize everything in bursts and sprints, and each realization is a loss: The children you imagine having someday will never have an aunt or uncle on your side. No cousins, no family gatherings or parties or holidays filled with the clamor of relatives. These were "someday" concepts you took for granted before you realized they were extraordinary blessings.

It will take a few weeks before you consider whether the timing of your sister's choice was coincidental, but when the question finally breaks through the immediate mist of dread, you're struck by an icepick. Did your sister mean to choose your birthday? Was it a message? Your mom holds strong that no, no, it's not possible. She was so out of it, she had no idea what day it was. You don't know, will never know, but either way the date is significant. One day you are sixteen and your sister is alive, but missing. The next day you are seventeen and she is gone. Sixteen will, even in the moment, sound *so very young*. You won't celebrate another birthday again, at least, never entirely.

Three days later (far too late), you ask the girls from your canceled party not to tell anyone else. You don't know this yet, but a screenshot of your message has already circulated, spreading from grade to grade, from someone's sibling to someone else's, all the way up to Kait's peers. Soon, you and your mom are fielding calls left and right from people who knew your sister —"We have a right to know what happened," they say. And they do (you all do), but it is hard to give anyone certainty when at the end of the day, you are only speculating yourself.

This is when your mask slips off — you are livid with whoever took the picture, sensationalized your life's complete and total devastation into petty gossip. You go on a witch hunt to find the girl who is making your mom's life more stressful than it already is (it is you, who sent the message, who is ultimately to blame, but it's easier to externalize the burning, heartburn-inducing panic). You can no longer protect your sister, you have failed at this in the greatest way there is to fail, but you can still try to shield your mom so you focus on this. You know, deep down that it's not the girl's fault, but for a moment, it's calming to have a target for your hatred, however misplaced. In retrospect, maybe you weren't so nice in your grief.

There is a smattering of similar incidents in the first week in which you lose it. Then, you resume life. You will be at a friend's house party by Saturday, planning for the SATs by Sunday. Some may debate whether this quality is strength or callousness, but only you know the truth: You are in a coma of inexpression. You forget so much of the following year, you come to wonder if you were ever even awake.

A day or so after *it* happened, a friend drops you off after school because your mom is incapacitated (a testament to her unwavering strength, this only happens once). You tell the girl not to worry about driving up your long driveway — you know it's a hassle to back out. She sighs, "When are you going to just get your license?"

You received your learner's permit right away — studied for the written portion of the exam and aced it on the first try, one hundred percent: your second favorite number. But you were so anxious about the road test that your parents hired a retired neighbor to drive around town with you, his foot resting a centimeter above an emergency brake. You follow his instructions to a precision that unnerves him. "There will come a moment when you have to trust your own instincts," he tells you in a gruff voice. When it's time to pull out into a busy intersection, he refuses to make the call for you. Cars whizz by, passing and passing, the gaps between them smaller and smaller. A parade of waiting vehicles lines up behind you, honking impatiently. The weight and power of the bulk of metal beneath your shaking hands makes you vibrate.

Your sister had the opposite experience — she kept failing and failing the written section, even igniting alarm from a DMV worker. "Is she okay?" the woman half whispered to your mom. "Has she been diagnosed with anything? Dyslexia or something?" Yet the physical test was no problem for her. Your sister would have jumped confidently into a pilot seat had she the opportunity. You can see her now, grabbing the wheel, hitting the dials with a reckless abandonment. "I've played video games like this before," she'd say nonchalantly. "I'm sure it's the same thing."

But your friend is right. You're seventeen now. You should have overcome your fears and scheduled a driver's test already. You're a burden, and self-hatred shreds away your self-will.

"I'll get my license when I stop wanting to drive into trees," you retort sharply before quickly, awkwardly, pulling your backpack out of the passenger seat, yanking the strap where it's caught on some lever or handle. You regret your outburst immediately — wish you could suck the words back into your body like the thin white puff of breath that escapes you.

You know this sentiment will disturb your friend, and maybe you want her to be disturbed. After all, it's the most honest thing you've said in years: Every time you get in a car, you have this sick fantasy that one of the long pine trees that crowd your neighborhood will fall on you. When you try to practice for the driving exam, the wheel slithers alive beneath your palms like the pulse of a snake. You sense it twitching, itching to spasm just a few feet to the left, off the road, into a ditch. You believe you deserve a violent ending — it was you who called your mom that night. Who pulled the lifeboat away from your sister when she needed it the most. Envisioning yourself trampled soothes you. Legally, this alone should prevent you from carrying a license.

You skate up the black ice of your driveway. Snow covers the lawn a foot deep. You remember the police telling your parents about the chunks of ice — the frozen river. You were sitting in the living room when your mom told you this — on the yellow armchairs near the front window, looking out into the slope of yard and the gathering of trees you used to pretend was a fort when you were young and everything was better. For some reason, you and your mom had never before sat in these chairs together, and you will never sit in them again. She closed her eyes and pinched the bridge of her nose as she explained. *It's unlikely we'll recover a body until the river melts.*

The harbor master described the blow of meeting the frozen water as equivalent to the devastating force of being hit by a freight train speeding at two hundred miles per hour. He said there may not be remains to be found.

Occasionally, you'll watch a film, study a history textbook, read a novel, and in it a body is discovered in a river (this, like the subject of suicide, is more common than you ever could have anticipated). The description is always uncovered, indecent: "The fish got to her." Or, "It's hard to identify the body because the face is so bloated." Each time you reflexively look for an escape: the rectangle of your classroom's door, a window, the cool lick of an imaginary gun pressed to your temple. You push it away from you; you disassociate.

The next unit in your AP American Literature class is *As I Lay Dying* by William Faulkner. The Southern Gothic details an impoverished family's journey to bury their mother in her hometown. The words disturb you to the point of needing to take frequent bathroom breaks — without explanation, you calmly grab the shiny laminated hallway pass. Once the door closes behind you, you sprint down the empty hallway. You lean your arms against the bathroom's sink, ignoring how the stray water seeps into the cotton fabric of your sleeves, weighing you down further. Again, you want to vomit. Again, nothing comes out.

Death in its most abstract form will never make much sense to you. How is it that we can occupy a body — interact with strangers, breathe, produce tears, stretch our muscles into a smile, scrape our knees, watch the skin cells stitch themselves back together again — and then vacate? You've witnessed it in nature: a leaf separated from its base, the green seeping out, the leaf twisting crisp and brown. You've seen food spoil. But you will never wrap your head around the idea that human consciousness can vanish. You remember your sister's Google searches, how easily placated she appeared to be. Even in death, you are so different.

Another time, the ninth of January, the day after it happened, sitting down for an Honors Physics exam, a full hour passes while your test remains blank. You are good at this subject, but every time you set your pencil's intention to start an equation, you pick it up again. Your brain goes static. The page is filled with graphite dots of failed beginnings. A second does not go by without you thinking, "My sister is missing." It expands into every crevice of your mind until there's no room for anything else. You cannot get through a minute without your sister's name intruding, a bulldozer in the spongy mounds of your brain tissue.

When the period bell rings, you wait behind a line of students asking last-minute questions. You want the room to empty so you can explain in private, but one classmate lingers. When it's your turn, you hand your teacher the blank test (not even your name is written on it), but instead of your well-prepared speech, an unhuman croak escapes your throat. You collapse into hysterics right then and there. The teacher, to his eternal credit, politely ushers the remaining student out of the classroom and spends the next period (his lunch break) consoling you.

For the rest of the school year, this man periodically asks how you are — he will be the one who notifies the guidance department, who then notifies your teachers. He will call your mom and check up on her. His wife is a poet and he'll gift you writing books, encourage you into a future you once wanted more than anything but has now spoiled, stale and acidic. You will never, ever forget his kindness: a reminder of the very best of human nature.

There are two charcoal portraits of you and your sister in your family's den: one atop the other. You are around eight in yours, while your sister is fourteen in hers. The drawings are in thick gold frames. You have always loved your sister's portrait, because the artist captured her likeness perfectly, how her smile reached the crinkles of her eyes. You hate yours; you were a brat that day, uncomfortable posing on the summer sidewalk, sweltering in the August heat. Your mom ended up mailing the artist a picture of you because you refused to sit still.

You stare at these images for a moment, letting fury slide in the absence of all coherent thought. For a second, you are angry at your sister — *why did she do this?* Then your real frustration begins — the kind directed at yourself. You never understood your sister's violent impulses before, but now you wish to destroy everything in sight — tear your heart out, rip your body from the inside out. You start punching the wall, smacking the portrait again and again with your fists. Each hit is a resounding why. *Why, why, why, why.*

When you've pounded every sap of energy from your body, you emerge back into yourself: the drawing of you hangs lopsided, but the glass isn't shattered. You are so incapable, so weak, you can't even break the stupid glass. Your sister smiles undisturbed, an ambivalent witness. For the rest of your days, she will only ever be an ambivalent witness —

she will only ever be the girl on the wall. You collapse onto the couch and roll into a ball, screaming and crying until your brain relents into a merciful sleep, as thick as death. Your knuckles have small circular bruises for the coming weeks, the only physical indication that you have changed at all. You periodically pinch the skin of your arm to remind yourself that you are still alive.

People tell you that it gets better — time heals all wounds and whatnot. This isn't necessarily true. The pain never lessens, you only grow around it, strong enough to carry it like a backpack until one day, you almost forget it's there. Grief is a muscle we strengthen, but if you dig deep enough, you'll find it present — a twinge in your knees, flesh cut to the bone.

At the end of the day, you will be grateful that in all of the gaps and wedges the English language forgot to fill, "grief" is not one of them: because grief is not loss, nor pain, nor absence, nor heartbreak, nor anger. Grief is its own entity: all-encompassing. Grief is the second person: outside of you. Grief defies logic. Grief takes "I" and "me" and turns everything into the lingering gray slush of snow at the edge of a highway that melts with spring but brings with it no resolution. You are disembodied. Taste — the fried rice takeout you order every night from the same restaurant — is dulled. Touch — those reassuring pats from friends and family — are bubble-wrapped. You and your mom watch endless reruns of comedy shows during silent dinners, missing the cue for laughter. You mutely consume all nine seasons and 187 episodes of *One Tree Hill*. You retain none of the plot.

There's something indecent about watching the human mind unravel. You felt this way when witnessing your sister's loosening sanity, but now it's you who has lost some hidden thread that connects you to the center of the universe. Who am "I" anymore? Did I ever exist? *Do I even want myself back?*

Twenty-nine

I had driven over the Benjamin Franklin Bridge hundreds of times before that night. I had driven by it, on it, near it, and never once thought anything of it. It was a Philadelphia landmark — a staple, framed in dramatic black-and-white photographs in hotel lobbies. It was always there, only a thirty-minute drive from our home, standing before us, a silent threat in the distance. If I were to look back on the past now, it would seem so obvious — omnipresent.

It was there when we first moved to Philadelphia, when we drove through the crowded streets and arrived at our new home. It was there when we went trick-or-treating. It watched as I did cartwheels on the streets. It watched as we moved to the green suburbs. It watched as my sister fell from the stoop, as she was rushed to the hospital.

At my high school crew practices, I listened, half-awake, in the early mornings to my teammates lament the pollution in the Schuylkill River where our practices were held.

"And if anyone jumps from the Benjamin Franklin Bridge," a girl in a race unitard said, "it could wash up *here*."

She wrinkled her nose, and her audience shuddered a chorus of "*Ew!*"

I thought nothing of this. I never bothered to fact-check her, to research for myself whether the river was downstream or upstream of the bridge. I thought it disturbing, especially when I found myself catapulted out of the boat, my body dipped halfway into the water. I thought of it when we pulled the boat out of the water after practice, lifting it above our heads. Droplets of the river running down my body, my hair, my mouth. But I never considered it deeply until it was my sister's body.

Until it was my *sister*.

A girl walks to the peak of the Benjamin Franklin Bridge.

In April of my junior year of high school, I attended a "paint party" EDM concert called Life in Color. It had been nearly four months since my sister disappeared. I was still going through the brushstrokes of life: going to the same parties I had always gone to, studying for the same tests, looking at colleges with the same feverous obsession.

I missed one day of school. It seemed appropriate to stay home — to seclude myself in privacy — but quickly I realized how little there was to actually *do*. How little there was to say. There was no body to have a funeral with, no planning necessary. My sister's clothes remained hanging in her closet. Her shoes waited by the door. There was nothing to clean, nothing to pack. There was no answer except for that one, elusive image.

Kait walking to the peak of the Benjamin Franklin Bridge.

I returned to school. I returned to the tests and the sports practices and after-school résumé-boosting clubs, and for anyone who has never grieved, how "well" I must have seemed. How polite, how contained. If only they knew I did not seem to be grieving, because I wasn't. I wasn't irate, I wasn't unraveling, because I was still waiting.

I was waiting for my sister to come back.

I decided to attend the concert because it was something I would have done before Kait disappeared, and I was determined to maintain everything as it once was. Perhaps if nothing changed, it would be as if it never happened at all. Maybe Kait would return.

How embarrassing it would be to have publicly mourned my sister when she walked through the entrance of our home the next weekend! How silly I would feel when she returned!

And how angry she would be to discover we had deceived everyone in reporting her death. How much harder it would be for her to readjust if there were digital memorials dedicated to her, candles lit and prayers recited.

"I was only gone for a few weeks!" She'd roll those green eyes. "You're so dramatic."

I woke a week after she disappeared to find one of her sticky notes attached to the shelf of my white desk. I was getting dressed in a hurry, throwing clothes on in the ten minutes I had before the first-period bell rang in my high school's linoleum hallway.

With my pants pulled halfway up my thighs, I spotted the bright orange square from the corner of my eye. My heart leapt up, getting caught somewhere in my throat. I twisted in horror and then relief: fear and desperate hope.

I love you Kyle, it said. Her nickname for me. Her girly script. Her. Kait. It was her. She was here. I ran down the stairs, nearly slipping on the polished wood, reminded of how as kids we used to propel ourselves in sliding contests in our freshly laundered socks.

A dozen scenarios ran through my head. Kait, alive, sending me a message. Waiting for me in the kitchen, a glass of orange juice in hand, the sheepish grin, the elfish look.

"I didn't want to wake you," she'd say.

"I'm home," she'd say.

Or maybe Kait was really gone, passed to the other side. Maybe this was her in spirit form, contacting me. Telling me she loved me still. Telling me she was okay.

"Mom!" I screamed, the words tripping over each other in a jumble, a highway pileup, syllables colliding and crashing in a line. "Mom, I found this on my desk."

I put the precious orange square on the black granite countertop of our kitchen island like a detective proudly displaying her evidence.

"Oh yeah! I found that behind the sofa the other day when I was cleaning up." She smiled the only smile she could muster these days: one that didn't reach her eyes but tried so hard to that it looked like a hook or a sideways comma.

"I thought it would cheer you up, give you something to hold on to."

I nodded slowly, trying not to cry.

"Oh, of course." I returned her hooked smile. "Thank you."

The night of April fifth was unseasonably cold, too cold for the tiny shirts and neon skirts we wore. Too cold to be drenched in paint by the spray guns blasting the crowd.

Before my sister's disappearance, I never drank alcohol. I couldn't afford to disorient my reality — what if even the smallest disturbance, the smallest eruption grew and swelled until I too heard whispers that weren't there, saw visions dance across the walls?

After Kait's disappearance, I still didn't drink often, but when I did, I liked the way the liquid slowed my brain, how it cushioned simple facts until they were impossible to process, like listening to someone talk with cotton balls stuffed in my ears. I could think horrible, horrible truths, and yet they wouldn't quite reach me. They floated and bounced around until they were almost absurd.

A girl walks to the peak of the Benjamin Franklin Bridge.

That night of the concert, I took a swig from a plastic pint of vodka with an off-brand label. I wasn't quite drunk, but I was numb enough not to mind how cold it was or that there would soon be paint splattered in my hair. Somebody had organized a school bus to take our friends there, and I found it unusually hilarious to be sitting in the brown, ripped vinyl seats as if I was traveling back in time, a little girl on her way to class. It was not until I arrived at the concert venue that I realized my grave mistake.

The Life in Color concert was held at Penn's Landing, a waterfront area of Center City Philadelphia situated alongside the Benjamin Franklin Bridge.

It confronted me then as I stepped out of the bus. It demanded to know what I was doing, where I had been. It stood before me a brutish beast, a dark, looming figure. It watched me as the techno beat blasted its way into my skull, rattling my bones and nerve endings until I believed I could maybe see a girl up there. A girl walking to the peak. A girl disappearing from the peak. Was it Kait up there? Could she see me now? Had she been waiting all this time, just hoping someone would dare to look up?

The nausea returned. I wanted to throw a rock at the bridge, to scream at it. It was so big, and my sister was so small. It took advantage of her. Let her walk its path, let her look over the edge and stare at the waves. It had misled her. Whispered lies in her ears. It was to blame then, and now here it was again — taunting me, mocking me.

Angry tears streamed down my face, loosening the stupid plastic gems I had glued to the corner of my eyes. Stupid. Everything was stupid. I was stupid, to be wearing a skirt on this freezing April night. To be at a concert with music I didn't even like. To be covered in paint, and to be staring at my sister's assassin ten days before what should have been her twenty-third birthday.

And, oh, *crap*, I realized. Kait's birthday was in ten days. The first birthday she would not celebrate. Stupid, stupid, stupid.

I texted my friends to tell them I was leaving and maneuvered my way past throngs of drunks in light-up sneakers and glowing plastic bracelets. I shivered on the busy city street and called my mom to ask if she could pick me up.

"Why so sad?" A man jumped in my face. "It's a concert! Cheer up!"

"My sister jumped from that bridge," I wanted to tell him.

When Mom arrived, I apologized and thanked her, but I didn't tell her why I had to leave early. I didn't tell her that the bridge threatened me. I told her I was cold, getting sick, and needed to be home. I didn't ask if the bridge threatened her, too — if it mocked her, too.

I sat on towels so my dripping body wouldn't stain the seats with paint. I blasted the hot air on my hands until the shaking wasn't from the cold.

I didn't turn around again, didn't look in the rearview mirror to check one last time if maybe there was a splash of red up there on the bridge's peak.

A girl in a red jacket and high boots. A girl walking.

And then, poof, gone.

Thirty

There's a common thought experiment known as the Trolley Problem. In the hypothetical dilemma, a train is hurtling toward five people stuck in the tracks. You have two options: pull the lever and move the train to a fork in the road down an alternative path, where there is only one person trapped, or do nothing at all and let the five die. The scenario was proposed in the name of the principle that morality necessitates creating maximum happiness for the largest number of people. Yet one option requires action while the other has the luxury of passivity. So what do you do — kill one to save five?

I imagined many alternate futures for our family of four. It was clear that tragedy was a train headed our way. I was prepared, in a distant sense, that something bad was going to happen soon. The unspoken thought that ran through my veins was *What could I survive?* A stranger killing Kait in self-defense. Kait accidentally killing us. If our lives were a Trolley Problem, a utilitarian experiment, then the latter was the most welcome of scenarios. One in which I didn't live to see the consequences.

The worst arrived when I considered the possibility of Kait killing both of my parents. I imagined the funeral she wouldn't attend. The remorse she'd feel when the heat of her psychosis broke. I envisioned walking to a metal picnic bench — my sneakers slapping against the concrete jail floor. From then on, it was just going to be her and me: the weight of her care residing solely on my shoulders as it had on our mom's before.

In developmental psychology research, play is understood as a learning tool by which children process the world and their place in it. Kids will practice certain behaviors or actions, mimicking and modeling adults as a means to prepare for their eventual roles in society. They play "doctor," placing plastic stethoscopes on your chest, or "house," cleaning and cooking in the confines of their miniature world.

As children, we also practice more complex emotions. We marry our dolls off to one another and then break them up the next day. We create narratives and act them out on the playground. We even practice grief.

At sleepovers, I lay in the dim light of my friend's room and played a game we called Who Would Cry at My Funeral?

It was a dark game for eight-year-olds to play — an elaborate imagined scenario in which we met a sudden, tragic demise and each of our classmates attended our memorial. We pictured the long lines flowing from our caskets. Our teachers falling to their knees before our lifeless, serene faces. Our biggest bullies with tears sprung, confessing how utterly and completely they had wronged us. Who would speak? What would they say?

So you see, I prepared. I considered the Trolley Problem. I played out the worst-case scenarios. But this — *suicide* — I forgot to factor in to the equation. I had imagined this end possibly for myself, but never for Kait — always so confident, so self-assured. How could I be so blind? I calculated for everything but never this.

I used to ask my sister for advice when texting a crush — she'd grab the phone from my hand, type up some witty, flirty comeback and send it before I could wrestle the device away. When she got sick, I worried that she might reach out to people I knew via Facebook, messaging a boy I liked something senseless and disturbing. I blocked her so that she couldn't see my contact list. I fretted over the possibility of her following me to college, knocking on my dorm room at three a.m., scaring my roommates.

It's ironic, in a morbid sense, the baseless fears we predict before we know what there really is to be afraid of. I wonder if grief is quite simply a failure of imagination, because no amount of planning can prepare you for the profound absence of a single person.

Thirty-one

A flash of retrospection: Eight days before my sister disappeared, I rang in the new year in a classmate's crowded basement. The large home had iron gates blocking the entrance. Her parents were out of town, and several grades packed into every crevice of the house, spewing into hallways and bedrooms, crouching in groups on stairways. We wore real dresses and heels for the occasion, shiny tiaras proclaiming 2014! and those plastic New Year's Eve glasses with two holes for your eyes that really only made sense in the first decade of the 2000s. We said, "2014 is going to be our year!" We said, "Oh my gosh, can you believe how fast high school is going by?" I bought and returned several dresses before landing on a simple black one with silver beads around the neckline. I borrowed my sister's eyeliner where she left it on our shared bathroom's vanity among a collection of lipsticks and hair scrunchies.

When the clock struck midnight, I was in that basement amid a sea of friends and acquaintances, all of us bouncing up and down with every dropping number, chanting for the ball in Times Square to make its descent: *five, four, three, two, one*. I was internally listing my resolutions for the next year, my hopes the same as every year before — never appreciating the moment for what it is, always asking for more: 2014 is going to be different, *better*. My sister will get it together. Everything will go back to normal. I'll get in to my dream college, somewhere even Kait would approve of. I made the only wish I knew how to make anymore: *I wish my sister gets better.*

As the new year was rung in, a girl in front of me spilled her drink backwards. The sickly sweet smell of green apple–flavored vodka splashed down on me, seeping into my hair, my eyes, my dress. Before anyone could notice, I searched for a bathroom, coming across locked handles at every corner. When I finally found one, I wet a small square of toilet paper and wiped my face. Without my knowing precisely why, tears thudded against my eyelids, leaking at the edges. It was only 12:02 a.m., two minutes in to 2014.

Many cultures have superstitions surrounding the new year, from taboos to good omens. In the southern United States, eating collards and black-eyed peas can bring good luck, or having a slice of king cake in New Orleans can do the same. In Latin America, carrying around an empty suitcase invites a year of travel. Other harbingers of future fortune: eating twelve grapes, wearing red underwear, putting cash in your wallet (a signifier of prosperity), kissing someone at midnight. Even firecrackers and noisemakers are rooted in a folklore that loud noises dispel evil spirits.

New Year's Eve is also historically disappointing, and there's a good reason why. In a 1999 study, "The Pursuit and Assessment of Happiness Can Be Self-Defeating," researchers found that people who planned for a big celebration were the most unsatisfied. The study discussed their findings within the Heisenberg uncertainty principle of physics — when trying to measure a particle's energy, you inherently influence it. By monitoring your happiness, actively seeking enjoyment, you inherently influence the experience of it.

I wanted to start 2014 right. I wanted a sign, a symbol that this was going to be *the* year, the year that everything was going to be okay. Instead, I spent the first few minutes alone, crying in a bathroom but unsure of why: Was it just a simple letdown? Or was my intuition ringing off in some distant hollow of my mind, a little red light blinking a warning? In eight days, my sister would die. I couldn't tell you where she was on that New Year's Eve, how she spent it. Did she already know? Had she begun planning? Was there no resolution, not even a dull glint, a buried hope that this could be "the best year yet"?

For as long as I had been alive, Kait and I relied on superstitions, signs, and myths to prevent losing each other. We avoided cracks on the sidewalk, jumping over splintered slabs. We made our 11:11 wishes. Had all those signs, all those superstitions, led to nothing?

On the last week of January 2014 — less than a month after my sister's disappearance — my friend Julia held a birthday party at her family's home. I walked the familiar walk to her bedroom upstairs, where my friends and I had covered the wall with our signatures and inside jokes. In her room, conversation bubbled easily. I left my present on her desk and sat on the corner of her bed.

There had been a moment, during a sports practice the week before, when my hand went limp in the middle of a point. Our squash team was playing at a facility nearby our public high school. We were required to wear all white — white skirt, white athletic polo, white sneakers — and goggles that looked like they belonged in a chemistry lab. I was rallying with a friend while our coach watched, evaluating our moves. The tight, cramped court, the brightness of the walls, the harsh red lines, the quick smack of the small black ball as it went back and forth, back and forth, relentless in its movement. As hard as I hit it, the harder it came back. It wouldn't stop coming, and suddenly the game felt as fruitless as everything I had ever done — all those years of suffering, of trying, signing up for counseling, admitting Kait into programs. No matter what we did, her disease kept coming back, getting worse and worse until inevitably we lost her for good. So much hope, so much effort, and *for what?*

I remembered a seminar about mental illness that my mom and I went to during my freshman year of high school. The talk was held in a drab community center basement, and we had to drive a few towns over to get there. I was exhausted after a long day of school, bone-tired, but the class was required to visit Kait in her most recent psychiatric facility.

We sat in plastic folding chairs in the farthest row in the back. A doctor lectured on a projected PowerPoint screen, his monotone voice slowly lulling me to sleep. Every few seconds, my head bobbed up and down like a buoy in waves, my chin meeting my cheek and then jolting back up as if an electric current ran through it. Up and down, up and down I went as a man explained the insidious neurological disease leisurely killing my sister.

Now, back and forth the little squash ball went. Back and forth, always coming back to me no matter how much force I put into my racket — it returned a boomerang. I just wanted it to stop coming, *please* just stop coming. I felt useless, pathetic. I remembered falling asleep at the seminar. I remembered Kait's delicate, childlike handwriting: *Kait goes to heaven*. I remembered her Google searches and the ten thousand ways, both large and small, that I had failed her. I remembered her standing over me one day as I studied for an exam, yelling that it didn't matter. None of it mattered, why couldn't I see that? Up and down, up and down, back and forth I always went, relentless in my pursuit. And now I found it impossible to return to this hazy reality, the way you forget a dream the next day. In the morning light, I couldn't seem to remember what I was so desperately chasing after — that thing that seemed so important in my sleep. Back and forth.

The ball rebounded off the tin line at the bottom of the court, stopping a sudden death. It rolled mute and dumb, and with it I felt my arm go lank. I touched my face and found water falling: a leaky faucet no one had turned on. My friend turned around, positioning herself to start a new point, but stood still when she saw me. "Are you hurt?" she asked. I shook my head no. "Are you okay?" She came closer. I shook my head again, a sob bubbling in the place of words.

"I think I'm going to faint," I told her as the court grew punctuated with little gray dots.

"Go to the locker room," she said immediately. "I'll explain to Coach and be right there."

I pushed past the heavy glass doors, angling my face away from our coach so he wouldn't see my tears. It distantly occurred to me that he probably assumed I was upset about losing the point and I felt embarrassed, ashamed of my own weakness. Upstairs, I splashed water on my forehead and sat in the wicker chair of the women's locker room absentmindedly staring at the neatly folded towels on the table next to me in dull displacement. The air conditioner in the corner blasted aggressively, sending goosebumps up my arms and making a buzzing sound like the reverberation of a hundred bees. When my friend came in, I apologized and thanked her. She sat with me, comforting and kind, as I tried to explain myself, excuse myself. Women from the club walked in and out, sometimes with looks of disdain, sometimes with pity.

"It's not just that she — she died," I stuttered. "There was more. There was a lot more before. She wasn't well. Wasn't well for a while."

I had known this girl since I was eight or nine. We were friends through it all, but I had never mentioned anything about mental illness to her. It seemed too late now. Far too late to convey everything, but I kept trying anyway, mumbling what defied comprehension, even to me.

When I calmed down, she walked me back to the practice, and I kept thanking her and saying I was sorry. Thank you, and I'm so sorry to bother you. *I'm so sorry.*

At my friend's birthday party, I listened as my closest friends planned out the weekend: who was coming tonight, where we would go tomorrow. I was an alien alone in a foreign landscape. I no longer spoke the language.

When it was time for dinner, we went downstairs to my friend's kitchen and sat around the island on stools. Her mother brought out a square white cake with pink and purple frosting.

"Look," Julia said, pointing to the words. "Because you had to cancel your party, I thought we could share mine."

The cake read, *Happy 17th Birthday, Kyleigh + Julia.*

The small gesture was quite possibly the nicest thing anyone had ever done for me, and I felt wholly unworthy. I didn't deserve to celebrate a birthday. No one realized what had really happened — that I felt complicit in my sister's illness and now in her death. In pictures from that night, we blow out the candles together and my eyes are glossy, my cheeks matching the burgundy shade of the tank-top I wore. It was the first time since I was seven that my wish was not for Kait to get better. In its place, my wish was a hollow chant of "I'm sorry."

I'msorryI'msorryI'msorry.

Afterward, I thanked my friend and her parents profusely, and then as soon as I could do so without being impolite, I escaped to a rarely used bathroom near their attic, sitting for some time on the cool tile floor, trying to catch my breath.

Eventually I rejoined everyone in the basement where the rest of the party had arrived — more kids from our class, friends we knew from nearby private schools. A boy I had a crush on for years appeared. As I looked at him, all I could think was that my sister had picked out the outfit I wore on a date we went on the summer prior. She paired the necklace with the shirt and the slightly heeled sandals, the gold-studded ones that gave me blisters and left scars — the white lines on my ankles a reminder to this day. Kait gave me the encouragement to go at all, called me a wimp, rolled her eyes, offered me a shot for some "liquid courage," which I promptly rejected, but the suggestion made me laugh and relax enough to go on the date at all.

Now she was gone.

When I walked around, mingled, looked into my peers' eyes, this singular thought rebounded against the interior of my skull like that doctor's pinball. Back and forth the ball went.

Do you know? I wanted to ask everyone around me. *Has the screenshot spread to you yet? Do you know that she is gone? Do you know what I have done?*

For many years, blowing out those candles was the last wish I ever made — I tucked my hopes into some imaginary box and left them to rot.

Thirty-two

I once had a therapist compare my loss to the passing of his dog. My knee-jerk reaction was to be offended. A sister is not a dog. The magnitude does not equate. I remembered the week after my sister's disappearance when a classmate left our calculus exam in tears because her pet was sick and she was too distracted. My own brain was a scattered galaxy, my thoughts disjointed and incomplete. I gritted my teeth, locked my jaw, and finished the test.

But now I understand what he meant.

Grief is implicitly tied to regret. I thought it was a symptom of suicide — the feeling of inadequacy and failure. And in some ways it is: Suicide grievers often fall into "complicated grief," the shame, the blame, the regret leaving us empty. But years later, when my own dog (my beloved Sailor from Marblehead) passed away from simple old age at seventeen years old — Mom and her neighbor wrapping him in a towel and taking him outside to our backyard where he could look at the wildflowers that sprouted between blades of grass as he faded in and out of consciousness — I remembered the therapist. (Two years after, when our other dog, Lilly, died, for the first time I had the excruciating, illogical, unbearably lonely thought of *Someday, I may be the only person alive who knew my sister, my parents, any of it.*)

With even a pet's death, you are swollen with self-blame. Did Sailor have a good enough life? Wouldn't he have liked to play outside more? Maybe go to some real dog parks — spread himself wild and free. Let him drink out of the shared water bowl, forget your fears about kennel cough. Should I have crafted my own dog food, committed to organic, all-natural grass-fed instead of kibble? (His stomach was too sensitive for this — when he was a puppy, he could only swallow Gerber's baby hot dogs, but you won't be able to reflect upon this logically.) Anytime one of us raised our voice, even when cheering along to a sports game, my dogs would shake, and I couldn't help but wonder if it was a by-product of those years of Kait's chaos: canine post-traumatic stress disorder. The thought sucked me dry.

Guilt is the cousin of suicide, irrevocably related. I called Mom and asked her to come home when she should've been with my sister. That is a tangible action, a physical regret. And yet, all loss carries with it some form of remorse or self-condemnation. Was I a good enough daughter? Should I have written to my grandparents more? Did I say "I love you" as often as I should have?

We never feel like we did enough. We regret what we said and what we didn't say. In the face of mourning, we are all insufficient. We are all impossibly small.

Thirty-three

A caveat. One day you learn about parallel universes.

It starts off simple, innocent, really, as most poisons begin. You're at a friend's party and someone mentions the show *Sex and the City.*

"*Wait!*" a girl says. "I thought it was called 'Sex *in* the City.'"

A discussion opens up, the Mandela effect is brought up — the phenomenon where mundane details of pop culture are misremembered — and somewhere along the way you fall into it headfirst.

Every girl pulls out her phone and now you're Googling the term, learning its origin story (how people gathered together in online chatrooms distinctly stating that they saw headlines reading that Nelson Mandela died in prison). You learn about the confusion around how to correctly spell the children's book series, *The Berenstain Bears,* and how some insist that it used to be called "The Berenstein Bears" with an "e" not an "a." How Oscar Meyer is actually spelled Oscar Mayer. And. okay, sure, these may be simple vowel swaps, but then things gets more interesting.

You could've sworn the Monopoly Man had a monocle, and wasn't it always Cheez-Itz (plural) not Cheez-*It*? And, damn it, you know for a fact that Curious George had a tail, because you saw him swinging from it in the cartoon. Right? *Right.*

The solution: multiverse theory.

You're no physicist, but you boil the science down to oversimplified nuggets you can grasp. The term "cosmological horizon" refers to the distance from which it is conceivable to gather information. Because the universe may be infinitely expanding, there comes a point when it is unknowable, unobservable.

You like this term immediately, because it reminds you of your former life on the water, where you watched the sun dip into the horizon of a red sky. You imagine the universe making this same motion, dropping into mystery.

When you were a preschooler during a long car ride with your family, you remember looking out the backseat window. It was night and you were driving somewhere near the mountains — perhaps you were going on a family skiing trip. You loved skiing back then: the whip of the wind, feeling the mountain move beneath your feet. You would sing songs, thinking no one could hear, thinking yourself free. This was before you became consumed by head injuries and the terrors of falling and cracking.

In the car, all was quiet, and you saw the moon between the branches of trees, like a face in the sky. As you sped down the road, it stayed the same distance apart like it was attached to you, a bad thought you couldn't quite drop. *The moon follows me*, you said, because you were young and silly and believed yourself special and mystical and logically the center of the universe. (Later, in elementary school when you learned about the heliocentric versus geocentric models of the cosmos, you admit you would've thought Copernicus mad.)

You once heard that there are more stars in the sky than grains of sand on all of the world's beaches. You also once heard that we know more about space than we do about the human brain. This upsets you, because the universe seems to you a blank canvas, too vast to comprehend — how could we know even less about our own minds? Then you think about your sister, about all the people who stared at her, dumbstruck, unable to help, and you know that sadly, it must be true. Never was there an emptier canvas than that.

According to some theories, if the universe goes on forever, it may start repeating itself because only so many patterns of particles exist.

Like seeing your doppelgänger on the street, there may be another universe where every choice you made is different in subtle and grand ways. In one universe, maybe the show really was called Sex *in* the City. Maybe you picked the blue sweater one morning instead of the red. Maybe in one universe, your sister is alive.

Yes, you think. *Yes*, this must be it.

Being vacuumed down this rabbit hole is seductive, effortless, the way you always imagined falling in love would be. It is easier than anything has been lately.

You are reasonable enough to know that much of this is speculative, and the Mandela effect can be explained by the suggestibility of our memory, because nothing about what we remember is immune to influence. But the world stopped making sense on January 8, 2014, and wishful thinking is the last lifeline of the grieving. Another world started three days before your seventeenth birthday, and who's to say that something didn't go wrong? Maybe the wires of the stars crossed, maybe there's a way to go back, to get her back. Maybe it was all a simple misunderstanding. This wasn't supposed to happen, you know it. You *know* it.

You learn about the variety of recordings on the *Voyager 1* and *Voyager 2* — spacecrafts sent to explore the outer edges of our heliosphere — and how the Golden Record contains sounds of Earth: laughter, greetings from many languages, the chirp of birds, the splash of dolphins, music, and a message from President Jimmy Carter. The concept of our human noise being blasted into space in the hopes of making contact with alien beings strikes a chord of familiarity. The recordings sing into the void just as you do.

You think, any day now, someone, something, out there will hear the tape. Maybe we can cross back into that other dimension, the better one, before it's too late.

You also recognize that if you continue down this path, if you become more entrenched in cosmic loopholes, you will lose your grasp on reality like your sister did. A part of you yearns for this release, to finally let go, let yourself crumble the way you feel, but you must stay grounded in this world, in the here and now. So you try to release it, but there it stands — a twinkling, intoxicating caveat.

Weeks later, on the back of a printout of "The Five Stages of Grief," you find a letter Mom penned to Kait on the day of her first birthday since her disappearance. It's an apology note and a love letter. After it, she writes to God, asking for a caveat of her own.

"God," she addresses him informally, an accusation in the hard three letters.

"Why would you let this happen? Why the pain? Why did you let her get sick? Why didn't you help me take better care of her? *Why?*"

She ends with one final question, somehow smaller than the others, meeker.

"Can I please have her back?"

Thirty-four

The day after Christmas in 2004, an undersea earthquake struck the coast of Indonesia, setting off the Indian Ocean tsunami and resulting in approximately 230,000 deaths.

Much has been written about the tragedy, including two incredibly powerful memoirs — *Wave* by Sonali Deraniyagala, who lost her parents, husband, and two young sons in an almost unspeakable devastation — and *Lives Other Than My Own* by Emmanuel Carrére, who bore witness to a grandfather's search for his missing grandchild. Both accounts center around Sri Lanka, one of the hardest hit countries, and both begin with similar shock at how average the day was before the catastrophe.

"I thought nothing of it at first. The ocean looked a little closer to our hotel than usual. That was all. A white foamy wave had climbed all the way up to the rim of sand where the beach fell abruptly down to the sea. You never saw water on that stretch of sand. . . . Steve was in the shower, or reading on the toilet more likely. Our two boys were on the back veranda, buzzing around their Christmas presents," writes Deraniyagala.

"Curiously enough, nothing seems amiss at first," says Carrére. "Everything appears normal. Then you start to notice how strange things really are. The water seems so far away. . . . Normally, there are about twenty yards of beach between the ocean's edge and the foot of the cliff. Now, however, the sand stretches off into the distance: flat, gray, glistening in the hazy sunshine, like Mont-Saint-Michel at low tide."

The 2004 tsunami fundamentally altered preparation and risk reduction for natural disasters. Now, there are seismometers, tidal gauges, and buoys to detect ocean tremors. The Indian Ocean Tsunami Warning and Mitigation System was opened in 2007. Sensors have been installed in the seafloor that can trigger early warnings.

Kerry Sieh, the director of the Earth Observatory of Singapore, told CBS News: "What the 2004 event showed very clearly was that there was nothing in the Indian Ocean, nothing whatsoever in terms of technology or people's awareness or infrastructure preparation."

The NOAA Tsunami Program runs the U.S. Tsunami Warning System, with two operating systems staffed twenty-four hours a day, seven days a week. There is still a great disparity and an underserving of certain communities. There are still lapses. Tragedy can still strike, but for the most part, the world is more alert. Coastal towns have more emergency training. The hope is that a calamity of such magnitude can be prevented in the future.

When something truly terrible happens, we fixate on the details, the minutiae, the chronology. Do these specifics ground us somehow? Do we focus on the quotidian because we know that nothing will ever be normal again? The water looked curious but not concerning, odd but not threatening. It was a beautiful day. Never again will it be a beautiful day in quite the same way. Never again will the sky hold the unblemished clarity of a life without loss.

Or is it the lack of a sign that really gets under our skin? Tragedy can strike without premonition. A natural disaster can arrive when the kids are playing with their Christmas presents. The narrative containers we use to impose structure and morality onto our lives no longer fit. Happy endings do not necessitate good deeds. Pain is immune to virtue.

The day my sister died, I was stressed, studying for an exam. It seemed important, imperative even, that I do well on the test. That night, I curled into my covers, warm and cozy, naïve to the fact that everything had fundamentally changed.

I was sixteen, almost seventeen. I still believed that misfortune dragged with it apprehension, a hunch. I still believed in superstitions and wishing on 11:11 and blind faith. I still believed in warning signs; some signal, a chance to fix history before it crushed you. I didn't yet understand that life is littered with random contingencies, chance encounters, unforeseeable complications.

Of course, there *had* been signs if we knew what to look for. There had been many signs: the childhood antics, the teenage rebellion, the partying, the shambles of violent beginnings, the hallucinations — the swastika in the front entrance hall in the tiled floor — the increasing tension. The head trauma, the doctor telling us, *She won't be the same.* There was Kait herself, writing in that notebook, saying she needed help before we had the opportunity to hear her. *I am stronger than I was before but so weak.*

There had likely been signs before the tsunami as well — a disturbance on the ocean's floor, sand displaced, a shuddering in the waves, vibrations that grew and grew. The problem lay in there not being measures in place to detect them. What good is a sign if the technology doesn't exist to capture it? What good is a warning if there's no infrastructure to sound the alarm?

We didn't have the education to know what to look for. And even if we had it, the systems did not exist to effectively help us. The hope here is that change is possible, that stories like Kait's can help serve as those warnings. The hope is that the alarm bells will be rung, next time, before it's too late.

Thirty-five

The rest of high school passes in strange spurts and trickles, slowly and then in a single breath.

Your junior-year prom is held in April — two months *after*. You wear a deep blue fit-and-flare dress with a cinched waist, v-cut neckline, and scalloped edges. You bought it on eBay — a gamble, but miraculously, it fits. You curl your long hair, throw on a pair of light gold heels your mom found the week before. Usually, your sister would have helped you pick out a dress. What will she think? Even now, *especially* now, you are fixated on what she thinks of you. When people say "Your sister is watching over you," the thought is not a comfort. You picture her up there for real, in some mystic cloud, surveying you from above, criticizing everything you do and say — the way you hold your spoon, the sound of your laugh. Her criticism used to be limited to a physical presence, but now you can imagine her everywhere.

A large majority of the juniors goes to a friend's house to take pictures before the dance while parents mingle in the backyard. "I'm sorry," Mom says before she drops you off. "I'm so sorry, I'm not ready to face everyone yet." When she goes to the grocery store, she still ducks between aisles, afraid someone might catch sight of her and express their condolences. Her mouth gone dry, her speech shriveled up.

When you look back, you wonder how she was able to keep supporting you through it all. Her weight drops rapidly. She loses bone density. Every step hurts. (You will be shocked continuously by this physical aspect of grief. Your chest pierced, your shoulders instinctually concaving around the hole in self-defense. You knew loss would be mentally, emotionally strenuous, but you never expected this.) Imagining your mom's suffering, a bottomless multiplication of your own, makes you wince. You wonder how anyone ever survived it.

When you think about this pain, the hungry hole where your heart used to be, you want to alert every philosopher, every neuroscientist, every academic who is at this very moment debating the nature of human consciousness in an overly air-conditioned lecture hall. You've heard their theories — the idea that the brain is akin to a computer, a machine that may be uploaded like a flash drive for eternal life. You want them to know that they've got it all wrong. You are seventeen, but you know this more certainly than anyone has ever known anything. The soul resides not in the brain, but right there between your rib cage. It might be possible to code technology to predict human speech patterns or program artificial intelligence to respond back to our questions. We might suffer a migraine when we're stressed — a dagger at our temple — but when our souls are irreparably damaged, it's not our minds that hurt. It's right there in the violent wanting of our chests. You know this because your soul has just broken.

At the pre-prom gathering, parents periodically stop to ask how you are, rubbing the bare skin of your exposed arm and patting your clammy hand reassuringly. They are incredibly well-intentioned, thoughtful, but each time the subject is brought up, your eyes cloud. Then you are whisked away for a photo. A condolence, a photo. A condolence, a photo. The repetition continues. The corsage around your wrist weighs heavy, leaving an angry red line on your sensitive skin. You wonder if your smile looks maniacal.

Weeks ago, your father left and your parents separated. He coped with your sister's death by finding himself a new future — leaving your mother (and you in the process) for a woman he knew from long ago, and moving out of your childhood home. Your parents will soon enter into a long, arduous divorce process that lasts five years, but you don't know this yet. In that time, you will only see your father twice, but you don't know this yet either.

Your life has seemed to close up on itself, every family gathering a little more intimate, the people around you decimated like dropped flies. And what a difference it makes — when four becomes two. It would almost be cozy if it weren't suffocating in its indistinct sadness.

You battle two camps: you hate the subject of your sister's disappearance, would rather bury it down, but at the same time, you are *desperate* for someone to ask you about it. You want everything to go back to normal, if it ever was normal, but you also want to acknowledge that it won't, cannot, will never be wholly normal again.

The next year, you attend a National Honor Society award ceremony. You stand in alphabetical order in a rigid line outside the door to your auditorium. You are about to enter the stage, to collect the certificate and small pin, but the vice principal — the one your sister once spilled bong water on — pauses when she reads your name on a printed-out list. "Leddy?" she says in high-pitched surprise. "Are you related to Kait?" You swallow a hard rock. Yes, you answer. "How is she doing?" the woman asks, not unkindly.

"She's okay." You try to arrange your mouth into a smile but your teeth no longer fit, like a misaligned jigsaw puzzle. Your heart beats rapidly. The boy before you proceeds toward the door. You hear the crowd erupt in applause.

"Where does she go to school, or did she graduate already?" the woman asks, still staring at her list of names. If she were to look up, would she see in your eyes the panic that runs through your veins — a deer caught in headlights, or rather, a deer already hit, ripped open and discarded on the side of the road? You are nothing in that moment but skin and bones and a beating heart.

Quickly, you do the mental calculation. Your sister passed away when she was twenty-two, meaning she would be twenty-three now, a year out of college.

"She went to Drexel," you respond. "She's working in fashion in the city now." You add this extra detail for good measure, hoping it will serve as a conversational plug.

"How wonderful!" The woman sounds pleased, relieved even. "That makes me so happy." She smiles genuinely, and you believe her. You try to match her expression, but beads of sweat prick your hairline. For a second, you let the possibility of this alternative reality envelop you. The life your sister could have had. Then you are on stage.

You shake the principal's hand, your knees clacking from the encounter. You realize what this achievement cost you — what you have sacrificed to stand in this line, praised for your crisp A's and perfect GPA. You remember the phone call you made to your mom, the one that took her away from your sister, and in its shadow this pin seems so small, the certificate impossibly thin. You feel an animalistic urge to rip it in two with your teeth.

You wonder if the boy in line behind you heard the conversation. If he knows your sister is gone and thinks you a pathological liar. You're not sure why you lied in the first place, but once you do, you can't stop. The truth refuses to come out smoothly, catches edges on the way up, spills out hoarse and crooked where the fiction is as smooth as melted butter.

Not long after, you sit in your AP Spanish class, practicing a conversational exercise, asking simple questions. "*¿Còmo se llama?*" What's your name? "*¿De dónde eres?*" Where are you from? "*¿A que colegio vas?*" What school do you go to? And then, "*¿Tienes hermanos?*" Do you have any siblings?

You tell the girl, no, *no tengo hermanos*. She says, *No, wait.* She says she thought you did — her sister was in your sister's grade. The vomit rises as you continue to shake your head no, the answer unintelligible in any language. Do you have a sister? You don't know.

It is technically a harmless question, but it harms you irreparably — countlessly and when you least expect it: at a job interview, on a date, during a teacher's office hours.

At a fitting for your senior prom dress, you watch your reflection in the three tilted mirrors of the podium. You are wearing a simple gown, floor length. You are here to have the dress trimmed so it doesn't drag when you walk.

Mom is sitting in an armchair in the corner. You avoid her eyes. If she notices the question, she doesn't react. You are both used to the verbal land mines, the polite lies.

You are wearing black — the color of the funeral garb you never wore. You don't like this tone on you, never have; you were the girl who once *loved* colors, remember. You were the girl who carried your sister's flag when she was unable to. In her absence, you are drained of any vibrancy she once lent you. The dress makes your already pale skin fainter. You look more like a ghost than your sister ever could.

You tell the woman, "I'm an only child." The words seep down your throat with an earthy taste, dirt swallowed, raw and dry.

In college, the question becomes a refrain, a constant companion. The first few weeks are filled with endless chatter, superficial ice-breakers, and vapid banter. But the question isn't simple, and every time, no matter the context, it startles you. Something in your chest is twisted and wrenched.

You decided to go to college in Boston. A part of you hoped that moving closer to your family's roots would bring back something good and right inside of you. Primarily, you grew up in Philadelphia, but it was never home to anyone in your family but you. Your mom moved to the shores of Nantucket Island, a New England beach town you used to visit in your childhood, finding comfort in being by the ocean and waves again. You worry obsessively about each other, the separation is a loss in and of itself. You survived so much as a duo, and now you are unan-chored, loose in the world.

You take turns saying to each other, "I need you to take care of your-self," in response to an admittance of stress or fear or in reply to nothing at all. You both know the coded message beneath this statement: I need you to stay alive. You make it your mission to keep her fed, expressing cravings you don't have because it seems the only tangible difference you can make. Keep her healthy, keep her alive. Some days, it is all she can do to take a shower and chauffeur you to school (you managed to finally get your license, but you still don't trust your mental health enough to get be-hind the wheel). Everything hurts — the pressure of the water, her legs sliding against the leather seats like there's sandpaper between her joints, but still, she does it for you. You pretend your friends have canceled par-ties and plans, feign groundings as an excuse for why you must stay home on the weekends with her. She says, "You swear they really did cancel?" You say, "Yes, I swear." You were never a liar before your sister died, but here you are.

It would be noble to say this is all for her own benefit, but you know she is the only support keeping you standing. You are both islands and your relationship is the sole bridge, an arm reaching out. Now, while you're at college, there is no one feeding her. There is no one making sure she gets outside. You call her four times a day at minimum, just to make sure she's breathing. You add each other's phone locations on GPS and spend hours staring at the bird's-eye view of your house, a little speck of gray, willing her to leave it. Letting yourselves give in would be the path of least resistance, but you don't because you need the other to live.

The year before you had a university interview in a local café chain, sitting under the harsh lighting and the laminated tabletops. The man reminded you of one of your friend's fathers: professional, put together, and vaguely intimidating. It was the one-year anniversary of your sister's death, and you still didn't know how to commemorate the occasion, but the interviewer asked to meet on this specific day at this specific time, and who were you to argue or ask to reschedule? After a few moments of gentle chatter, he proposes a question you're not expecting but probably should have been.

"Who is your biggest role model?"

The first thought that dashes through your brain is of your mom, so you tell the man this in all honesty. He looks disappointed, or rather a bit snarky, self-satisfied at your ignorance and his comparative age and infinite wisdom.

"That's a classic mistake," he says. "When you grow up, you'll realize there's a whole world of people you should look up to instead of your parents, but you're young. You don't have much life experience yet."

Maybe it's the smothering press of the day and the long list of things you should be doing instead of being at this interview that triggers you: buying your mom flowers, creating a memorial for your sister, volunteering in her name, or at the very least having a night of quiet reflection and memory. Or maybe it's just the interviewer's smug face and his dismissal of a woman he has never met. Either way, you enter into a monologue. You tell the man that yes, there's a whole host of more academically impressive names you could have conjured: your favorite writers, humanitarians you admire, activists, and researchers.

You say that despite their incredible careers, you don't know how these people interact with the world on a daily basis. You don't know whether they say thank you to servers or smile at strangers, you don't know how they treat their kids or spouses or pets. What you do know is that your mom has suffered more than anyone you have ever met: She has lost enough to warrant any behavior she may choose. Yet every day, she is kind to each person she meets. Every day, she wakes up and stretches the pain from her limbs and the grief from her bones and puts one foot in front of the other when thousands of others would have just stayed in bed. You say to the man that *this* is what you aspire to be: strong like your mom, kind like your mom.

Unsurprisingly, the interview ends not long after in jilted waves and failed starts at normality. When he asks if you have any siblings, more to change the topic you assume than for any other intentional reason, you tell him no, your sister died exactly one year ago today. You don't cry when you say this, you don't even feel the urge to cry. Frustration has emblazoned you. A dark part of you relishes in the whip of your harsh words. You imagine your pain as a palpable thing you can viciously lob at him. *Feel my heartbreak*, you think. *Know what I have lost, what I must live forevermore without.*

You don't get into the college, and you don't wonder why.

In Boston, you move into a quad, a small square room with four desks and four twin beds tucked into each corner. Besides at sleepaway camp, you have never shared a room with anyone but your sister. Mom and you go through the chaos of carrying large trunks and suitcases and bedding up three cramped flights of stairs in the humid August air. You are both so filled with dread and fear, you hardly speak at all. She is your best friend, your favorite person in the world. This was true before Kait's illness, before her death, but there's something uniquely bonding about going through so many life-and-death moments together — only so many times you can sacrifice yourself for each other until you are tied together permanently. And now you are each only half alive with grief. It seems a cruel fate to leave each other now.

At night, you lay awake, staring at an unfamiliar ceiling and the unfamiliar shadows that dance across it. You become a wind-up toy, coiled and wrought, waiting for the first sunbeams of morning to appear. You gulp down thick sleeping pills and then imagine the hot energy of your bloodstream burning and disintegrating them before they can work their sweet relief. Your mind refuses to turn off like the never-ending stream of prattle from a late-night sitcom. You hear the sounds of birds chirping to one another before unconsciousness reaches you.

The next day, you hang a picture of your sister and you on the uneven brick alongside your bed like a dreamcatcher. You are around two or three in it, wearing an elaborate yellow and black polka-dotted outfit your sister costumed you in. She stands behind you, hunched over so her hands rest on your shoulders, displaying her work proudly. Your tiny feet are in a pair of her bubblegum-pink Disney princess dress-up shoes, several sizes too big.

The problem is that you didn't have a game plan before you got here. So for a while, you answer the question inconsistently, depending on your emotional bandwidth and the demands of the moment. Mostly, you say you're an only child. Once, a boy responded with a smirk and told you that this "made sense." You *seem* like an only child. You were standing on a bus on the way to the main academic campus, and you felt so fundamentally misunderstood in the moment that you wondered if it was possible for anyone to ever truly know you again. You held on to the plastic hanging handrail while your knees went numb.

A few times, when you're especially caught off-guard — midbite into a sandwich, your stomach somersaulting while you chew — you nod reflexively, *yes*. Then come more questions. How old is she? What is she doing? Are you close? Even if she hadn't disappeared, this line of questioning would be impossible to answer without scaring someone: Where is she? Likely in a psychiatric ward. Are you close? She was your whole world, until you had to wall yourself off from her. You wonder if everyday conversations are as much a riddle for the rest of society. You worry about who you may have unintentionally maimed in your own blind ignorance.

Eventually, your discrepancies catch up to you.

A few weeks into school, you're sitting in a packed dorm room with a handful of new friends. The topic of celebrity encounters comes up, and everyone is laughing. Without thinking, you mention your sister meeting that actor in Martha's Vineyard when she was still a teen. Remembering the story makes you smile, and for a second, you relish in being your sister's sibling once again. The legendary Kaitlyn Lantz Leddy.

The boy from the bus responds first. "Wait," he says sharply, a smug detective. "You told me you were an only child." Your extremities go cold as the blood of your body rushes to your cheeks. "We were actually talking about this the other night," he continues. "You told Tommy you had a sister, but told me you didn't. Why would you lie about something like that?" Everyone in the room turns to face you.

You laugh nervously — a half cough. Tears well in the triangles of your eyes, and inexplicably, you are reminded of the only time you were ever chastised by a teacher. (It was the sixth grade, and you had forgotten to get a permission slip signed in time, so you forged your mom's cursive signature in shaky loops. You erased and then rewrote it at least three times, leaving a hard lead trace in the paper; your efforts so obtuse it hurts to remember. The teacher pulled you aside in the hallway, confronting you in a soft voice, his arms crossed. He was likely suppressing a laugh at your foolish attempt at espionage, but his stern expression made you wish you could pool into a puddle and sink into the blue tiled floor beneath his feet.)

"Well, um." You try to keep your voice light, nonchalant, airy. It cracks in odd rhythms. "Well, yes, I'm sorry, I did have a sister, but I don't anymore."

Somewhere in your consciousness, your brain knows a more eloquent way to word this, but the polite phrasing escapes you now. Besides, this is the crude truth, isn't it? You had a sister and now you don't. The loss contained in this simple fact reignites the hot iron in your chest.

When you moved to Boston, you had the strangest sense that you were leaving her behind. As little girls, you concocted a plan to one day buy a mansion large enough for two separate wings. Each of your families would be housed in either side, meeting in the shared kitchen for breakfast. Your parents would, of course, be in the home across the street.

It dawns over you that she never wanted to be in Philly. She always wanted to leave, to return to New England, to the beaches and blueness of before, but now she would never get the chance. Perhaps in another universe, if you had a body, you would have sprinkled her ashes on the rocky rough shore of your childhood, or would have taken her with you. But now she is stuck, forever, in the city she despised.

In these instances, you feel there are two versions of you existing at once. The girl you present to the world — who keeps her cool, stays composed — and a fainter, imaginary version of you who falls to the ground, curls into a ball on the floor, wretches and wretches on her hands and knees. This alternative reality seems so real that you can almost feel the would-be rug burn on your palms, the edges of the rough fabric marking your legs with angry lines.

After the boy does his due diligence of stumbling through a mumbled apology, after the moment breaks and the whole day seems shattered by it, after you want to tell the guy, "Don't worry, it's not your fault," because really, it isn't, but to speak would be to cry — your roommate mercifully changes the subject. Everyone continues as they were, and you sit there for the rest of the night in silence. Your hands are slick around the beer you cradle like a blanket. When you finally get up to leave, your muscles ache as if you've just returned from a long run. You realize that you've been unwittingly clenching them for hours.

Time and time again, you are amazed that the lines of your sister's endless influences are not etched into your forehead. It shocks you that no one can intuit that you are wearing this color because Kait once remarked that you looked pretty in it. You use her vernacular, her culture, a country of one, and no one knows its origin. Your sister lived five years without you, but she is all you've ever known. It concerns you how easy it is to publicly erase her.

You were a sister for *seventeen* years (you take to rounding up by three days). You were born a sister, willed into existence a sister. You borrowed clothes and shared rooms and beds and secrets and heartbreaks. You held hands, built sandcastles. You collected buckets of sea glass, burrowing your fingers carefully into the fine sand until the texture turned chunky like wet concrete, pools of water appearing in the shallow hole as if by magic. You used to be a siphon for secrets, but now you swallow them whole. When your sister was old enough that she realistically shouldn't have believed you, you convinced her that brown cows produce chocolate milk. She repaid the favor a few months later by persuading you that you were adopted and the Australian singer Cody Simpson (who you share a birthday with) was actually your twin brother.

You've screamed, "I *hate* you."

Slammed doors, cried, wished you weren't a sister at all.

You've giggled, "I *love* you."

Spilled tears from being tickled so hard, it pained you.

You wish there was an adequate term for what you are — like orphan or widower — a term that says "I once meant something to somebody." When you were a little girl, you went mute from lack of need, but now you are mute with grief.

Phase III, Recovery
Pale Yellow

Thirty-six

My sophomore year of college, I began volunteering at a men's homeless center, Pine Street Inn, with a campus group. Once a week, we would take the train to an unassuming industrial building in downtown Boston. We walked by men lined up single-file, waiting to enter a security checkpoint with metal detectors and a bag scanner. To get to the employee entrance, we had to pass by these men and go through a side door. I always felt guilty doing so — the privilege of not having to wait made me feel I was intruding, as did much of my presence in the shelter.

Occasionally, we would help serve meals, wearing hairnets and scooping the day's menu onto plastic trays. Afterward, we cleaned tables, wiping down debris and sweeping the floor of dropped napkins with smears of food stains in the corners. Leading up to holidays, the dining room was filled with makeshift decorations: paper snowflakes, hanging banners, wreaths with big red bows. One day, I spent my full shift upstairs in the staff office with a large glass window overlooking the scene as I sorted clothing donations by size and category, but mostly our group's role resided in the waiting area.

Walking down a narrow ramp, we were met by rows of blue lockers, cafeteria-style benches, and dingy tile floors, the smell of unwashed bodies permeating the air. A handful of television screens were planted on the walls, displaying the news, a sports game, or a series of movies broadcasted in different languages with subtitles running across the bottom.

Pine Street Inn offers many services. It's the largest homeless services provider in New England and has a turnover of nearly two thousand homeless men and women every day. There are long-term housing programs, recovery services, and workforce development training. We dealt with the daily influx of visitors, spending our evenings talking to guests, sitting beside them and playing a game of Dominoes before dinner or making casual conversation.

All too often, individuals experiencing homelessness are overlooked. We walk by the man on the street with the cardboard sign and the open cup filled with the clang of too few coins. We turn the other way when we see a woman digging through the trash at a subway station or carrying a cart full of miscellaneous objects up the tightly packed staircase. Perhaps we stop to search our wallets for some cash, or maybe we grant a small head nod and say an equally small, "Good morning," but mostly, we go on with our days.

I don't believe the average person does this to be cruel. I believe we do it out of survival. Our natural instincts and our learned behaviors encourage us to keep our guard up. The man on the corner could be dangerous. The woman muttering to herself on the train about the second coming of Jesus could be deranged. She could be my sister. We let fear get the best of us.

It is also hard not to be struck by the sheer vastness of the challenge that homelessness presents. In 2019, a total of 567,715 Americans were found to be experiencing homelessness in a single night. That's seventeen out of 10,000 citizens. Hearing this number can be demoralizing and dehumanizing, can make us feel hopeless.

As volunteers, however, my and my colleagues' role at Pine Street Inn was to make these men feel *seen*. We stopped to shake hands, asked about their families and interests. One visitor always wanted to share his favorite music with our group, pulling out Spotify and blasting "Zombie," by the Cranberries a little too loud for the guests at the neighboring table. A few taught me card games: hearts, blackjack, gin rummy. Sometimes, a guest would stop me before I left and say thank you — admitting he felt "normal" for the first time in ages. Other times, our efforts to mingle were met with glares or grunts. Almost always, I was thankful when we were eventually called to the kitchen, when I could pull on rubber gloves, an apron, and do something tangibly useful. Just listening didn't feel like enough.

Besides, who were we — a bunch of privileged college students — to sit among these men and pretend to understand their plight? At the end of our shifts, we walked back to our dorm rooms, studied for our exams, went to the local bars on the weekends, and neatly packed it all away until the following week.

When I applied to colleges, I was franker in my application essays than I had been with any of my friends. I outlined the basics of what had happened to my sister. I wrote that I wished "to use writing and the study of psychology to illuminate misconceptions about mental illness." The difference, I believed, was between a vocation and a passion. Why couldn't I combine both?

And while I followed through on my double major, the writing fell to the wayside. I entered into the clinical track, studying abnormal psychology, neuroscience, and mental healthcare.

In crowded auditoriums, I saw my sister everywhere. I partook in class discussions and intellectual debates about schizophrenia. I suppressed a shudder when I answered test questions about the chemical reactions that likely took place in my sister's brain. I tried to be indifferent, distant. My sister's changing personality ordered before me as a simple algebraic equation in the cramped text of my professor's PowerPoint.

There was the prodromal phase, characterized by the American Psychiatric Association as "barely noticeable changes in the way a person thinks, feels, and behaves." This involves a decrease in performance at school or work, difficulty concentrating, and withdrawal.

Next comes the acute or active phase, where clearly psychotic symptoms can be seen and a formal thought disorder diagnosed. If schizophrenia were a Shakespearean drama, such a moment would be described as the "falling action" — the instant everything comes undone. The point of no return.

Finally, the recovery phase, also known as the residual phase. Psychotic symptoms decrease, leaving the individual with "residual" depression. The term conjures images of a Windex commercial, a streak of filmy white residue left behind the brush of a paper towel. Leftovers: simple and erasable. During this final stage, the final act, the ability to function regularly returns. The patient may experience a temporary recovery.

It was all so neat: a clear beginning, middle, and end. Tidy, organized, condensed. Except, it wasn't at all. In the moment, it was anything but — impossible to contain in a narrative arc. Too immediate to see clearly: a picture held close to your face — the smell of the page, the metallic kick of ink, the image itself indistinguishable like a Rorschach inkblot test.

When my sister first became sick, Mom wrote a series of bullet points and tucked them into the glossy pages of *Chicken Noodle Soup for the Soul.* In changing pens, she chronicled what we knew and what we may never know. She tried to answer two big questions: What happened and why?

She listed in chronological order the escalating tensions of the last ten or so years.

Caught for underaged drinking — 3 times.
Kait hits her head, is hospitalized.
Dr. admitted her (302?)
Takes real-estate course!

The list continues for several pages, the black cursive scrawl occasionally interrupted by a blue pen, crossing out and then adding details in the margins as if she has just returned and remembered something crucial.

"I don't know how many times she was hospitalized," the blue pen writes.

Already, our mom was trying to make sense of the senseless, to infuse the chaos with a cohesive narrative. How did we get so off-course? What went wrong and why?

In her timeline, she searched for the answer to an unanswerable question, because there was no singular event, no hidden clue waiting to be discovered. Kait was sick, and her illness was of the worst kind — in her own mind, invisible and untraceable.

The bullets grow more dramatic, more desperate. Childhood mischief transcends to abuse and danger. The violence becomes erratic and unpredictable.

How do you make meaning of disorder?

How do you create a narrative of entropy?

Faced with the depths of Kait's madness, my family wanted so desperately to impose structure onto our lives, but it was shapeless. It took and took until the bowl was scraped empty and so were we.

More than a clinical definition, Kait's life was as messy and beautiful and painful as any life is. It was real and human: vague scenes flashing by in succession. Her old tie-dye sweatshirt, worn and tattered. The crochet top she never let me borrow. The blue waves of a childhood by the sea. The river she disappeared into, the tides that swept her away, never to return. The pool we used to play in with its terra-cotta outline. And the white caps that encroach on our old beach, moving closer every year. I see the seal we named Tappadingo, one summer, his gray head bobbing in the deep water like a friendly nod.

There's the emerald green of leaves on treetops: the landlocked Pennsylvania of our adolescence. Light sparkling and trickling through branches, creating patterns on cars and shadows on warm, sizzling pavement.

Then, there's the redness of the incident itself — violent and halting. The blur of a stop sign blown by too quickly. The color of the jacket she was last seen in. How in Kait's worst moments, her most tumultuous blood rushed to her cheeks, the shade of the cherry-flavored lip balm she used to adore.

And finally a period of lapse, a dulled lavender, the color of my sister's bedspread left in the light of the sun too long: time passing, healing and loss, as pale as yellow light. A "residual" depression of our own.

Isn't that at the core struggle of mental healthcare after all? The juggle between the human (the soul, relationships, what makes us who we are) and the coldness of medicine (objectivity, distance, the classification of diagnosis) — the very antithesis to individuality, designed to clump as a collective.

I kept feeling like my professors didn't understand. I listened mutely as one made a joke about schizophrenia, gesturing wildly with his hands: "The walls are talking to me!" The class laughed along, appreciative of the break from the monotony of the lecture. I quietly went to an empty bathroom in the basement and kicked the turquoise tile wall, swallowing a scream.

I watched documentaries and read case studies, seeing my sister everywhere. Never before had I realized how common our experience was. The symptoms and chaos that once seemed so otherworldly were riddled in every textbook I read. We were not alone. We had never been alone.

At the first sign of my sister's burgeoning mental illness, Mom began an impressive collection of self-help books. They piled in stacks under her bed, spiraling on top of one another, threatening to fall. There were religious books of all faiths, stories of loss and survival, testimonials from neurologists. She believed she may find something between the black print and white pages — a rhyme or reason we hadn't thought of before. The stacks formed a fortress under her bed and around her dresser, a mini barricade between her and the world.

"Listen," she said to me once, "I finally figured it out: We're textbook. It's us. We're right there." She let out a long breath. And then, "I wish I had known sooner."

I tried to understand her. How could our lives, so unique to us, so full of loss and hurt, be "textbook"? Nothing about our situation was textbook. And if it had been, then why hadn't we been able to fix it? If the dysfunction was common, of the everyday garden variety, then where was the easy solution? At least if it was our own, it could be held without blame, without comparison. Besides, I reasoned at the time, there is something demeaning in being told that your extraordinary pain is actually quite ordinary.

But now I understand what Mom meant.

I saw Kait frequently in the homeless shelter. She was the man with shaggy hair who pulled me aside and confessed that aliens had abducted him and left a chip in the blue veins of his arm. She was the older gentleman muttering to himself in the corner, some one-sided argument getting the best of him. Once, a guest told me that his hair was being cut in his sleep, and I felt my breath snag in my windpipe, reminded of my sister confessing to me the almost verbatim conviction.

According to the latest statistics, about 1.2 percent of Americans are diagnosed with the disorder, but I saw schizophrenia everywhere. Perhaps because the disorder causes so many of its victims to fall on the fringes of society, diagnosis grows oblique. Or perhaps I was just more alert to the symptoms than the average person around me — my nerve endings cued for the slightest reminder, my very genetic code a kind of magnet.

There are many other reasons for homelessness: lack of affordable housing, systemic racism and cyclical poverty, unemployment, low wages, and the failure of our foster services, but mental illness and substance abuse are an undeniable part of the equation. The point of the volunteers' role at Pine Street Inn was to make these men feel seen, and sometimes I felt I saw them all too clearly. Other times, I confess, I wondered if maybe I only saw Kait.

The next summer, I worked at a group home in Nantucket for women diagnosed with psychiatric disorders, primarily the collected schizophrenias. By this point, I had given up on writing and was pursuing my clinical studies instead. I was dedicating myself to studying the disease that killed my sister, as if that pursuit could somehow serve as penance, a chance to redo the past. I believed I had escaped our cycle of tragedy, but even so I was forcing myself to relive it. Mom had a similar coping mechanism: volunteering with National Alliance on Mental Illness, domestic abuse shelters, and Alliance for Substance Abuse Prevention. Looking back, I ask myself now: Were we genuinely trying to use our experience to serve others, or were we really just punishing ourselves?

The patients at the facility I worked at were older, all in their late fifties or sixties. There were five in total, each suffering from delusions and hallucinations, but most of them as sweet as can be. Unlike the halfway homes I had visited my sister in, this facility was more long-term care oriented.

Occasionally we would go for an outing, and I'd drive a rusted van that looked like a small bus and rattled over the cobblestone streets of the charming, historical town, threatening to break. We watched the whales emerge from the water at a nearby beach — their flat shiny backs like boulders in the distance. We went out for homemade ice cream on a hot July day. We browsed the local thrift store, sorting through mismatched rows of clothing. We did a daily hour of drawing, sitting at the wooden living room table and coloring in the soothing, geometric shape of mandalas while an old radio crooned in and out of focus in the corner.

There weren't enough recovery support workers available at our location, so, unlike at similar properties under the same umbrella organization, I was the only personnel present during my shift. I spent weeks in training, becoming certified by the state in their medication administration program and learning how to provide basic treatment. Still, I never felt fully prepared. I was always terrified of slipping up, saying the wrong thing, making a mistake I couldn't take back. I knew too well the consequence of my actions, knew too well the fragility of my clients. I worked days, evenings, and overnight, driving the women to their appointments, providing individual daily rehabilitation routines, administering and documenting antipsychotics, and managing all group programming.

I saw Kait often there. I heard her, too — when a patient insisted that there were spies trying to break in to the home, and I had to explain to her that the sound she heard was the ordinary clamor of a family passing by on a nearby sidewalk. I felt my sister when one of the women whispered to me conspiratorially that a man in the grocery store aisle had evil thoughts. Together these moments formed a painful keyhole into the future my sister likely would have led.

The women frequently went outside for a cigarette break, sitting on the small wooden bench in the front yard facing the street, or in the backyard on the slowly eroding, rarely used swing set. Watching the smoke exhale in the thick summer air, I saw Kait sitting on our roof, sneaking out through the small alcove of her bedroom she once fell from, burning through packs of cigarettes. I can see the outline of her back now, slightly sloped as she leans over her bent legs and looks across the green yard and the birds that flit from tree to tree with a soft *twee twee* sound. I used to squint at the back of her skull when she wasn't looking, wishing I had x-ray goggles. What hid behind those wild, blond waves?

My sister was everywhere that summer, just as she had been at the homeless shelter, but there was an important distinction: None of the patients was violent. There were many safety measures in place at the home: a locked drawer in the file cabinet where the sharp knives were kept (the women had to request access to obtain one when making dinner), another key for a sealed lockbox where medications were stored so no one could overdose. And yet I never once felt afraid or threatened. This natural mellowing was likely a quality of age: positive symptoms of schizophrenia (hallucinations, delusions) tend to decrease while negative symptoms (apathy, anhedonia, reduced social interest) remain the same or increase. Or, perhaps my sister's head injuries were what made her more prone to violence. There is also a great deal of cognitive decline in older populations, and adverse health effects such as higher rates of congestive heart failure, hypothyroidism, and chronic obstructive pulmonary disease.

One day, I asked a patient what she was reading and she eagerly thrust the book into my hand with a huge smile. "Take it!" she said. I spent the next half an hour convincing her that I didn't need her copy and drove to the bookstore the next day to buy my own so that we could read it together. She wrote me thank-you notes and poems on printer paper, sometimes slipping money into them. I was confused until another staff member warned me that this was her way of testing us: If we accepted the money, she was convinced we were government agents paid to spy on her. Each time I politely handed the money back to her, a reassured smile would split across her face.

The patient walked into the dusty, overcrowded staff office several times a day to tell me about a new "invention" she had thought of. Usually it was an item that already existed but had been reimagined in ambiguous terms like a "portable bed that you could inflate like a pool raft." Some days, she sat still for hours, staring blankly at the wall and pausing only to stand up and bend her knees or move her arms in small circles.

As I was an inexperienced driver and terrified of denting the company van, the women helped me back out of tricky spots — craning their necks to look out the rearview window. When I administered one patient a Dixie cup of her morning medication and asked how she was, every day she replied with the same dismissive wave: "Oh, I'm fine! Just thankful to be here." I nearly fell to my knees when I learned about the depression and suicidal ideations she suffered from.

I relied on one of the patients most consistently, because she was a calming figure for the others: level-headed, patient, and above all, unflaggingly kind. Where some of the other household members had clear cognitive deficits and impairments, she was sharp, quick-witted, and always game for a laugh. However, every time we left the sanctuary of the house to go for a short errand or activity, she would be seized by panic, and I would have to remind her of how charming, intelligent, and capable she was.

"You have every tool you need," I said. "I get nervous too, even when I have to make a phone call or ask for help at a store, but if I can do it, you certainly can. You help me all day long!"

One lazy afternoon in the sticky heat, my back pressed against the air conditioner unit, I read the client's case file and discovered an autobiography she had written in the third person. In it, she explained the voices she heard during our every outing, and I realized the inner turmoil she must be suppressing on a daily basis. I was reminded of my sister's scribbled messages — the radio with its messages, Edie Sedgwick, her own insecurities and doubts — and about how much truly lurks beneath the surface of mental illness, unseen and unheard. I sat for a while on the office chair, breathing in the musty smell of the files and leaning my forehead into my hand; feeling naïve, insensitive, and excruciatingly sad.

My other part-time gig that summer was as a sales assistant at a high-end boutique catering to the rich vacationers who could afford such splurges as a four-hundred-dollar cashmere sweater. My boss spent the entirety of the day in a broom closet turned makeshift office, crunching numbers, obsessing over the newest designer products and the credit card traffic of the elite. The place, with its constant dusting, refolding, and arranging of display windows, felt more maddening, more abnormal than any of the women in the group home. When my boss asked about my other job, she stared at me in confusion.

"I think . . . I think I've seen those women wandering the grocery store before," she half whispered like it was a conspiracy — something she was ashamed to admit existed in her town. "They're crazy, right?"

I was reminded of my own fear of stigma, my cowardice, our desire to protect Kait's reputation costing us all in the end. Despite the higher pay, I quit the sales job shortly after our conversation, picking up more hours at the group home instead.

I felt perhaps too much kinship for the patients I worked with. My heart broke twice an hour, every hour. Like at the homeless shelter, it disturbed me when I finally left my shift, replaced by a new employee. Every time I walked out the door and into the summer breeze, I was sick with guilt and relief. With my sister, there had been no walking away. Her illness consumed our family, became part of us, swallowed us whole. How could I now stroll so easily into the blue dusk, away from these women who reminded me so very much of her?

In each of my experiences in clinical and academic settings, I was astonished by the universality of our story, a story that as we were living it felt so singular, suffocating, and isolating. Back in Boston, when I stood on the MBTA subway platform and heard a man's incoherent preaching, I looked at my phone screen like the rest of the commuters around me, but inside, my chest ballooned and then deflated, pressing violently against my rib cage like a second heartbeat. *That could be Kait*, I thought. I was paralyzed with my inability to help, as I had been paralyzed by my inability to help my sister. When I exited the train, it always took me a few moments to regain normal breathing, squeezing my eyelids shut in the elevator until my pulse steadied.

When Mom first left Philadelphia and lay alone in her new bed and eerily quiet home, she says she slept for what felt like the first time in eight years. She couldn't believe that there was no phone call ringing her awake, no jolt in the door testing the hinges, no new hospitalization, no threat banging at her bedside. She was not half awake waiting for crisis: bags already packed, emergency numbers at the ready. There was only the rushing roar of the ocean, the waves hitting the sand, pulling in the tide with a gentle lulling.

In the morning, she was sure that if she had just gotten *one* full night of true rest when Kait was sick, she could've done something differently (she did everything there was to do, but it's impossible to convince a mother of this). The thought halved her.

Even now, she tells me that she often wakes up angry — several years later and before the day can be anything else. It is at first just another day without her daughter.

Sometimes I worry that locked deep inside of me is relief for this cease-fire. The peace. No longer having to worry. In my waking state, I think in soft, flippant caresses like "She's in a better place." Or "At least she's no longer suffering." I think about the women in the group home, about the life that my sister likely would have led if she had survived. But when I dream and Kait appears, as she does nearly every night, I feel no dread, not even a drop.

I'm walking through a crowded street. Faces pass me in a blur: colors, shapes, the sharp ring of a whistle, the smell of baked concrete and day-old hot dogs boiling in their stands. Taxis speed by as I struggle to pass. The air is thick with exhaust. Every step I take feels like I'm stepping on melted, sticky gum, clinging to my soles and begging me not to go further, but I have to go. I'm on a mission. I can't remember why or who I'm trying to get to, but I know it's important. Nothing can stop me.

I make a sharp turn down a brick alleyway. I see a sliver of the bright blue-jay sky some hundred yards away. I'm close. That's when Kait walks by.

I'm never expecting it, but there she is, clear as day, walking toward me: the face in the crowd, the girl I never expected to see again, as familiar to me as my own reflection.

She's never well in my dreams — not even my unconscious is hopeful enough to imagine finding her well. She's crippled with a druglike stupor. She's too skinny, sickly-looking, covered in filth or pocked with heroin needles, but I don't care. She is *alive.*

I forget my plan, and I run as fast as I can.

Mom rarely dreams, but when she does, she dreams of the Salem Witch Trials.

The town of Salem borders Marblehead. We spent the occasional Halloween there as girls, visiting haunted houses and tours of "ghost ships." On school trips, we learned about the trials. Later, Kait and I both read *The Crucible* for a high school literature class.

It is a place we really once occupied — familiar in the present, accessible — but in my mom's dreams we are not there now: We are there in the late 1600s and Kait is being persecuted for witchcraft. It's her schizophrenic symptoms that make her a target in these dreams. The way she screams and writhes when others are quiet and content. It's her hallucinations, the people she sees that no one else can.

In Mom's dream, we watch as Kait is thrown into a pit and burned alive for witchcraft. We are frozen, held back, twisting and screaming while the town condemns her, circling the scene. Eventually, Mom looks up and watches as I'm torn with grief, lost somewhere in a madness of my own — two children gone in one blink.

When she tells me about this nightmare, she wonders about reincarnation: "Do you think it's possible? Maybe we really were there. Maybe we're doomed to repeat our mistakes, to lose Kait over and over again."

Her blond hair is curled inward, framing her face. When I was a little girl, before I discovered curling irons, I believed her to be the luckiest woman in the world to wake up with such perfect hair. I also thought her invincible before we lost Kait.

I tell her it's impossible. Reincarnation is about your soul, and what was wrong with Kait was purely physical: neurochemical. If reincarnation is real, then my sister will come back healthy and happy, and we will find her again, but she won't need saving this time.

Mom blinks away tears.

"You're right," she tells me. "Thank you."

I nod, self-assured, but that night in my own sleep, I feel as though every misunderstood instance of schizophrenia from all of human history is rising to meet me: the horrific misguided trends of trephination (removing a part of the skull to cast away "evil spirits") first discovered in the remains of prehistoric people, bloodletting and purging in ancient Greek medicine, the isolations and asylums of the nineteenth century, the lobotomies of the 1950s, the eyes of the homeless of today.

I see Kait and her silent suffering, my own ignorance and misunderstandings. I recall the time an officer pulled me aside on our long, steep, cracked driveway and asked me what was wrong, what had happened to instigate yet another domestic violence call.

This is never going to stop, I thought. *I am going to spend my whole life running from my sister. I am going to spend my whole life afraid.*

"You want to know what's wrong? *Nothing* is wrong," I screamed into the air, at the world, at Kait, at the officer, at the detached callousness of the sleepy blades of grass beneath my feet and the chirping, tireless birds above my head who didn't care whether we lived or died or suffered. What gall they had to continue on as if our lives were not yet again in smithereens, cracked open like the pottery Kait threw at our heads. "It's simple! The only thing wrong is that she's *crazy*. She's insane."

The man ushered me further up the driveway and away from Kait, explaining under the green canopy of trees in our backyard how hurtful the word *crazy* is. I listened to the lecture, and of course, I knew he was right. I knew it was wrong and cruel and even dangerous of me to say. The word was like a slur, a label I had thrown at my sister viciously with the intent to hurt. I wished to take it back immediately, but there it was: vibrating in the still air along with the rest of our mistakes.

The regret is palpable: a hand pressing firmly on my chest, weighing me down like clothes in water. We were not perfect angels, and because of that, we would never be perfect victims. I hate myself for my own foolishness, the words and actions I must have piled against my sister, creating a bed of evidence that might have factored into her final decision. Had Kait returned to this moment when she thought of staying in this life — or going?

This is what recovery was like for us — the supposed third phase of schizophrenia. There was no recovery for Kait: only us, her family, trying to gather together the remains she left behind and make something better with them. Trying to move on but always pulled by the magnet of the past, knowing we'd surrender it all for a chance to make amends. With recovery, you learn that peace can feel like freedom, and freedom can feel an awful lot like guilt.

Thirty-seven

A few months after I started volunteering at the homeless shelter, I found myself at the psychic's doorstep.

I was twenty and my sister had been missing, presumed deceased for three years. By year three of grieving you are expected to be "at peace." You should have "overcome" your loss and depression by now. You should be stronger for it, hardened by the pain and yet still soft with love and remembrance. I was none of the above, and I was desperate to change this.

The Swiss American psychiatrist Elizabeth Kübler-Ross outlines this emotional frame in her 1969 book *On Death and Dying* — the five stages of grief being denial, anger, bargaining, depression, and acceptance.

It's a pervasive theory, engulfing nearly every corner of society. And while many of the stages make quite a bit of sense, the recurring problem is that grief is rarely predictable and almost never linear, and its lie is the emphasis on the last stage, acceptance. This focus on "getting over it," moving on, deftly hopping over the steps of grief as if it's a land mine, belies the reality of what grief is, which is its own form of insanity.

At the church that first week after Kait disappeared, I knelt and I offered God my left hand. I took this imagined conversation seriously, a high-powered lawyer with a poker face, acutely aware of every concession I made. I could learn to tie my shoes with my left hand, strengthen my finger muscles enough to grip a pencil, I reasoned.

When nothing happened, I surrendered my arm, and then my leg, and then both my legs. Finally, I offered my life, a fair exchange, I thought: an eye for an eye. I told Him that everything would be different. I'll get Kait help. I'll fix this, *please.*

I was not bargaining out of spite. I was bargaining because I truly believed that my thoughts could effect a change, redo the past. I believed someone could hear me with the certainty of my sister's once-upon-a-time delusions.

I found myself shuffling through the stages of grief, moving forward and then falling backwards again. I was often angry, simmering beneath a façade of cheeriness. I was jealous when my roommates' sisters visited our college, and I watched them tease each other the way my sister and I had as children, the way we hadn't since she fell sick. I found myself crying in the clogged stall of a club bathroom on my sister's birthday that weekend, feeling like the loneliest, most despicable being on this planet: as small and inconsequential as a piece of lint, as crushed and lonely as the loneliest ant. Most of the time, I bottled up such feelings, but on that particular night, I spilled open to my other roommate and her boyfriend on the dirty gray carpet of our freshman hallway.

"It was never going to be like that for us," I sobbed in hiccups and gasps, failing to explain myself properly. "We were never going to be sisters like that. Why couldn't we be like that?"

I watched my friends fight with their siblings, suppressed resentment churning inside of me. Of course they fought. All siblings fight. My sister and I bickered ruthlessly — but did they know what they had?

The real question, the meat of the problem, hurt too much to approach directly. I had to walk around it, deflect it onto others: How had *I* not known what I had? How had *I* taken my sister for granted?

The irony of the five stages of grief is that they were not originally intended for those grieving a death — Kübler-Ross was writing about her experiences caring for patients as they came to terms with their own terminal illnesses. Her later book, *On Grief and Grieving: Finding the Meaning of Grief Through the Five Stages of Loss,* focuses on applying these stages to loss.

It can be comforting to have a linear progression — to feel your strangest, most absurd thoughts identified and explained — but there's also a danger in believing we are not grieving "correctly." As a modern society, we have largely abandoned traditional mourning rituals. We are as eager to hear someone say they are "okay" as we are to say it ourselves. I used to wish that I could wear all black like a Victorian widow — a veil over my face that said, "Be gentle with me." I used to wish there was an etiquette book for grief: a protective formality written into the code of our society, a temporary insanity clause defendable in the court of life.

I suppressed my sister's illness for years, internalizing the panic, the fear, the heartbreak, and letting the cells of my being absorb it. Afterward, I did the same to my grief. I packaged the pain away, never dealing with it properly so that now it rose up inside me, bubbling up at the most inconvenient of moments. I wanted so desperately to go back to who I was before her death — so terrified of being labeled as anything other than the cheery girl of my youth — that I submerged my grief rather than process it. I largely fell out of touch with many of my high school friends, rejected my former life. I wanted to be someone unmarred by grief, so I invented her.

When you experience severe loss at a young age — the kind of loss that makes you think your own life no longer worth living — it is as if a gulf has appeared, dividing the world into two separate, insurmountable cliffs: those who understand, who have lost someone truly dear to them, and those who do not understand. I looked at my friends and all I could think was *You don't know.* You *think* you know, you believe yourself capable of imagining, but you don't know, cannot truly know until you do, and then it's too late.

I could feel it in the silence that fell over my conversations sometimes, like the sudden deadening in the woods before a storm. The blankness, the drifting eyes and thoughts. The way words seemed to escape me, run away like tendrils of loose smoke from a burning candle.

A group of my high school friends expressed frustration the summer after my sister died. I was acting moody, they said, and everyone was sick of it. We were spending the weekend down at the Jersey shore, and on the way there, the girl driving took a wrong turn. One minute we were on the highway and then the next, there we were — driving over the Benjamin Franklin Bridge. I saw the seashell blue beams like an iron cage outside my window. Every organ in my body flipped. I had to close my eyes just to keep the vomit down.

They didn't know this of course, because I kept it to myself and because everyone assumed the worst would be over by now; I should be back to normal, shiny and new. I was not. I was a crumpled, discarded mess. I was acting odd, because I wanted to die. *I want to die, I want to die, I want to die* was the chant in my head at all hours of the day while I studied and laughed and smiled and played along with the motions of living. My body used to move on its own accord, but with grief, the smallest actions required an exhausting amount of discipline and strength. I had to consciously tell the muscles of my mouth to rise at the appropriate cues. I had to direct my arm to brush back my hair.

With every month that flew by, so too did any hope of finding my sister dead or alive. As the days and weeks and years stacked upon each other and as I dealt with my parents' separation and the fallout that came with it — the court dates, the legal bills, the stress headaches and brutal arguments — I declined rather than improved. Life was too painful, and I had not saved my sister. I wanted to die, and even worse, I believed I *deserved* to die. All of my effort, all of my concentration, was focused on this singular end: *trying not to die.*

I learned that looking the grieving in the eyes can be painful. A layer of protection has been lost, and more than uncomfortable, the vulnerability is repelling. I felt like my face was too open: a diary page plastered on my forehead — wide and defenseless. I was jolted when someone said my name, surprised that anyone could still recognize me, surprised I still had a name and the responsibility to answer to it.

One year in college, my roommates and I were watching a medical drama when one of our friends broached the question of whether you imagine yourself as the patient or the doctor in such scenes. The room was divided. Myself and a few others full-heartedly identified as the patient every time — felt the scalpel cut open the taut skin of our own abdomens, subconsciously cradled our arms around our bodies as if to protect ourselves from a real threat. Others imagined themselves the doctors, responsible for the life-saving surgeries and culpable if anything went wrong. All of us were empathizing, but through a different lens.

This sensation can be at least partially explained by research being done on "mirror neurons." When we witness others suffering, our emotional circuits are activated and "mirror neurons" are set off that allow us to feel as if we are experiencing the pain firsthand.

Looking grief in the eyes is like looking at a dissected human body: the sight of blood, needles, torn ligaments, and open wounds. The same driving force operates in both scenarios, and sometimes it's easier not to think about how easily we can come apart — how abruptly, a full, complex human being can be reduced to a series of strung-together memories or parts on an operating table. Delving into the interior depths of mental illness and grief can make our own self-proclaimed sanity seem a delicate, serendipitous accident. How easily we too could come undone if only our fates took one wrong turn.

I didn't want to be one of those people it hurt to look at. I masked my pain so no one else would have to feel it. Subsequently, "strong" was an adjective thrown around me often. I was strong because I hadn't asked anyone else to be.

Three years after my sister's disappearance, I sat in my grandparents' home — the same home where we had spent almost every Christmas together, enacting the same traditions we always did.

We still exchanged gifts, and I still forgot to wrap mine, resorting to a loosely veiled bag I scavenged in the dusty clutter of the basement storage room. We still ate baked shrimp with the buttery Ritz cracker filling my grandma knows I love. We even still had "green mold": a gelatin concoction the color of the Statue of Liberty, filled with nuts, pineapples, and the miscellaneous mystery of my grandma's imagination.

Everything was the same, except Kait's absence hung about the room like a physical presence — her ghost as large in passing as her laugh was in life.

During what would be our final holiday season with my sister, she missed Thanksgiving. She had gone out drinking the night before, gotten into a fight with a girl, and was punched in the face. The sweeping bone of her cheek was swollen and garish — the bruise blossomed the color of the deep purple hydrangea bushes that used to line the Massachusetts neighborhood of our girlhood. She was hung over, unintelligible, incapable of making the long drive to dinner.

I remember looking at her empty seat in the candlelight of my grandparents' home amid the clang of utensils and excited conversation, thinking how wrong it felt for her to be absent. Never before had my sister and I not spent a holiday together. That Christmas, she was in a state institution once again. The holiday season after that, gone forever. Little did I know that there would be many more holidays, countless holidays, a lifetime of holidays with the same sinking, loose feeling in my chest. Little did I know that the chair would remain empty.

Every holiday since, my Poppy still played his Bocelli and he still sung along to the deep operatic tones with his eyes closed and a glass of red wine swishing in his hand. And I still laughed. And we still said grace, but everything was different: Topics seem to swallow themselves when there is one unutterable truth permeating the air. Like little kids commanded not to say a curse, the more my family resisted, the more Kait's name bubbled up inside of us, threatening to spill, red wine splattering across the white tablecloth.

The morning after that Thanksgiving, my Poppy turned to me as we sipped coffee in the bright light of the atrium, the sun and the heated tile floors warming the leather couch I sat on.

"Do you ever think Kait could still be alive?" he asked in a hushed voice.

My heart broke as I had to tell him that no, I didn't *think* it was possible. Because I couldn't say that I *knew*; I could only say *think*. If he had asked if I hoped, I would have said yes, but no, I didn't believe. My verb choice was a remnant of the ever-elusive dream that perhaps it wasn't true. The way Mom closed Kait's bedroom door immediately after it happened, because it was too easy to imagine my sister out of the corner of our eye, rummaging through her drawers: the trick of the light and our desperate wanting creating a kind of brief, fluttering peripheral hope.

A popular fraud has taken hold in which impersonators will call grandparents and pretend to be their grandchildren, insisting that they have gotten into a car crash or are spending the night in jail. "Grandma," the scammers will say. "Can you please mail me some money?"

It happened to a great-uncle of mine, leaving him out five hundred in cash. Afterward, my own grandparents were cognizant of the possibility.

Still, when the phone inevitably rang and a female voice spoke to Poppy, saying "Hi, Grandpa, it's me," I know that for him the fabric of everything split open with the force of a single wish.

It's the moment when we see a girl in a yellow bikini lounging near the waves of a beach — her face in profile. "That kind of looks like Kait," Mom says aloud, and I wonder: Is she saying this as a casual observation, or has her heart just hiccupped, like mine, because for a moment she really thought it could be her? Did she feel everything in the world rise and fall in a single spasm when she realized that no, Kait's chin was more prominent, her eyes greenish-blue, not brown? Every minuscule difference a new heartbreak as the possibility faded further away.

It's when a friend of Kait's from high school reaches out to me (as often happens) and tells me that every six to twelve months he'll go through her old social media posts, police records, and missing persons reports, holding out hope that one day she'll reappear "with some story that explains everything, wearing new designer gear and three times the freckles."

It's when Mom gets a phone call from an unfamiliar number, and she pauses what she's doing: chopping a pepper in the kitchen, her jacket still on from our winter walk. "A Pennsylvania number," she notices curiously.

As she answers, the person on the other line remains silent. She says "hello" a few times, first normally, then in a singsong pitch, and finally with an air of urgency. The caller hangs up.

"I hate that," she says. "They just hung up."

I want to ask why she hates this; if she's afraid of robot hackers or prank phone calls, or if she's like me. Even when I *know* it's not Kait, my heart lifts at the idea that maybe it could be. My brain draws an image for me instinctually — a Philly payphone. A girl, a woman now, dialing the number she knows by heart. Her fingers are cold; her gloves held bunched together in one hand as she holds the phone in the other. She's not sure why she's calling. Maybe she just wants to hear our mom's voice.

I don't ask Mom if this is what she sees too, because I know what she'll tell me.

"It's never going to be her. She's gone."

"I know," I always say, emphasizing the words unnaturally. "But don't you ever sometimes wonder?" It is easier to give our Poppy closure than it is to provide that same reassurance for myself.

"I know she's gone, Ky. I'm her mom. I know."

Her "know" sounds different from mine; less forced, more permanent.

While the rest of us had no premonition, no sibling superstitious warning in my case, Mom did. When Kait was upset, our mom used to hear a ringing in her left ear, a mechanical buzzing like a fly buzzing too close, or an overheated microwave — no matter how far away she was, she knew my sister was unwell, a kind of maternal sixth sense. When my sister went missing, it rang constantly and then it stopped altogether. The deafening silence was its own mourning song.

That's the thing — you can know and know and *know* without really ever fully believing or accepting it. For better and for worse, hope proves itself to be surprisingly resilient.

For three long years, I swam in this loop of denial, anger, bargaining, and depression. If grief is an odyssey, then the psychic was my last, desperate stop: my final chance at returning home.

Thirty-eight

When the psychic asked me what the number eleven meant to me, I felt my body tense. I saw my sister and me as little girls, making a wish on 11:11 twice a day, every day. I saw how she had willed me into existence on January 11. I saw myself slightly older, praying for my sister to get better. I saw our superstitions and every sign we had looked for along the way, and every sign we had missed. I wanted to scream out, to tell the woman all of this, but instead I remained quiet — aware that she would be reading my reaction.

"It's my birthday," I said quite simply, trying to steady my voice.

Internally, I was saying something quite different. I was thinking, *Kait, Kait, Kait*. I was thinking, *Please let it be you.* Staring at the neon lights and the crystal balls, and the bright cards and the moons and stars of the tablecloth, I begged the universe for it to somehow be true.

When the woman spoke again, she claimed that the number eleven was someone on the other side's way of trying to guide me along my path. She told me it was like a gentle nudge, a squeeze of the palm that meant to say, "I'm with you. Keep going."

The woman advised me to stop blaming myself for the past. She cautioned me against visiting further psychics and asked me not to come back to her own shop. "Stop looking for answers," she said in a tone that truly did sound a touch omniscient.

When I left the shop, I described to my friend everything the woman said, quickly committing it in a text to my mom so I wouldn't forget. She found the psychic trips a bit excessive, but she was also desperate for the same confirmation I was. Kait believed in psychics, so why not try it (within reason)? we thought. What was twenty bucks if it brought closure?

Devin and I walked in circles around the Boston suburb, past a dismal-looking park with cracked sidewalks and a chain-link fence. We walked and talked in loops, with no destination. I told her what I had always been afraid to tell people: how my sister had died, what her diagnosis meant, the years of turmoil we lived through before it all. My limbs shook, jittery and alive. I wanted to cry.

I didn't know if I believed the psychic or if this had only been a random lucky guess: strange and fortuitous timing. Many people wish at 11:11. Did I detect a taste of surprise on the psychic's face when I said that yes, the number eleven did mean something to me? Did her eyebrows not raise ever so lightly?

But did it really matter if the psychic was a fraud or a prophet?

My sister believed the universe spoke in codes and signs. When we were little girls, Kait told me to hold my breath whenever we drove past a cemetery. "Pretend you're underwater," she advised.

Over time, I learned that the key is to swallow the air, let it puff your cheeks out, focus on something else, anything else — the pebbled back of the leather seat in front of you or the stray wrapper on the floor crinkling beneath your shoe. It helps to pinch your nostrils like you're about to do a cannonball. Your chest will burn — ignore it. Gray headstones will stare at you, slick with rain or burned by the sun, poking out from the ground like prairie dogs or sunflowers turning their heads toward the light. Ignore these, too. Because if you dare inhale, you'll be consuming more than oxygen — you run the risk of swallowing a lost soul.

The same goes for tunnels: You must hold your breath for the entirety of the journey through the dark passage, touch one hand to the ceiling, and make a wish.

When Kait developed schizophrenia, these signs took on new meanings. Suddenly, every song lyric, every television show, was a message just for her.

Folie à deux, or shared mental symptoms, is defined as an identical mental disorder affecting two or more individuals, usually of the same family. It was first described in 1860 by the French neurologist Julies Baillarger. The message is not that madness is contagious, but that it's easy to plant a delusion and watch it spurt legs, especially between close relatives.

But this wasn't a folie à deux — no more than any sense of faith is. I actively chose to believe in the psychic's words, because it was as good as believing in anything else. Was the woman plugging in to some kind of psychic radio? Most likely not.

Most likely she was feeding me exactly what I wanted to hear, because what I wanted to hear is what everyone wants: to be liberated from blame, to feel loved and supported, to know that there is life after death and hope after loss. I wanted meaning, and she placed it in my open palms like a talisman.

From that day on, when I saw the number eleven — in the white letters on a green highway sign, the small print of an expiration date, the price on an old receipt — I stopped what I was doing and I remembered my sister. It was as if every day without Kait was one long car ride: a stretch of road past a cemetery. I had been holding my breath for so long, I almost forgot what it was like to breathe.

The psychic's emphasis on the number eleven touched something primal in me — it brought me back to who my sister and I had been before she got sick: little girls who occupied a world of our own creation together. I began to remember *that* Kait, the one who chose me, the one who believed in wishes and dreams and possibility. I began to forgive myself a little more.

A year or so later, when I suffered my first real romantic heartbreak, I pulled into our driveway, parked in front of the white gardening shed, and let my head rest against the leather wheel. A screw in my chest untightened, and the faint echo of pain reminded me of how I felt when Kait had gone. *I just want my sister,* I thought as tears punched my eyelids. *I just want to talk to my sister about this.* It was late afternoon, but when I looked up, the dashboard of the car's radio read, *11:11 p.m.* in crisp, undeniable lines. The system had malfunctioned, rewinding us backward several hours.

Was this a message from my sister or a simple mechanical error? Did it matter? It was a lifeboat and I clung to it.

Maybe an insistence on cosmic meaning is futile. Life may never fit into a coherent pattern. There may not be a grand scheme at play, a larger picture on the horizon. Given probability, the psychic could have chosen any number or symbol or image and I would likely see it often, because I'd be paying attention to it, seeking it out.

This is a natural extension of our shared humanity — patterns are the fabrics of stories: the disjointed signs that weave us into narratives. An event is just an event until it leads to an outcome. We instinctually look for causality between variables, which is to say we look for meaning. We see structure where there is none, feel the illusion of control in the face of unpredictable chance.

In mental healthcare, grouping symptoms serves a similar purpose — it allows us to seek connections, similarities, potential causes and treatments. We can outline the phases of a disease, commit the trajectory of it to the bulky pages of the DSM-5. Our brains are hardwired to recognize repetitions, and there's a good reason for this: In the wild, finding a commonality between the berries you pick and the ones that make you sick is the difference between life and death. Still, there comes a point when patterns fail us. With schizophrenia, seeing signs, messages, clues where there are none, is a hallmark of the disease. It can become poisonous, even obsessive.

Still, if delusional comfort it is, then it is a comfort I share with others just the same.

A friend of mine finds ladybugs crawling in unlikely places — the crook of her arm, the windowsill by her bed, and each time she does, she believes it's a message from her deceased grandfather. My aunt sees blue jays, and every fluttering of wings or flash of color in a tree feels like a hug from her father. People smell perfume in the wind or hear their old wedding song in a moment of distress.

On October 29, 2019, the *Today Show* posted an essay by Andrea Remke, a writer who lost her husband suddenly, about seeing butterflies as a symbol of his ongoing presence. The post went viral, gathering around 5,900 likes and 3,600 shares. The 1,400 comments are mostly from readers expressing their own spiritual experiences: white feathers fluttering from trees, hummingbirds and cardinals appearing at family gatherings, a cactus blooming coral flowers, a passed loved one's favorite color. Some call these slivers of reminders "angel winks."

While researching for this book, I searched into Google, "Signs we see after someone dies," and the first suggested link was titled: "11 Signs of After Death Communication." I'd be lying if I said the coincidence didn't momentarily startle me.

The refusal to believe in the afterlife is as stubborn and desperate as the desire to. People are even affronted by the claim, which begs the question: What is it about someone else's belief that is so polarizing? It is as impossible to prove the existence of life after death as it is to disprove it. All that is left in the graveyard of this intellectual stalemate is personal choice. If you are forced to spend the rest of your life without someone, if you are brave enough to keep living despite this singular, crushing fact, then who is to judge how you find strength?

A therapist could have expressed the same sentiment to me as the psychic did; and afterward, when I decided I deserved to feel better, many did. I was lucky: Unlike my sister's illness, my mental health issues had a mostly treatable, cognitive basis. While I suffered from anxiety attacks and depressive episodes, they were based in action and traced easily to causal events.

I was depressed because my sister died. I was depressed because I believed I had failed her and subsequently believed in my own unworthiness to live. I was anxious, because life proved itself to be unpredictable; because I had lived in a household since I was eight years old that was poked through with trauma, violence, and my sister's mercurial moods.

In the mental health community, such chronic stress is referred to as adverse childhood experiences, or ACEs. It's been found that people with ACEs are more likely to develop autoimmune diseases, heart disease, and even cancer. When a stress response is triggered routinely, such as in the flight-or-fight response, the brain is inflamed with chemicals that change the very shape and size of the hippocampus (the region of the brain responsible for how we respond to emotions), as well as the synaptic connections in the brain's circuitry.

On a neurological level, I was, as the psychic put it, quite literally always waiting for the next catastrophe to strike.

My depression was like a terrible, incapacitating flu. Even when I could consciously remember a happier time, even when I knew deep down that this too shall pass, I didn't believe it. Then, when I recovered, I forgot how it felt to be sick, so that every instance, every re-immersion, was a shock.

But once I started seeking help, I found my mind supple to the improvements brought by exercise, nutrition, and dialectic behavioral therapy. I leaned in to the methods I learned about in my studies: reframing thought patterns, restructuring my belief systems. When I thought negatively about myself or remembered something negative my sister had once said about me, I didn't let the thought reach completion. I interrupted it, replaced the insult with a positive trait. I made a list of eleven reasons to keep going and kept it as the screensaver of my phone, writing in neat bullet points everything I had to be thankful for. I collected compliments like wildflowers, preserving them for a rainy day. This is how youth should be measured, I thought, by how badly you allow yourself to be treated and for how long — even, or perhaps especially, by yourself.

I used to look around me and only see what was missing. My life was consumed by holes, until I started seeing everything I *do* have instead.

I have a mom who loves and supports me with a genuine, never-ending stream of patience. I have a mom like a best friend, and who is lucky enough to say this? I have friends who stuck by me, who ask me how I am and genuinely wish to know the answer. Who make me laugh on my darkest days, who turn on the lights when I forget how to. I have a Poppy, a tall Swede who will sigh, glance around the table, and say, "Look how lucky I am. Surrounded by the three most beautiful ladies." We all roll our eyes, but how nice it feels anyway. A grandmother who texts me goodnight and I love you, every single evening without fail. I had a sister worth having — someone who brought me up, tended the garden.

I once thought that loss made me bereft, but I am swollen with fortune.

This is also the beauty of a healthy brain unfolding: It is plastic, adaptive, always learning from and adjusting to our world. A King's College London study found that cognitive behavioral therapy (CBT) can lead to heightened connectivity between key brain regions. To put it simply, replacing negative thought patterns with positive ones rewires our brains with lasting effects and creates detectable, physical changes.

The psychic helped me down this path. Was it a grief treatment that I recommend? No. Was it scientific? Absolutely not. And do I believe that the number eleven was truly my sister communicating with me, tapping in to some karmic spiritual energy? Probably not. Magic it may not have been, but it did do something truly magical for me.

Every time I saw the two lines of 11 — on a subway car, on a license plate, on the hanging, wobbly sign of a storefront's work hours — I took a breath and remembered my sister. This has made every difference.

Back to Blue

Thirty-nine

I wrote an essay about my sister's disappearance during the spring semester of my senior year of college. I had long abandoned the hopes of being a writer: submitted a few articles for our university paper, published a satirical short story under a pseudonym, always keeping the dream in a secret back pocket, until my sister's death snapped it in two.

Afterwards, I decided to pursue clinical psychology, because I needed to help people like my sister in all the ways I failed to help her. I was admitted to Columbia University's master's in social work program and accepted my place in their class.

I continued to write, but only for myself. I took a handful of creative workshops in undergrad just for fun. It was in one of these classes that I wrote the essay that changed my life.

The piece centered around grieving in the digital age.

When Kait first disappeared, I looked at her Facebook page constantly, waiting for the hollow dot next to her name to suddenly fill in green, an indication that she was active on her account. I imagined her at some dusty, faraway public library, logging in to message a confidant. I'd seize the moment, send something fast and furious. *Kait*, I'd type. *It's me. Just tell me you're okay.*

When the bubble remained gray and opaque, I hesitantly began rereading our old conversations, scrolling through the gaps between messages sometimes several months long. I recoiled at the sight of every unanswered text she sent. I withdrew my hand from the touchpad, and then returned to it gingerly, as if shocked by some electric current. My sister was preserved on Facebook, but so too were my many, many mistakes.

Our family has no gravestone to visit, no memorial, not even a symbolic garden. Where once grievers would speak aloud at a cemetery, telling the hard unfeeling earth about life milestones and everyday disappointments, all I had was the device in my hand.

For a while, every minor cultural or political event that transpired was a loss. The more the world changed, moved on without my sister, the farther away she felt. An illogical thought consumed me: If my sister were to return, she'd feel left out. It would be difficult to readjust if she remained uninformed. I took it upon myself to remedy this.

After all, if I could still see her, hear her, and text her, was she really gone? If Facebook still reminded me annually of her birthday, calculating the passing years into her current age, then her death wasn't a period or an end but more of an ellipsis, and I could still imagine the ". . ." of a chat bubble popping up at any moment.

I felt like I was coming to know my sister in aftereffect — discovering that we had been to the same restaurant and sat in the same seat when I found a grainy cell phone photo of her in a tagged picture. I realized how much I had truly looked at her through the glorified lens of a little sister when I began watching *Gossip Girl* or *The O.C.* and discovered that Kait's old "indie" playlist (which I still listened to on repeat) was riddled with songs from the shows' soundtracks.

There was still so much to learn about my sister.

With a new age of technology in which our every keystroke is documented, a living part of all of us — our Google searches, our private thoughts misspelled in our Notes section, our impulsive texts, our unflattering photos — has been recorded to unknown ends. In this gray area, there is a danger of too much holding on and not enough letting go. The question is no longer what's possible but what's morally permissible.

Mom tells me that the day before my sister died, Kait turned to her in the front seat of our car with fear in the waning crescent of her eyes.

"If anything ever happens, don't post any bad pictures of me," she begged.

Mom laughed away the dread that settled in her core.

"You've never taken a bad photo in your life," she assured her.

I wonder now, was Kait thinking of the potential missing person posters plastered on trees, stapled on telephone poles, and jostled and crumpled by the wind — the ones we would never end up needing? Was she thinking of the milk carton kids of the eighties? The missing faces smiling over your morning cereal. Had she already made her final decision?

And what had she meant when she asked us not to post any bad photos of her? Which photos did she deem "bad," especially among the ones she had posted online herself? If she was gone, did she even care? How much holding on is too much, and how much of ourselves are we leaving behind as a digital legacy?

One day I received a reply from my sister.

I was at an Irish pub in downtown Boston. A live band was playing one of Kait's favorite songs, and the room expanded with the memory of her. I wanted nothing more in that moment than to talk to my sister.

"I miss you," I texted at 11:02 p.m. "I'm sorry."

Almost immediately, a singular question mark was sent back.

My heart did a violent somersault, an unpleasant torque of my innards. I rushed to the bathroom, pushing through the crowd, spilling drinks in the process, a chorus of indignant *Hey!*s following in my wake. I entered an open stall, leaning against the graffiti-scattered wall.

I typed, "I'm sorry who's this's?" My hands were shaking so much that I worried I might accidentally drop my phone in the toilet. I went back to correct the error: "this?*"

My thought process was simple: If this was just someone messing with me, a cruel hacker or a sadistic stranger, I didn't want to give away too much information. Say it first, I thought, as I had thought at the psychic's office. Say her name. *Tell me it's you, Kait.*

Fast, mercifully fast, within the very same minute, the person responded: "I think u got the wrong number."

"Is this Kaitlyn Leddy?" I asked directly, hope caving my willpower. *Please*, Kait. Please.

"Nope sorry."

Everything in the room seemed to deflate.

I dialed the woman's number, and the answering voice mail confirmed the truth. The woman's pitch was lower than Kait's and it lacked her musical quality — the inflection went down where Kait's would have risen. The number, sitting unused for two years, had been forfeited and recycled. No longer could I delude myself into thinking that Kait may one day respond. She was gone in a new way.

My essay centered around this discovery and my accompanying grief.

A writing professor suggested I submit the piece to the *New York Times* Modern Love college contest. The odds of being accepted were laughingly low — the last round in 2017 saw two thousand submissions, making my likelihood of winning roughly one in two thousand or .05 percent.

On the lofted twin bed of my dorm room, I said a prayer to Kait. "If you don't want me to write about you, then don't let this essay be accepted. Crash my computer. Let it go. I'll drop it, I promise."

On the week of my sister's birthday, I won the contest.

Call it kismet. Call it dumb luck. All I know is that the essay led to inquiries from agents, which led to a publishing contract, which led to this book. I wanted to be a writer so desperately that the desire made my veins ache, but after Kait died, I abandoned it all. Writing about her opened this world back up for me.

For the first time since I was twelve, I began to talk more freely about my sister to friends and family again. People who never knew I once had a sibling now asked questions about her life. Gradually, I began to feel like myself again.

Forty

It's a Tuesday when I happen across a paragraph that drains the blood from my body.

In a study published in *Frontiers in Psychiatry*, researchers examined the link between mild encephalitis and schizophrenia:

> One of the most promising new research concepts is the mild encephalitis hypothesis of schizophrenia, developed mainly by Karl Bechter and Norbert Müller. According to this hypothesis, a significant subgroup of schizophrenia patients suffer from a mild, but chronic, form of encephalitis with markedly different etiologies ranging from viral infections, traumas to autoimmune diseases ... The mild encephalitis hypothesis implies that schizophrenia would no longer be considered an incurable psychiatric disorder. Instead, it would be considered a chronic, but treatable, neurological disease.

A treatable neurological disease.

When I read this phrase, my nausea returns with a viciousness that unnerves me. It rises inside me, alive and lethal. I want to roll into a ball until my muscles ache. I want to close my eyes, but I can't. I owe it to my sister to keep reading and researching no matter how difficult the truth is to face.

Encephalitis is inflammation of the brain, and it's not unique to head trauma: neuroinflammation can be caused by bacterial or viral infections, as well as autoimmune disorders such as tick-borne diseases. In each instance, the brain swells.

Susannah Cahalan, author of *Brain on Fire*, was ultimately diagnosed with anti-NMDA receptor encephalitis after an arduous medical drama. At first, a doctor insisted that her test results were normal: EEG, MRI, neurological exam, bloodwork. He explained away her symptoms as "alcohol withdrawal," despite Calahan neither being a heavy drinker nor having a history of substance abuse. Another doctor diagnosed her with bipolar disorder and prescribed heavy psychiatric medication.

This happened to my sister, as well. A series of exams with no noticeable abnormalities.

It is only after Dr. Souhel Najjar discovers Cahalan's elevated white blood cell count that he suspects an infection, eventually leading to the diagnosis of encephalitis.

Cahalan was diagnosed in 2009. The neurologic disease was first identified by Dr. Joseph Dalmau at the University of Pennsylvania in 2007. This small, quiet detail makes my heart skip a beat.

In 2010, my sister was in the University of Pennsylvania's psychiatric ward and Psychiatry and Neurology unit. We were in the hospital frequently, Mom begging doctors to consider alternative, creative procedures and diagnoses. She was asking about autoimmune disorders, explaining my sister's potential history of Lyme disease, her traumatic brain injury, the underlying hormonal regulation issues, and her diagnosis of polycystic ovarian syndrome (PCOS). My sister was screaming in the hallway, convinced our father was going to kill her. Cahalan was screaming that her father had already killed her mother and was after her next. They were much the same, but Cahalan was in the autoimmune unit and my sister was ushered into the psychiatric ward, sealing their fates and careening the two down vastly different journeys.

Did we cross paths? Is it possible that we were in the same place at the same time, some invisible string tethering us? Cahalan was only the two hundred and seventeenth person in the world to be diagnosed with anti-NMDA receptor encephalitis. A 2019 study by Dr. Dalmau and colleagues found the disease most common in women (80 percent) and triggered often by herpes simplex virus or ovarian teratomas. Again the PCOS diagnosis returns.

When I learned about this, I thought back to the bridge: the figure that always punctuates my thoughts. I wished again that we had recovered a body, but this time, the morbid regret was tied to a different form of closure. If there had been an autopsy, would my sister's brain look like those of the NFL players — atrophied, clumps of tau protein and a ventricular enlargement in the center of the two hemispheres like a black butterfly? Would it have the characteristic inflammation of anti-NMDA receptor encephalitis? Or, would it be eerily, inexplicably perfectly intact?

Doctors still aren't sure how it all began for Cahalan either — what pathogen instigated her brain to attack itself. It could have been a bite from a bed bug, some parasite in a meal, a common viral infection.

That's the thing about schizophrenia and mental illness in general — looking for one origin is like looking for a singular origin of every cancer at once. There are many different kinds of cancer — carcinoma, sarcoma, leukemia, lymphoma, melanoma — and they each require their own treatments. Besides, a new theory of mental illness is gaining traction now — one that wholeheartedly dismisses such reductive fallacies: the microglial universal theory of disease.

In 2020, Donna Jackson Nakazawa published *The Angel and the Assassin: The Tiny Brain Cell That Changed the Course of Medicine*. Inspired by her own string of autoimmune diseases, including the paralyzing Guillain-Barré syndrome, that led to cognitive glitches and shifts in mood, Nakazawa embarked on a mission to understand the connection between immunology and brain-based disorders. In 2012, scientists discovered that the once overlooked tiny brain cells called microglia held the power to protect, repair, and repopulate neurons and synapses. Although the brain was previously considered to have immune privilege, this groundbreaking research showed that the cells work much in the same way as white blood cells do, protecting the brain against infectious diseases and foreign invaders when working correctly, and attacking its own cells and tissues when misfired.

When this immune response went into overdrive, the microglia over-pruned synapses, leading to neuroinflammation and neuropsychiatric and cognitive disorders such as Alzheimer's disease, depression, and schizophrenia (researchers have estimated that a third of people diagnosed with schizophrenia have some immune dysfunction).

Microglia may go haywire when the fight-or-flight is chronically activated, as happens with adverse childhood experiences, or by some combination of genetics and epigenetic shifts. When on the attack, microglia prune synapses, destroying neurons in the hippocampus that would otherwise be capable of adaptation and regeneration. Researchers have proposed that this may be why the hippocampus is shrunken in individuals diagnosed with depression and developmental trauma.

I wonder if I peeked into my scalp, what I would see, and if there's anything else I could be doing to heal my own brain health.

With Alzheimer's, this neuroinflammation, or mild encephalitis, prevents microglia from doing what they're designed to do — clearing up amyloid plaques and tangles. With traumatic brain injuries or CTE, a single, moderate traumatic brain injury can cause cognitive decline, mood changes, and memory loss, as well as age the brain by as much as five years. In brain autopsies of those who have traumatic brain injuries, an unusual level of microglial activity has been found.

This is all relatively new research — discovered between 2012 and 2020. During that time, my sister, exhausted, terrified, and worn down by the fight for her sanity, took her own life. While it can take years for cutting-edge science to make its way to the doctor's office, my sister shows us just how high the stakes are. We don't have years to sit around and wait.

The field of brain-based disorders is steadily growing, creating a world of new possibilities in treatments, gene detection, and autoimmune therapies. As Nakazawa puts it, this new hope comes down to the promise and peril of microglia and a better understanding of the bidirectional feedback loop between neuroinflammation and psychiatric disorders.

And yet, in my own opinion, the biggest difference we can make lies entirely outside the field of scientific innovation and is rather a pro-foundly simple shift in public opinion and conversation.

What a different direction this story of ours could have taken if the psychologists, doctors, friends, family members, my own father, school officials involved (and Kait herself) understood mental illness as the po-tentially treatable, physical brain disorder that it is. If we were not told that it was "all in her head." If her diagnosis was met with compassion, creativity, and open dialogue. How much my life would have been altered for the better if I could have told my friends, teachers, and peers about my sister's struggles without fear of their reaction or judgment.

Kait and millions like her are battling a neurological condition. I know this now, but God, what I would give to have known it sooner.

Forty-one

I'm twenty-three years old as I finish writing this book. This number is significant for two key reasons. For one, schizophrenic symptoms on average tend to emerge in women between the ages of eighteen and twenty-five.

During my twenty-third year, I began questioning whether or not I was starting to develop the onset of psychosis.

In the minutes of spare time I had, I researched incessantly. I read dense psychological texts on the train to work, interviewed professors and clinicians between meetings, and learned about all the ways you can lose your grasp on perception.

I was also living in New York City for the first time and experiencing how people, shadows, animals, and objects flit across the street—the constant movement creating an abstract zoo. Street vents churn with condensed pools of steam smelling like chlorine. Quick black rats scurry from beneath cars and trash cans and jump over the metal ridges of dirty subway tracks. Honking cars, traffic, a fragment of a passerby's cell phone conversation. Miscellaneous meat bakes in the heat of vendor stands, creating clouds of smoke so thick you can *see* the smell.

New York is filled with discordant perspectives: snippets and loose strands. The city never stands still long enough to give anyone a chance to see the whole picture.

I convinced myself sometimes that I was losing my mind. I was wholly overstimulated, overwhelmed: living in a new city, taking on a new job, meeting new friends, while reliving the worst, most suffocating moments of my life in these pages. I often felt like I couldn't breathe. My college boyfriend and I broke up, and before I could feel the inevitable heartbreak, all I felt was relief. *One less thing to worry about.* I found myself battling a newfound claustrophobia — my whole body tensing in the crowded bustle of my commute or the packed corners of restaurants and bars.

One evening in March 2020, after a particularly long day of work and writing, I sat down on the couch of my living room, exhausted. With vague curiosity, I looked up my horoscope on my iPhone.

The words were harsher than I had ever seen on the website before. "The key for you is to minimize your daily drama as much as possible, Capricorn," it read. "You may not realize how much you cripple yourself by the way you exaggerate every aspect of your life."

Jeez, I thought. *That was a little blunter than usual.* I went to send a screenshot to my mom to share a laugh, but when I picked up my phone again, the words had changed to some generic, optimistic cliché advice about how to take control of my career.

Was this a hallucination?

I without a doubt read those words. I saw them on my screen a minute before, each letter, each sentence. I double-checked the date, refreshed the website. Where did it go? Panic spread in my veins.

I'd had a terrible day at work earlier. While trying to juggle everything, I felt I was failing at it all. I was working as an editorial assistant at a national magazine, and I was writing this book every off moment I had, scribbling thoughts on sticky notes at my desk. Every morning, I walked across the shiny, speckled floor of the office building, past floor-to-ceiling glassed offices and larger-than-life black-and-white framed prints of historical fashion moments that reminded me of the vintage *Vogue* covers my sister used to keep in her room.

We shared the office space with titles under the same umbrella company, including the brands *InStyle*, *Better Homes and Gardens*, *People*, *Real Simple*, *Time*, and *Sports Illustrated*. Fresh out of my undergraduate degree where I had virtually no editorial experience, I found myself in over my head — showing up to my first day of work in a navy tweed dress with gold buttons while my coworkers stared at me in confusion, clad in jeans and heels. Although most often I was reporting, editing, and fact-checking fluff pieces on such glamorous subjects as stomach bugs and pacifiers, I couldn't help but think of my sister.

To get to work, I walked through the World Trade Center Oculus, underneath the vaulted roof and long stretches of white ribs that re-minded me of the bones of some ancient beached whale. I thought of my sister in all of the places I never imagined myself — as I pushed through the bustling crowd of commuters and stood waiting in the steamed heat of the subway tract or walked beside the looming figures of illuminated skyscrapers. In all the places she would be surprised to find me, living a life neither of us could have predicted.

Where I was lucky if my hair didn't frizz in the mornings, I could eas-ily imagine my sister fitting in with the glossy world of magazines. What would she have worn to work? Would her modeling career have taken off?

I saw Kait everywhere, and her presence wasn't just a vague notion; it was visceral. I could sense her on every page I wrote. I saw the num-ber eleven with every step I took — on a street sign, the decimals of my coffee order receipt, above the door of the subway car I was on, on the time stamp of an important email — until looking for these "signs" be-came no more conducive to my well-being than Kait's insistence on the coded messages of a radio show had been for her.

So did this mean I had been hallucinating those words on the horo-scope? I knew enough about psychosis and my sister's delusions to un-derstand that it was possible to suffer such an intense, convincing visual delusion.

Sweating slightly, I sat down and then stood back up. Down and then back up. I walked to my bedroom and stared at the large mirror attached to the white dresser, probing my reflection. The same girl as ever stared back at me — long blond hair slightly disheveled from a chaotic commute home, two wide blue eyes looking more panic-stricken than usual, the bump on my nose that my sister used to tease me about, my pale cheeks flushed with energy. Could I trust this image? Could I trust anything I saw? Did the shadows behind me not look sinister? The oblong lights of the city traffic outside my window scattered across the wall, gathering in bunches and then dissipating like rain on a windshield. I could hear the light bulb on my dresser corner buzzing slightly, humming with a singing sound. *Could I always hear that, or was this new too?*

I knew firsthand how fragile sanity is — how quickly it can come undone like the thread of your favorite sweater pulled at just the right angle. Looking around my room, wondering if I had hallucinated the horoscope, I felt the urgency of this delicate balance — my age and genetic history.

Taking a few deep breaths to steady myself, I pulled out my laptop from a cluttered bag and typed in the URL of the horoscope website. I scoured the page, poring over other signs and dates with a seriousness not usually dedicated to cosmic predictions, until finally, with a long exhale of relief, I found it. This time, the same text was filed under the Leo category. There had been a glitch in the system.

To be sure, I sent a picture to Mom. "Can you read this back to me?" I asked on the phone, trying to mask my urgency with an air of nonchalance.

When she read the sentences with perfect precision, I laughed with gratitude, closing my eyes in relief. *Just a false alarm*, I thought.

Today my mind was still my own, but would there come a day when it wasn't?

A course I took my sophomore year of college called Developmental Psychopathology chronicled the manifestation of mental health issues in youth. One day, we watched a documentary series about childhood schizophrenia called *Born Schizophrenic*.

On the screen, a woman in her thirties discusses her daughter's psychosis. She's only six years old but has been suffering from schizophrenic symptoms for nearly all of her life. Her imaginary friends are so ingrained in her worldview that her mom begins to suspect they are beyond the range of normal childhood imagination.

"I have been stabbed with forks, tomato stakes," her mother tells the camera.

"Seven" is the name of one of these hallucinations. As described by the child's mother, Seven is violent and reclusive.

"Can you draw Seven for us?" the mother asks the little girl.

The child, petite, pale, self-contained, begins to draw a block number colored in striped lines while the mother describes the girl's other hallucinations: spiders crawling on her skin, causing the child to scratch and pick at her arms, rats running across the floor, keeping her awake at night.

The camera pans to the sister. She looks slightly older but with a similarly vulnerable demeanor, like that of a baby bird.

"Sometimes I'm really scared of her," she admits.

"Why do you help her then?" the mother prompts.

"Because she's my sister, and I love her." The girl shrugs. "Like, that's what any other big sister would do, even if she has that illness."

Her delicate shoulders hunch toward the camera, protective and defeated at the same time, and I felt as though I have never been more connected to a stranger in all my life.

After my sister died, I made a habit of keeping checks on my sanity, such as performing a routine breast cancer self-exam in the shower. I feel for the lumps and bumps. I do my due diligence of taking care of my mental health, myself. I wear helmets when I ski. My hands rise automatically to protect my head when I trip.

But somehow, before I listened to that mother speak about her daughter, there was one big piece of the family puzzle I had somehow never thought to consider. When we lost Kait, despite the trauma and grief, at the very least I believed myself free of loving someone with schizophrenia once and for all.

For the first time, in the dark cloak of the classroom, I worried not about Kait, who was gone, and not about the vulnerability of my own mind, but about a future child. I imagined a life in which my mind remained my own, I found the right partner to marry, and we had a baby — only to discover that child had the same condition as my sister. I imagined watching the signs creep in slowly, until the recognition ripped across my chest like a yanked-back shower curtain in a horror movie, the feared monster revealed to have been hiding there all along.

Could I bring a child into the world, knowing this was a possibility? Knowing I could be condemning them to the same brutal suffering Kait endured?

"Isn't that *fascinating?*" my professor said as the movie ended.

She was a small woman, well into her late sixties, with a distinctly academic look: cardigan sweaters, clear tights, and orthopedic shoes. She looked like a grandma: sweet, motherly, fragile. I wanted to smack her.

I took several deep breaths while the class engaged in a heated discussion of genetics and mental health. I had a flyaway impulse to shield my face.

That could be me, I thought. *That likely won't be any of you, but it could be me.*

When the class finally ended, I went to sit by a drained fountain in the school's courtyard. The air was chipped and cold. Soon enough I would slide on the mask I knew too well — the one I carried with me my entire life to avoid revealing Kait's condition to others. Smile wide, eyes bright. I would face my roommates and say nothing. I would listen to their days, and I would laugh and I would offer reassuring words, not telling a soul that it took every ounce of strength in my body to remain tied together before them. But for these few minutes alone in the winter night, I let the reality settle around me like the taste of snow in the cold January air.

Would I risk passing my sister's diagnosis to my children?

It was a question that hurt to even consider. I had to dance around it, approach it at arm's length.

When I thought of Kait, of everything that made her who she was, I knew I was more than thankful that she existed. The violence, the chaos, the shattered glass and threats, were not enough to wish that none of it had happened. To have her in my life at all — the good, the bad, the childhood pranks and teenage mentorship — was so essential to my being that the thought of anything else was unfathomable.

But what about Kait? Would she have asked for this life? If before we are born, we are given a slideshow preview of what will happen, would Kait have chosen to stay, cozy, warm, and blissfully naïve in our mom's womb? Would she have volunteered for this? Did the good outweigh the bad for *her*?

And what about Mom? My own pain was one thing — the pain of watching a fallen idol, the pain of witnessing loss and violence at a young age — but Mom's grief was something I couldn't bear to think of for very long, a place so unpleasant it hurt to visit.

I walked back to my dorm fundamentally changed by the evening but without the words or wherewithal to explain why. Although I had spent my life copying Kait, wishing I could become her, the thought of this particular replication filled me with a suffocating terror.

This, then, is why I write. It is too late to help Kait, but there are others like her who are actively suffering. There are others like me who love someone with a mental illness, who are lost and confused and helpless and also actively suffering in our own way.

I write for the little girl on the video. I write for the men at the homeless shelter, my beloved patients at the group home — sweet, isolated, and so unbearably vulnerable. I write for the children I may or may not have someday and for their children's children. I write for myself, so if I do eventually develop schizophrenia, the world will be gentler on me.

I thought we were the only people in the world to go through what we did, but this was a falsehood. We were silent, so very silent, because others were silent. We swallowed our truth, our loss. We lied and lied and lied, thinking we were protecting something, but what good has silence ever done to change anything?

Forty-two

Twenty-three is also significant for a very different reason.

My sister died at age twenty-two.

I was born a little sister. I came into this world with a twin flame already five or six steps ahead of me. She was my timeline, my touchpoint, the marking in the woods that let me know all wasn't lost.

What did Kait look like when she turned thirteen? *Would I ever be that beautiful?* What was she wearing at sixteen? *Could I borrow it?* When did she date her first boyfriend? When did she get her ears pierced? Who was her teacher in the seventh grade?

After her head injury, these comparisons brought more guilt than comfort. When Kait was twenty, she was in and out of psychiatric care. When I was twenty, I found an old license of hers and used it to get into a bar. The action felt wrong even as I did it, but my friends were all using their older siblings' IDs, and I knew that Kait would have insisted on giving me hers had she the opportunity. The idea of her little sister, the type-A, the goody-two-shoes, doing anything illegal, would thrill her. "Kyle!" she would have hollered. "Oh Mylanta, what a rule breaker we have here!" Having her license made me feel like she was still passing things down to me, like we were still engaging in sibling rituals.

I only used it the one time. I stood shaking in a huddled line, waiting to hand the flimsy plastic to the bouncer. The man looked at it for a while, and then back at me, and I knew that he didn't believe it was me in the photo, because my sister was a model; four inches taller than me and tanner and infinitely more beautiful.

"What's your birthday?" he asked in a gruff voice.

"April sixteenth, 1991," I said automatically, tears springing against my will.

"How old are you?" He narrowed his eyes slightly, searching.

"I'm twenty-six," I lied.

Twenty-six. It hit me then that I could not imagine my sister at twenty-six. A twenty-six-year-old Kait was someone entirely foreign to me. What would she be doing? Who would she be had this whole tragedy not transpired? Would she be happy? Engaged? A career woman? Would I visit her in her city apartment, meet her friends, learn her ways?

"Go in," the bouncer said. "You need a new license. This is expired."

Flushed and broken and beating, I slid past the bulky man and into the crowded bar where my friends were waiting. I smiled and joined them, but beneath the veneer a single thought coursed under my skin with a pressing insistence. *I passed for Kait.*

I never tried the license again, because it was a rare, precious object, and seeing its delicate shape in the bouncer's meaty hand made me realize that I could not bear to lose it; but I kept it in my wallet just the same. Every time I saw the familiar gleam of plastic, I felt as though I was taking my sister with me. The bureaucratic, official, government-issued rectangle proved that she was real, that she had lived and existed and mattered.

When I turned twenty-three, the script went blank. For the first time in my life, I was surpassing my sister. One day, I will look back on her and think her so very young, her life so very short. I'll move onward into new stages and she will stay frozen, always twenty-two years old. This is what mental illness stole from my sister — not just the joys of aging but also the lessons and hardships and grit that come with it. The *possibility* of better days, of moving to new cities and meeting new people, of having children and making mistakes and miracles.

When I was a little girl, I'd ask my mom, "If you were my age, would you be my friend?"

She'd respond every time, "I'd be lucky to have a friend like you."

Now I wonder the same about my sister. If we had the chance to grow into adulthood together without the burden of schizophrenia, would we be closer for it? Would we have left behind the petty jealousies of adolescence and emerged as a team? Would she want to be my friend?

After my seventeenth birthday, I forfeited celebrations. The date would always remind me of my sister, and death anniversaries are windowless days: purposeless and listless. I tried a few times to celebrate my birthday, but each failed in predictable ways. I went out for a dinner with a handful of friends on my twentieth, posed for pictures with a champagne bottle on my twenty-first. And yet no matter how hard I tried, the night ended the same: me, alone in some unfamiliar bathroom, remembering my sister, feeling guilty and tired and nauseous and wishing I could evaporate. The next morning, all I felt was relief that the day was over.

But twenty-three, I decided, would be different. I was older, wiser. I had spent most of the previous year remembering my sister, writing these pages, chronicling what had happened so that now I could leave it all behind in a tidy box and move on to the stage of quiet acceptance.

And yet I found myself in a bathroom once again, unable to stop the tears, the feverish persistence of which surprised me. Two friends were staying at my apartment from out of town, but I couldn't leave my bathroom to face them. I tried to curl my hair and line my eyes with mascara, but the tears kept coming and coming, erasing my work until any attempt to wipe them away became fruitless. I texted an apology from behind the protection of a closed door like a little kid afraid to meet my parents' eyes.

"I'm sorry," I said. "I didn't expect this. I wouldn't have invited you over if I knew this would happen."

My friends were comforting and kind, leaving me alone until I finally calmed down enough to join them. I thought I had grown so much, overcome so very much, but I was shocked to discover that it still lurked beneath the surface, waiting to submerge me. That's the thing about grief — you can plan and reflect and set timelines and expectations, but sometimes you find yourself right back where you started, crying unexpectedly in yet another bathroom.

I'm a year older than my sister now, but she still feels older to me. Maybe she will always feel this way — even when I'm thirty-three or forty-three or fifty-three. I still want her to check under my bed for monsters and tell me that everything is going to be okay.

My friends joke that I am everyone's big sister, because I make an effort to befriend their younger siblings. I can sense, even if their little sisters would deny it, this same wanting from them. I can see the bedroom doors that were closed to them in their youth; I can see how fast they tried to grow just to catch up — each inch on the wall an inch closer to their goal; I can see the fleeting look from the corner of their eye that hunts for the face of their sibling, hungry for confirmation that yes, they are doing just fine.

I was on the subway recently and across from me were two little girls with approximately the same age difference as Kait and me. The older girl was around eight or nine years old, while the younger trotted after her at three or four. Their mother was distracted, looking at something on her phone.

The girls played on the smooth blue bench across from me, occasionally standing up and jostling between the silver pole that separated them. The older sister was sharing her toys with the younger one — a boy and girl doll with plastic, chunky hair.

"We have to have a wedding for them," the older girl announced. "Because they love each other, and when people love each other, that's what they do. They get married, got it?"

The little sister looked up with a vacant, easy smile. They were strikingly similar to my sister and me, except their hair color was inverted — the little sister had darker curls while the older sister's hair was lighter and more tamed, held back by barrettes. Still I could see in the little girl's face the magnitude of her utter faith. Anything her sister told her was gospel, the law of the land, the official doctrine. *Got it?* the sister asked, and she did. She was soaking up every word.

Did the older sister know her power? Do siblings ever know the hold they have over us?

I saw the world through my sister's eyes for twenty-two years. I wrote this book seeking her perspective. And now the page is empty. For once, there are no comparisons to be made.

Kait never made it to twenty-three, but here I am. Her parallel line abruptly ends, but mine continues on. I carry her with me like the license in my wallet.

The question is: What shall I make with what remains?

Forty-three

Two weeks after my disastrous twenty-third birthday, I went to a friend's apartment for a house-warming party. Because we're in our early twenties and broke and live in tiny, cramped New York City apartments, the event involved little ceremony beyond the opening of some lukewarm cases of beer and hard seltzer. Lazy after a long week of work, I almost bailed on attending, but it was my friends' first weekend in the city, and inspired by my sister's influence, I was trying to be more spontaneous when it came to making plans. I wanted to spend my first year in the city having as many different experiences as possible, opening myself up to opportunities — I could hear what my sister used to tell me, what she would likely tell me now: *Kyle, you never know who you'll meet.*

The boys lived in an East Village walk-up above a small, unassuming diner with a dingy navy blue awning and large red sign. When we exited our taxi, my two friends and I hopped up the steps and stood shivering before the building's intercom system. As we bounced in place under the short overhang with our hands stuffed in our too thin jackets, I turned to a silver call box next to the front door, looking for the right apartment number to click. I skimmed the web of black typeface and unfamiliar names. That's when I saw it:

Kaitlyn Leddy. #60.

With cold wonder, I reached out to touch it, tracing my sister's exact spelling with my index finger as if to make sure it was real: her full, legal name. It had been so long since I had seen this name anywhere. I met many Kates, some Cates, a few Caits, but never a *Kait*, and certainly never a Kait*lyn*. As she had with my own name, my grandmother had intervened to make the spelling flow with our surname, adding the "y." Kaitlyn Leddy and Kyleigh Leddy. Two K. L.'s, a duo.

An icy thread looped up my shoulders, tying my insides in knots. "Ugh! They're not listed yet," one of my friends complained.

"That's my sister's name," I said in a quiet voice.

Pointing toward the list, I forced a soft laugh, my voice growing louder as I explained, "Look. It says, 'Kaitlyn Leddy.' That was my sister's name, how weird is this?"

"Wait, what? That's such a funny coincidence."

I agreed — weird, funny, random, and a coincidence, clearly.

The conversation shifted, the boys buzzed us in, and we walked into a narrow hallway with a steep staircase to the left and metal mailboxes to the right.

"Hold on," I said. "I want to check something fast."

Scanning the boxes, I saw it again — this time written in pencil with childishly large letters was my last name on a white sticker. It looked quite impossibly like my sister's handwriting.

"Wow, this is so weird," I called over to my friends, who were waiting by the staircase. "Such a small world."

Something was beginning to plant itself in my core, pulling on the sides of my intestines with razor-sharp claws. Was it possible for it to really be *such* a small world?

We began our ascent up the six flights of stairs, our thighs aching from the effort. With every step I climbed, a sense of wrongness enveloped me. When we reached our friends' door, I realized that their apartment was directly across from this "Kaitlyn Leddy." Out of all the buildings in Manhattan, out of all the doors in this building, how was this happening?

I let my stare linger for a moment on the red door. Resting outside was a dirty pineapple-patterned welcome mat with a bright pink background. The white tile floors of the hallway were aged and cracked. I surprised myself by thinking, *What is my sister doing here?*

I tore my gaze from the door reluctantly and followed my friends into the small party. For the first fifteen minutes, I arranged my face into a smile, held a spiked seltzer in my lap, tried to banter good-naturedly. Yet the gold numbers of the apartment blinked against my eyelids, a beacon. *Six zero.*

Excusing myself to the bathroom, I sat down on the edge of the tub gingerly and pulled out my phone. I checked Google first, Facebook next, LinkedIn and Instagram as a last resort, searching for someone named Kaitlyn Leddy who was not my sister. I only found two in our country — neither of whom were listed as living in New York City.

The first thought was propulsive. *What if my sister is alive?* Then logic took over. If she had been hiding out all this time, wouldn't she change her name? But . . . maybe she had amnesia and all she could remember was this last shred of her old life? Fate drew me here to find her, catapulted me onto her doorstep.

Fact and desperate fiction battled each other like this for several minutes.

Finally, I looked at myself in the dirty mirror, trying to steady my breathing. I leaned against the cool sink. I knew my sister was gone. I *knew* it. But how effortlessly easy it was to fall back into old rhythms of magical thinking.

Leaving the bathroom, I wove my way into the hallway. I sat on the first step of the stairs, angling my body so that I could stare directly at the door labeled with the wobbly six and zero.

For a while, I stayed like this, hoping the apartment door would fly itself open. Out would walk my sister, or perhaps someone distinctly not my sister. Either way, the mystery would be solved. The more I stared at the door, the more out of focus it grew. A red jacket, a red door. The pattern was not lost on me.

I did what I always do in moments of stress and called my mom. "So, don't freak out, but . . ."

Mom agreed that it was a strange coincidence. I asked if I should knock. She wondered what that would accomplish but diplomatically said yes, knock if it will make you feel better.

"I mean, I feel like I have to *see* for myself, to make sure it's not her or it'll haunt us, right?"

There was a pause. "Ky, it's not her. It's never going to be her."

Out of nowhere, I burst into tears violently. A sunny day, and then a tsunami. A friend and his girlfriend, late to the party, scooted by me up the stairs. "Hey!" the boy said, but despite my best efforts to smile, something on my face sent him scurrying by without further ado.

Mom waited for my breath to steady on the phone. She apologized profusely for upsetting me, and I could hear tears in her voice as well. "No, *I'm* sorry," I said. Back and forth we went, jockeying the placeless blame.

"It is a weird coincidence, though. Maybe it's a sign?" Mom asked on the phone. "Maybe we're going to find something out, maybe even find her body . . . Or . . ." Another pause, a whisper. "Do you think someone stole her identity?"

I hadn't thought about this.

Three years ago, if someone asked me if I thought my sister was still "with me," I'd have said no, but recently the answer had changed to a definitive, rock-solid yes. She was everywhere. Like that prickly feeling you get on the back of your neck without needing to turn around when someone is staring at you — I felt my sister's presence to an uncanny degree.

But this was not a knock, not a nudging or a reassuring fragment of my own bereavement process. This was a shove. If previous "signs" had been arbitrary signals of my own healthy grieving, open for interpretation — this encounter was startlingly explicit.

If my sister was sending me a message, then it wasn't a gentle urging. Rather, it was a push headfirst down the stairs. It didn't say, "I'm with you," metaphorically, spiritually. It said, "I am here *now*." But then again, that was Kait's style. She always made space for herself.

As for someone having stolen her identity, the more I thought about this, the more plausible the possibility seemed. Any Google search of her name turned up missing persons reports. In the back of my brain, I recalled a computer science teacher once remarking that missing people are the perfect targets for identity theft, because personal information is readily available. Was this the answer, then? Had I been somehow drawn to this exact door because my sister knew someone was using her name? Was it my fault for having written about her disappearance, for making it so public?

I imagined how angry it would make my sister — how much weight she put into being *Kaitlyn Leddy* — and I felt rage boil up inside me, too. The more I looked at the deep red scratched paint of the door, the more certain I was that I would ultimately have to knock. And yet, I also knew that the second I made contact, the moment the door creaked open, I would have to abandon the last remnants of any hope that it would ever be my sister behind it. The opening of the door would be an end to something, a finality. I wasn't sure why I knew this, but I knew.

Mom and I hung up the phone. She asked if I wanted her to come down to the city tomorrow and knock on the door with me. I told her no, don't be silly, that's ridiculous. I can handle it.

Still, I stayed put, imagining a life for my sister in which she did live behind the red door with the pineapple doormat. Nausea came over me. I leaned on the cool staircase railing for support, tucking my forehead into the crook of my bent arm. How could I have come so far, only to be back where I started?

After some time, my friend Kate came outside to check up on me. When I explained the situation, she volunteered to help me knock before everyone left to go to a bar. "Don't worry, Kyles," she said cheerily. "You don't have to do this alone."

Only one other person on this planet besides her ever called me "Kyles."

She gave me a hug and went back inside, but when the time came, everyone from the party exited in a long wave, flooding the small staircase. I was swept up in the movement, left alone on the top step, while someone called out, "Are you coming?" The doors were closing — I would lose track of everyone, be left here alone with the ghost of my sister or the threat of her impersonator.

I couldn't do it.

With one last glance at the red door, I hurried after them, regret thudding through me all the way down the long stairs.

I didn't sleep for the next three days.

All night images of the red rectangle consumed my dreams. I dreamed with a literal, transparent consistency — of doors and villains with stolen identities, and of my sister chasing after me, stepping on the back of my heels like a shadow.

Two days later, a Sunday, I texted my friend to ask if he was around and if he could buzz me into the building. He said no, he and his roommate were out all day. I considered lying, saying that I had forgotten something at his place, but I didn't want to risk having him search for the item himself or asking me to go inside and look. So I told him the truth in the vaguest, least threatening terms I could think of. Understanding the problem, he sent me his weekly schedule and suggested I come by after work on Monday.

That day I dressed with extra care, spending more time than usual on my makeup. My hands shook with sleep deprivation. For a reason I couldn't pinpoint, I wanted to look my best.

At the office, I used my lunch break to slip into one of the small, two-person conference rooms and research identity theft on my moon-bright laptop screen. I even called a USA.gov number for advice. The woman suggested we declare my sister deceased. I told her yes, yes, we would, but I knew that the procedure would be too much for Mom.

On my way out of work, I bought my friends cupcakes and wrote, *Thank you so so much. I promise I will never ask you for something this weird again*, in black Sharpie. I took the subway to Washington Square Park. Underneath my thick winter jacket, I was sweating with nerves.

What if no one was home and I was left standing there like an idiot? Or, what if only Kaitlyn Leddy's roommate was home? The next time I went, they would surely recognize me, and I would lose my chance forever. Or, what if this person really did steal my sister's identity and they were a dangerous criminal? What if they knew what I looked like from Kait's Facebook page and knocked me over the head with a candlestick? Would a "Kyleigh Leddy" pop up next?

A quieter what-if hissed beneath it all. What if it *was* Kait? This explained the extra minutes added to my morning routine, of course. I wanted to look my best for her. As if that would do it — she'd have to come home if she saw that I was wearing my best boots, a suede pair handed down from our mom. She'd say, *Look how much you've grown.*

When I reached the building, I was out of breath. I texted my friend and he buzzed me in. A small girl about the same age as me was getting her mail in the front entrance. I peeked over her shoulder to make sure it wasn't the number 60 mailbox. At the end of the six flights of stairs, I placed the box of cupcakes delicately on my friends' doorstep, pushed my hair out of my face, dialed 911, tucked my phone into my pocket, and kept my hand close to the call button just in case.

I knocked on the door — two sharp raps.

A blond woman answered. Before I could register anything else, all I saw was that she was about a foot too short to be my sister. I arranged my face into my best imitation of a cheery smile and entered into a well-practiced monologue.

"Hi!" I said, "Are you Kaitlyn?"

The girl smiled back enthusiastically, raising her eyebrows only slightly. "Yes," she told me. "I am!"

I told her that I was visiting my friend in the building and happened across the name Kaitlyn Leddy on the call log. "I went to high school with a girl with the same name," I lied. "And I just had to check if it was her, because I haven't seen her in *forever!*"

I willed my skin not to blush. A bead of sweat was gathering near my right temple. The straps of my work bag dug deep into the skin of my shoulder.

"Oh my gosh, that's so funny!" The girl opened the door wider, laughing with an effortless, effusive charm, as if she had been expecting me. She was wearing pajamas, and I could hear the theme music of the *Bachelor* franchise behind her. "I've actually never met anyone with the same exact spelling. Do you mind if I ask, where did you go to high school?"

My mouth spoke the truth automatically. "Right outside of Philadelphia."

"Oh, wow. I'm from a small town in Massachusetts," she offered in response.

"Where in Massachusetts?" I asked out of curiosity, adding despite myself. "I used to live in Marblehead."

Part of me wanted to kick myself for revealing too many personal details, but something about the girl's presence was comforting. It was like catching up with a friend I hadn't seen in a long time, as if my excuse for being there was true. Talking to her was easy.

"Wait, that's such a weird coincidence!" she blurted out. "My family lives right nearby. We played you guys in a lot of sports. Wow, what a small world, huh?"

I apologized for bothering her, she apologized for disappointing me and for not being my long-lost high school friend. She said she couldn't wait to tell her mother about this. "She thought she was so original with the spelling." Yes, I responded, my friend used to say the same thing.

The door closed, and I walked back down the stairs. And then I kept walking, up the twenty blocks and two avenues to my apartment. With each step I took past crowded restaurants and cans of garbage, I shed something unnamed.

I breathed in the cold air of the February day. Even at the time, I knew that this would be a moment that mattered.

I love places that change colors depending on the season — watching burnt grass spring to life, the vitality of green seeping into its core like a clock running backwards. New York is such a place, but February is a limbo month, held between the palms of winter holidays and the expectation of spring. The yellow bulbs of Christmas lights still hang in some windows. Pharmacies turn red and pink with Valentine's Day commercialization fever. You wear your winter jacket, but you unzip it just so, and sometimes, while walking under the tunnel of construction piping or across the red light of an intersection, you feel a slightly warmer waft — the color of March and April in the air.

The more I walked, the more I felt this promise. Skipping over the white lines of street crossings and the gum-splattered sidewalks, I knew spring would come.

I had no answer as to why I'd lost three nights of sleep over a nice, harmless girl — a common coincidence, a wink of the universe.

Maybe that was the point, though — there doesn't necessarily always need to be a reason. Sometimes life hands you improbable moments of astonishment. Sometimes a coincidence is just that: *a coincidence.* I had to stop looking for my sister. It was never going to be her. I had to stop searching for her everywhere. I had to release her.

That night I slept a deep, forgetful sleep. For the first time in months, my sister did not visit my dreams. All was quiet.

Forty-four

On the beach nearby the house where my mom now lives on Nantucket Island, we take long walks. We wear athletic clothing — Spandex and nylon — with running sneakers. We trudge through the sand, sinking deeper, sometimes bent toward the wind, other times propelled forward by it. We used to walk this same path with Kait when we came here on family vacations. She always walked faster than we did. *Slow down*, we called after her, as she sped ahead on her long legs, but she was not one to stroll casually. She went from one point to another; she sought out the finish line. Sometimes, if the light bounces against the fog at just the right angle, I still see her there in the mist, barreling ahead of us.

When the tide is high, the path becomes thin and winding, so we walk single-file until inevitably we are drawn into the green-dotted dunes that line the edge. Sometimes Mom goes first, carefully avoiding the protected brush, finding clear patches of sand and stepping gingerly over the roots of wild grass with blades that slice our ankles. I delicately fill in the footsteps behind her like I'm walking a tightrope. Other times, I'll forge ahead. A stray wave can find us here, hitting against the cliff and spraying ocean breeze. We yelp, startled, running backwards like little kids, tripping over the tangled vegetation.

"Can you believe this is real?" Mom will often say. "Can you believe that we're here?"

She walks the beach by herself when I'm not around. When she first began living alone, she forced herself to come here every day, no matter the weather. She would scream — scream into the water that churned and churned and churned, drowning her sound, sending a flutter of seagulls flying. Or she would stand atop the rickety public-access staircase and pause for a moment. When you're this close to the ocean, it's like it's in your chest, your bloodstream, pulling the tides of you closer and closer. She would stand and listen, straining to hear whatever the wind was telling her.

In the winter, we wear ski jackets, lined leggings, and thick knitted beanies. Mom's favorite hat has flaps on the ends that protect her ears from frostbite, and each time she wears it, I tease her by calling her Holden Caulfield, and she sticks her tongue out at me in response.

Sea levels are rising with climate change, eroding the shorelines. There used to be a veteran's association at our nearby park, but when the water rose, the ocean swallowed it in one bite. After some time, the remains were buried by sand and age, but it's starting to reemerge. Bulky pipes poke through the beach like needles through fabric. Old wires, frayed and impotent, coil in the jagged cliff. A large cement foundation peeks through the mounds as waves crash upon it. Loose bricks scatter near the darker dirt. It looks like an apocalyptic landscape.

Each time we walk this path, I am reminded of how nature reclaims, burying our monuments and our memories and ourselves. I am also reminded of the power of memory, how it resurfaces no matter how hard we might try to push it down. The past fights for a chance to be remembered.

Mom will abruptly stop walking, spotting something in the smooth sea glass and shells by the water's edge. Picking up a rock and carefully brushing wet sand from it, she asks, "Doesn't this look like a heart?" and it does, slightly.

She puts the keepsake in her pocket for now and then later places it on our front porch with the rest of her collection. There are colors of all shades: light orange, gray, blue, speckled and black, greenish like seaweed or sun-drenched red like old brick. Some are heavy and distorted, while others are skinny and triangular — flat as a pancake or curved like a cashew. She places the special ones, the most perfect ones, on the windowsill above our sink, directly in the sunlight. They remind her of Kait, she tells me, and I know I am not the only one looking for signs, seeking presence in the void.

My sister's old boyfriend reached out to me by Facebook after my essay was published in the *New York Times*. He told me my words brought him closure and clarity. He knew something "had gone wrong" but never exactly what. It made sense now. People will always remember her, he assured me, long after social media platforms are gone, for her "infectious smile and laugh, her charm, her generosity, her innocent youth, and most of all how much she looked up to you."

Despite myself, my hand covered my mouth when I read this line — a suppressed sob of surprise choking my breath.

"We had countless conversations about how she couldn't have had a better sibling and best friend. She always felt you were the one who was going to make your parents proud," he told me. "Congratulations on turning out to be everything she hoped you'd be, it's the best way you could have ever honored her."

Here was a gift I didn't know I could still receive — my sister speaking to me again in a way, bestowing upon me that pat on the back I still craved.

Another friend of hers contacted me and shared a different kind of memory:

"Kait was the biggest on not splitting the pole, like walking down the street. If you split the pole, then eventually you would not be friends. So we NEVER split the pole. Also we always looked at the clock (if my memory is right) at 4:16 . . . which was Kait's birthday. (Right?)"

I was shocked that he remembered the pole and still thought of my sister in his daily life — the pole, the time on the clock. I was also stunned to realize that yes, he was right. Kait and I shared 11:11, but she also made a separate wish on the numbers of her birthday. How could I have forgotten this?

"She was the Edie Sedgwick to my Andy Warhol," the boy told me.

Edie Sedgwick—the socialite, the protagonist of her last desperate scribbled and incoherent message. He knew about Edie Sedgwick. I had not.

Kait goes to heaven. Edie in heaven.

I went on a first date recently, and when the guy asked me what this book was about, I told him frankly that it centered around my sister's death and her battle with schizophrenia, and I didn't care what he thought. My voice didn't shake, and I didn't feel ashamed or embarrassed or broken. I didn't wonder if he was wondering about my genetic susceptibility.

I said it, and I think that means something. I hope every time I say the term out loud, the barrier of stigma will quiver just an inch.

So can there be a happy ending after grief, beyond that life goes on? There's no way to undo the past or redeem it, only to commemorate it. Make it count. My happy ending is coming to terms with what happened. In doing my part to honor my sister and bring awareness to her heartbreak in the hopes that it'll save someone else. My happy ending is this book. That I had the opportunity to write it, that I felt my sister more in these pages than I have since the day she left. And by letting this story go, I am learning how to be again.

I thought I was writing this to make my sister's life matter, but it already does. There are people who split a pole and think of her. She was a sister, certainly, but she was also a daughter, a friend, a patient, a comedian, an artist, a muse. She was someone's Edie.

Kait loved butterflies, so now I think back to the Butterfly Effect and the ripples of her life that I will never know. My sister mattered like everyone in this world matters, whether or not there are books written or buildings named in memoriam. The notion that we are capable of changing the world is both arrogant and obvious. Of course we change every life we meet, just not always in the grand gestures we expect.

In the morning, Mom takes her coffee by the front windows, or outside on the deck, and looks upon the stretch of green bushes and sliver of blue where the sky meets the sea. She hopes to someday start a kind of retreat center, building a community so no one has to feel as alone as we did. She wants families to know that they must help themselves before they can help their loved ones. She wishes to create a vacuum away from the chaos, if even just for a day of respite.

Whether or not she ever opens this foundation, my sister lives on through her. She is in the heart-shaped rocks and shells and bits of sea glass on the front steps. She is in the careful way my mom and I still, between us, call the spare bedroom "Kait's room" and not the guest room, even though my sister did not know this house long enough to make it her own. She is in the rosebush we planted on a trellis near her window. The wind is too strong for the pink flowers to fully prosper, but still she is there.

My sister is in the way I dress, the colors I choose, how I am challenged to be a more original, truer version of myself. She is in the moments where I say yes to an adventure instead of no. I feel her when that song is playing in the car and everyone is singing along, and I'm reminded of what it is to be alive — or when the fog rolls in, turning the trees into skinny silhouettes and the sun hangs low in a red summer sky. I see her in what is beautiful or interesting or sad, which is to say that I see her in everything. She is nowhere tangible, which is to say that she is everywhere.

We keep and keep and keep. We remember and remember and remember. We collect heart-shaped shells and signs and old notebooks and recollections. We hold on, memorize the lines of her tan, slender hands and the sound of her laugh, engraving ourselves with the smallest details, lest we ever forget. We try to make amends, reason with ghosts, explain ourselves to the wind.

And then, there comes a time when we must let go.

This is the end goal, after all. This is what the grief self-help books and psychologists and religious advisors and experts of many cultures tell us is necessary.

Only after we relinquish what is lost are we truly healed.

I must let her run in front of me, stop chasing after her footsteps in the sand. Or maybe it is me who must surpass her now.

This book cannot resurrect or preserve as I once thought the point of literature. All it can do is bury.

This is the true meaning of rest in peace. Let her rest, let her be gone. Stop calling her back; let her finally have some peace.

After everything, she deserves to be at peace.

So I let her go.

Still, she goes on.

Acknowledgments

It would be impossible to write acknowledgments without beginning with the most obvious event: the *New York Times* Modern Love College Contest that catapulted my career and made every word of this book possible. Thank you to my wonderful Creative Nonfiction professor, Suzanne Berne — an unparalleled writer, editor, teacher, and mentor. If not for your encouragement and sincere belief in your students and in the power of storytelling, I would never have known about the contest, let alone had the guts to actually submit to it. You are the truest testament to the profound impact teachers have on this world.

To Dan Jones and Miya Lee at the *New York Times*, thank you for taking a chance on me. In my mind's eye, I've reenacted a scene of Miya pulling my essay from the pile of submissions, and thought: *Yes, that was it.* That was the moment that changed everything. Thank you, Dan, for handling my family's story with patience, sensitivity, and empathy. It was a thrill of a lifetime to work with you.

To my brilliant and fearless literary agent, Eve Attermann, thank you for championing this book at every stage and for doing it all while bringing your adorable daughter into this world. I hope to be half as cool as you someday. I am also eternally grateful for my editor, Millicent Bennett, who immediately recognized what I wanted to accomplish and helped me realize the dream with such vision and conviction, elevating the project with every careful edit. Many people come together to create a book, and I am so fortunate to have worked with everyone at Mariner Books — including Alison Kerr Miller, a tremendously thorough and meticulous copyeditor.

Acknowledgments

While *The Perfect Other* was undoubtedly my miracle, writing it was terribly difficult at times. Reliving the trauma, trying to make meaning and beauty of it, was in many ways harder than living through the actual grief itself. And the burden wasn't mine alone to face; it affected everyone around me. To my New York City roommates — Kate Farabaugh, Caroline Kopfler, Julia Martin — thank you for the many nights spent consoling my anxieties with laughter and patience, listening to every internal debate I had about titles, covers, and content. To my dear friends Katherine Tague and Madison Semarjian: You both inspire me with your boundless grace, kindness, intelligence, and humor. I wish everyone in this world could be so lucky as to have friends like you. To Grandma and Poppy, thank you for the goodnight texts (that come every single night without fail!) and for being my biggest cheerleaders. *I love you to pieces!*

I couldn't in good faith dedicate this book to my mom, knowing the personal bravery it required to allow our story to become public. However, I do dedicate my life to her, because without her, I wouldn't be here today. Sustaining me throughout the years chronicled in this book, while writing it, and well beyond it, took tremendous sacrifice and strength. I live *because* of her and *for* her. If it wasn't clear yet, she is my very favorite person on this planet.

And finally, to my sister, Kaitlyn Lantz Leddy. Lately, I've been thinking a lot about the concept of irreplaceability. In a lot of ways, we're all replaceable. At one point or another, we will all likely have a new best friend, a new significant other, a new favorite restaurant, a new home. It's uncomfortable to think about — how easily we slide in and out of each other's lives. Yet I will have only ever had one sister. I will have only ever grown up beside one person in such an elemental way.

We should've gotten a lifetime together of this growing, but all things considered — however fraught and painful and short the time we had together was — I'm very thankful for the sister I had. She was, and will always be, the very definition of irreplaceable.

Kait, this book is a love letter to you.

A Note on Sources

For statistics related to the disproportionate mental health burdens faced by minorities, I consulted the following sources:

Adichie, Chimamanda Ngozi. "The Danger of a Single Story." TED video, filmed July 2009. https://www.ted.com/talks/chimamanda_ngozi_adichie_the_danger _of_a_single_story.

Centers for Disease Control and Prevention. "Suicide and Violence Prevention Among Gay and Bisexual Men," February 29, 2016. https://www.cdc.gov/ msmhealth/suicide-violence-prevention.htm.

National Alliance on Mental Illness (NAMI). "Mental Health by the Numbers," March 2021. https://www.nami.org/mhstats.

Office of Minority Health. "Mental and Behavioral Health — African Americans," last modified May 18, 2021. https://www.minorityhealth.hhs.gov/omh/ browse.aspx?lvl=4&lvlid=24.

Substance Abuse and Mental Health Services Administration, "2018 National Survey on Drug Use and Health: Detailed Tables." SAMHSA.gov. August 20, 2019. https://www.samhsa.gov/data/report/2018-nsduh-detailed-tables.

When discussing my sister's head trauma and the effects it may have had on her mental health, I relied on recent CTE research, such as this:

Ward, Joe, Josh Williams, and Sam Manchester. "111 NFL Brains: All but One Had CTE." New York Times, July 25, 2017. https://www.nytimes.com/ interactive/2017/07/25/sports/football/nfl-cte.html.

A Note on Sources

In the early stages of my sister's battle with mental illness, our family searched for potential connections between other ailments, including PCOS and substance abuse:

Cizza, Giovanni, Svetlana Primma, and Gyorgy Csako. "Depression as a Risk Factor for Osteoporosis." Trends in Endocrinology and Metabolism 20, no. 8 (October 2009): 367–73; U.S. National Library of Medicine: https://www.ncbi.nlm.nih.gov/pmc/articles/PMC2764354.

MacDonald, Ann. "Teens Who Smoke Pot at Risk for Later Schizophrenia, Psychosis." Harvard Health, March 7, 2011. https://www.health.harvard.edu/blog/teens-who-smoke-pot-at-risk-for-later-schizophrenia-psychosis-201103071676.

Office on Women's Health. "Polycystic Ovary Syndrome," last updated April 1, 2019. https://www.womenshealth.gov/a-z-topics/polycystic-ovary-syndrome.

Pearson, Michele L., Joseph V. Selby, Kenneth A. Katz, Virginia Cantrell, Christopher R. Braden, Monica E. Parise, Christopher D. Paddock, et al. "Clinical, Epidemiologic, Histopathologic and Molecular Features of an Unexplained Dermopathy." PLOS ONE: Public Library of Science, January 25, 2012. https://journals.plos.org/plosone/article?id=10.1371%2Fjournal.pone.0029908.

University of Oxford. "Small Risk of Violence in Schizophrenia Unless Drugs and Alcohol Are Involved," May 20, 2009. Oxford University website: https://www.ox.ac.uk/news/2009-05-20-small-risk-violence-schizophrenia-unless-drugs-and-alcohol-are-involved.

I used evidence from A. Eden Evins (2008) to shed light on the connection between schizophrenia and cigarette use:

Evins, A. Eden. "Nicotine Dependence in Schizophrenia: Prevalence, Mechanisms, and Implications for Treatment." Psychiatric Times 25, no. 3 (March 1, 2008). https://www.psychiatrictimes.com/view/nicotine-dependence-schizophrenia-prevalence-mechanisms-and-implications-treatment.

For research about the effect of PTSD on memory, I included the following study:

Northwestern University. "How Traumatic Memories Hide in the Brain, and How to Retrieve Them: Special Brain Mechanism Discovered to Store Stress-Related, Unconscious Memories." ScienceDaily, August 17, 2015. www.sciencedaily .com/releases/2015/08/150817132325.htm.

These resources present compelling neurological data on the mechanisms of schizophrenia, as well as the relation between mental illness and police violence:

Blakemore, S. J., J. Smith, R. Steel, C. E. Johnstone, and C. D. Frith. "The Perception of Self-Produced Sensory Stimuli in Patients with Auditory Hallucinations and Passivity Experiences: Evidence for a Breakdown in Self-Monitoring." Psychological Medicine 30, no. 5 (September 2000): 1131–39. https://pubmed.ncbi .nlm.nih.gov/12027049.

Carroll, Heather. "People with Untreated Mental Illness 16 Times More Likely to Be Killed by Law Enforcement." Treatment Advocacy Center. https://www .treatmentadvocacycenter.org/key-issues/criminalization-of-mental-illness/2976 -people-with-untreated-mental-illness-16-times-more-likely-to-be-killed-by-law -enforcement; accessed June 8, 2021.

Garrison, Jane R., Charles Fernyhough, Simon McCarthy-Jones, Mark Haggard, and Jon S. Simons. "Paracingulate Sulcus Morphology Is Associated with Hallucinations in the Human Brain." Nature Communications 6, no. 8956 (2015). https://www.nature.com/articles/ncomms9956.

Kochunov, Peter, Artemis Zavaliangos-Petropulu, Neda Jahanshad, Paul M. Thompson, Meghann C. Ryan, Joshua Chiappelli, Shuo Chen, et al. "White Matter Connection of Schizophrenia and Alzheimer's Disease." Schizophrenia Bulletin 47, no. 1 (January 2021): 197–201. https://academic.oup.com/schizophrenia bulletin/article/47/1/197/5873334.

An interesting examination into why seeking out happiness can have the opposite effect:

Schooler, Jonathan W., Dan Ariely, and George Loewenstein. "The Pursuit and Assessment of Happiness Can Be Self-Defeating." In The Psychology of Economic Decisions, edited by Isabelle Brocas and Juan D. Carillo Oxford: Oxford Univer-

sity Press, 2003. https://www.cmu.edu/dietrich/sds/docs/loewenstein/Pursuit AssessmentHappiness.pdf.

The National Alliance to End Homelessness cites the latest numbers on homelessness in the United States:

National Alliance to End Homelessness. "State of Homelessness: 2020 Edition." February 9, 2021. https://endhomelessness.org/homelessness-in-america/ homelessness-statistics/state-of-homelessness-2020.

The below source states that 1.2 percent of Americans are diagnosed with schizophrenia and includes additional resources for those suffering from the disorder:

"Schizophrenia Symptoms, Patterns and Statistics and Patterns." MentalHelp .net: An American Addiction Centers Resource. https://www.mentalhelp.net/ schizophrenia/statistics; accessed June 8, 2021.

A King's College London study provides hopeful evidence pointing to the lasting effects of CBT on neurological health:

Mason, L., E. Peters, S. C. Williams, and V. Kumari. "Brain Connectivity Changes Occurring Following Cognitive Behavioural Therapy for Psychosis Predict Long-Term Recovery." Translational Psychiatry 7 (2017). https://www .nature.com/articles/tp2016263.

Rita Riedmueller and Sabine Müller examine a promising new research concept, the mild encephalitis hypothesis of schizophrenia developed by Karl Bechter and Nobert Müller:

Riedmueller, Rita, and Sabine Müller. "Ethical Implications of the Mild Encephalitis Hypothesis of Schizophrenia." Frontiers in Psychiatry, 8, no. 9 (March 2017). https://www.researchgate.net/publication/314870048_Ethical_Implications_of _the_Mild_Encephalitis_Hypothesis_of_Schizophrenia.